EFFECTIVE LIBRARY AND INFORMATION CENTRE MANAGEMENT

Second Edition

Effective Library and Information Centre Management

Second Edition

Jo Bryson

Gower

Published by
Gower Publishing Limited
Gower House
Croft Road
Aldershot
Hampshire GU11 3HR
England

Gower
Old Post Road
Brookfield
Vermont 05036
USA

Jo Bryson has asserted her right under the Copyright, Designs and Patents Act 1988 to be identified as the author of this work.

British Library Cataloguing in Publication Data
Bryson, Jo, 1950–
    Effective Library and Information Centre Management
    1. Information services – Management
    I. Title
    025.5'2'068

ISBN 0 566 07691 8

Bryson, Jo, 1950–
    Effective Library and Information Centre Management / Jo Bryson.
        p.   cm.
    Includes index.
    ISBN 0–566–07691–8 (paperback)
    1. Information resources management—Handbooks, manuals, etc.
    2. Corporate libraries—Administration—Handbooks, manuals, etc.
    3. Information services—Management—Handbooks, manuals, etc.
    I. Title.
    T58.64.B795   1997
    658.4'038dc21   96–52110
                                                                              CIP

Typeset in Palatino by Bournemouth Colour Press, Parkstone, Poole, Dorset and Printed and bound in Great Britain by MPG Books Ltd, Bodmin, Cornwall

Contents

Figures

Tables

Preface

The objective

This book has been written as a management handbook for people working in information services in small- to medium-sized organizations and a management textbook for students in librarianship and information studies. It focuses on managing information services in dynamic environments where information is critical to maintaining organizational competitiveness through customer satisfaction and retention, increased productivity and performance, and financial viability.

This second edition reflects modern management trends in bringing together the disciplines of librarianship, records management and archives, information systems, computing and telecommunications with a view to promoting an integrated approach. Traditionally these disciplines have been managed and operated as discrete work units based on the format of the information. In recent times the importance of managing the content (the information resource) rather than the format has gained prominence and, as a result, the trend is towards managing these work units as an integrated information service.

The role of chief librarian has also been redefined as information service manager, reflecting the trend towards an integrated approach. The role has been extended with added responsibilities for the management of records, archives, information systems, computing and telecommunications. This new role builds upon the librarian's existing information organization and management knowledge and expertise, and applies these assets to the management of the technology and other types of corporate record to ensure competitive advantage.

It should be noted that competitive advantage is a notion that is not just restricted to profit-making or private sector organizations, but also refers to the efficient use of resources and the ability of the information service to create and match existing and potential customers' demands for services before other information services or information outlets.

The book focuses on strategic management issues that face individuals managing and working in information services today. The roles and activities of the information services manager and the forces that impact upon them are often interrelated and so an integrated management approach is used. For example, interrelationships can be found between the internal and external environments, the manager's ability to get things done through people and their interpersonal roles, and between the corporate culture of the organization and the way in which it uses information. An integrated approach is also a necessary mechanism for managing changing and competitive environments in organizations today.

Many management strategies can be undertaken at the individual level as well as at the organizational level. Strategies for planning and managing human, information and financial resources take place at the micro and macro level. The people interaction activities of managing change and conflict, motivation, stress management, personal development and training require management strategies at personal and organizational levels.

Many of the chapters are wide-ranging and include management issues at different levels within the parent organization. For example, the chapters can be used for reference to assist in the day-to-day management activities of the information service. They can also be used to provide an understanding of the wider organizational management issues that occur in the parent organization.

The concept of the parent organization is used throughout the book, and refers to the corporate environment in which the information service operates. It may be the local government authority, government department, private sector organization, research centre or academic institution. It is an important concept as the environment of the parent organization often shapes the environment of the information service.

Each chapter has been written with the intention of considering the topic in a manner that reflects modern management trends in dynamic and changing environments. Relevant examples in information services are then applied to the topic concerned. The examples have been selected to be most applicable to assist those who are recently qualified and working in small to medium-sized organizational environments with little or no access to others for support or advice on management issues, or for those with very little or no management training.

As information services can vary in function and customer base, the book uses a generic approach. Any underlying theme is to manage the service to meet the business needs of the parent organization, the information needs of its customers and other stakeholders' information requirements. For example, the parent organization for a public library and information service is usually the local authority. The public library supports the business needs of the local authority through the provision of information, education and recreation services to the local community, and its customers are a cross-section of people who vary in age, interests and lifestyle. The library may also provide specialist information services to the staff and elected members of the local authority, as well as accepting responsibility for records management and archives within the local authority.

In contrast, an information service in a small entrepreneurial organization may focus on supporting the research needs of management and employees of the organization as their primary customers. The primary objective being to manage the information systems and deliver research services in such a manner so as to assist the management and employees in maintaining the parent organization's competitiveness. A secondary role in the information service's contribution to this competitiveness could be to deliver information or services to customers of the entrepreneurial organization.

An analogy can be drawn between the information services and the heart. Information and its supporting technologies are the lifeblood and arteries of the organization. They are not only critical to its success, they can provide competitive advantage in business operations.

To position the information service at the leading and competitive edge so as to maintain the parent organization's competitiveness, the information services manager must be able to:

- understand their role as manager;
- understand the strategic influences and internal and external environments in which they operate;
- profitably and productively manage this environment through the integrated planning of human, information, technology and financial resources;
- create a corporate environment that fosters creativity and values expertise;
- inspire and get things done through people interaction skills;
- manage the information resource within the corporate environment;
- care for and manage themselves and others as individuals;
- assess risk and manage accordingly; and, finally,
- deliver services to meet customer needs.

These management requisites are used as the themes for the nine parts of the book. The chapters are grouped around these nine themes (see Figure P0.1). Each chapter is devoted to a topic that supports the underlying theme. The chapters compromise a mix of traditional topics that form the basis of

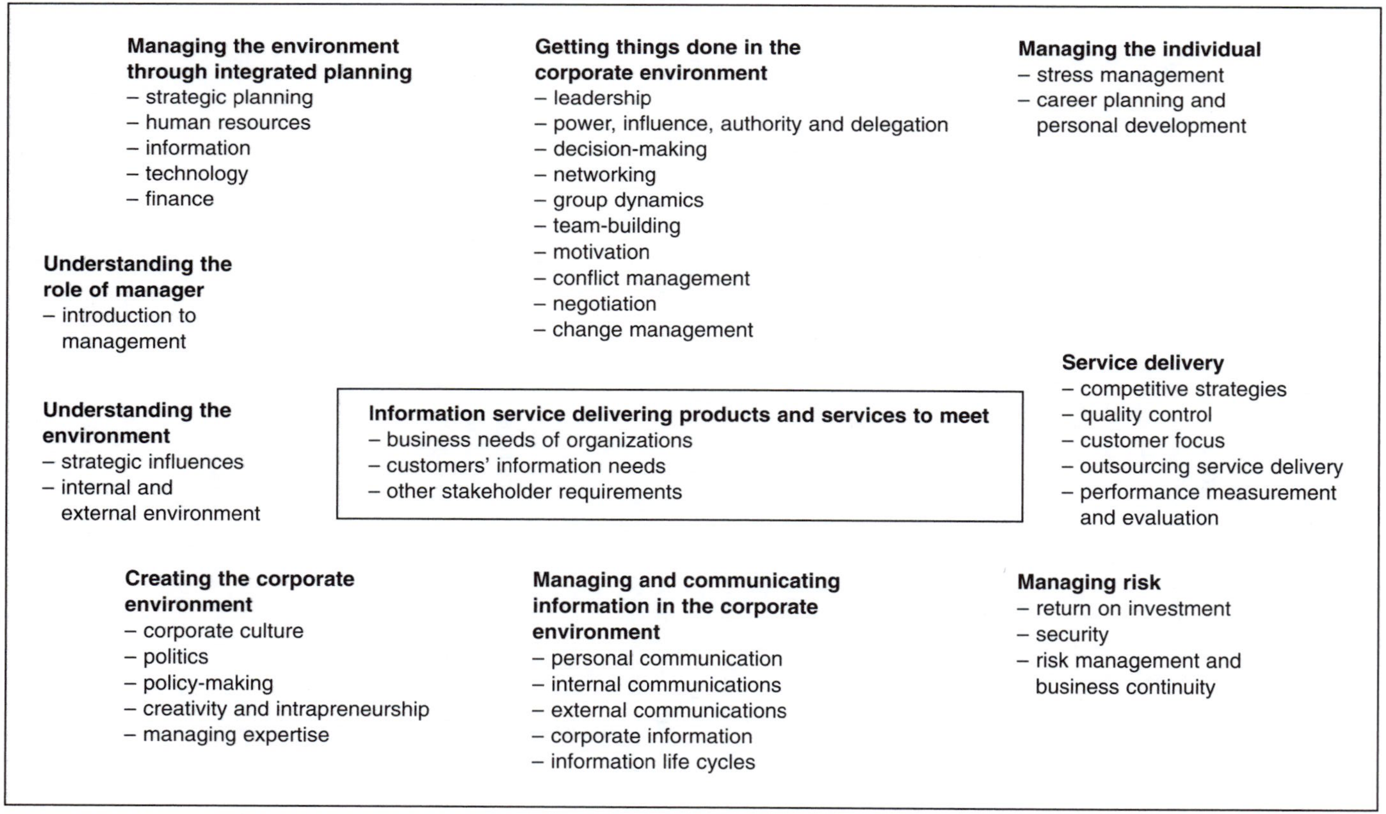

**Managing the environment
through integrated planning**
 – strategic planning
 – human resources
 – information
 – technology
 – finance

**Understanding the
role of manager**
 – introduction to
   management

**Understanding the
environment**
 – strategic influences
 – internal and
   external environment

**Creating the corporate
environment**
 – corporate culture
 – politics
 – policy-making
 – creativity and intrapreneurship
 – managing expertise

**Getting things done in the
corporate environment**
 – leadership
 – power, influence, authority and delegation
 – decision-making
 – networking
 – group dynamics
 – team-building
 – motivation
 – conflict management
 – negotiation
 – change management

Information service delivering products and services to meet
 – business needs of organizations
 – customers' information needs
 – other stakeholder requirements

**Managing and communicating
information in the corporate
environment**
 – personal communication
 – internal communications
 – external communications
 – corporate information
 – information life cycles

Managing the individual
 – stress management
 – career planning and
   personal development

Service delivery
 – competitive strategies
 – quality control
 – customer focus
 – outsourcing service delivery
 – performance measurement
   and evaluation

Managing risk
 – return on investment
 – security
 – risk management and
   business continuity

Figure P0.1   Managing information services: an integrated approach

management theory and new issues that reflect the current environment.

Structure

Part 1, 'Understanding the role of manager', provides the reader with some basic concepts of the functions of leadership and management. It describes the various managerial roles, the levels of management that can be found in organizations and their managerial skills.

Part 2, 'Understanding the environment', provides an integrated approach to understanding the strategic influences, and the internal and external environments in which an information services manager operates. It considers the necessary leadership styles and competences to lead today's organization into tomorrow's world. The need effectively to understand and manage the information service in the context of the changing environment is a basic requisite of the strategic planning function that is considered in the next part of the book.

In Part 3, 'Managing the environment through integrated planning', the competitive and changing environment is managed through an integrated approach to human, information, technology and financial resource planning. Whilst there is a chapter devoted to each of the resources, the underlying approach is that they are planned as an integral part of the strategic planning process. The strategic planning process establishes the objectives that drive the organization and results in the correct allocation of resources to the selected programmes. It develops the strategies that make it possible for the information service and its parent organization to deliver competitive and profitable services and products in changing times.

Organizations that survive in the competitive and changing environment are those which are able to create a corporate environment that reflects the external environment. Successful organizations display characteristics of being innovative, adaptable to change and creative in their problem-solving. Part 4 of the book, 'Creating the corporate environment', considers strategies that create an innovative corporate environment for the information service and its parent organization. There are chapters on developing and managing a strong, ethical and high-performance corporate culture, the use of politics and political behaviour, policy-making, creating an innovative environment and managing different expertise for the common good.

Having established the foundation for the information service and its parent organization in terms of its future direction and corporate environment, the manager must now get things done through people. Part 5 of the book, 'Getting things done in the corporate environment', considers the interpersonal aspects of management that builds teamwork to achieve outcomes and manage change. It contains chapters on leadership and the closely related behavioural processes of power, influence, authority and delegation.

Goals are achieved through decision-making and change. Part 5 of the book has chapters on decision-making and change management, as well as the skills of negotiation, conflict management and networking. These are the skills that are necessary to implement change in the least disruptive way.

Traditional organizational structures are changing. They are moving towards work environments where people operate in groups (where there is still a leader) or as a team (where everyone is a leader). The management of groups and teams require different management skills than the management of individuals. This change is reflected in the chapters on group dynamics and team-building.

Motivation is a key driver in getting other people to do things. A chapter on motivation is included that outlines strategies at the organizational and individual levels to motivate people.

A key role for the information service within the corporate environment is to manage the information resource and its supporting technologies to support the business needs of the organization and the information needs of customers. Part 6, 'Managing and communicating information in the corporate environment', is the cornerstone of the book. This is what the information service is about. It must provide information products and services to the internal customers (the students and employees of the parent organization such as university staff, management or research officers), to the external customers (such as students or staff from other universities) and to the stakeholders of the parent organization (members of the governing bodies, suppliers, etc.).

Communication is the process through which information (the message) is imparted to others. This part of the book has chapters devoted to strategies for managing personal communication, internal communications and communications with external bodies. This latter chapter includes the important issues of communicating the organization's image and obtaining competitive information from the external environment.

Part 6 also discusses the management of the information resource as a competitive tool and as an information utility. These two issues are covered in chapters on corporate information and information life cycles.

Part 7, 'Managing the individual', concentrates on managing the well-being of the people who work in the information service. It includes chapters on stress management, and career planning and personal development. Each chapter contains strategies that can be used at the personal level and at the organizational level.

The competitive and changing environment introduces a comparatively high level of risk for any organization. Risk factors can have financial, political, competitive, legal, human or technological origins. Part 8,

'Managing risk', concentrates on strategies that can be used to identify and manage potential risk factors so that their impacts are either minimized or neutralized. Part 8 contains chapters on return on investment, security, and risk management and business continuity.

The final and most important outcome of the managerial value chain is the enabling of product and service delivery. Part 9, 'Service delivery', deals with the reason for all the other parts, the service delivery aspects of the information service. It contains chapters on strategic marketing strategies to increase the competitiveness of the information service and its parent organization, and on quality control and customer focus. These ensure that services and products are delivered that meet the needs of customers.

Increasingly, organizations are concentrating their efforts on their core business and outsourcing other activities. Information services are often immediate targets for outsourcing, so a chapter on outsourcing service delivery is included in this part of the book. Finally, feedback on service delivery is covered in the chapter on performance measurement and evaluation.

The 'Epilogue' brings all of the parts of the book together in explaining the integrated approach.

Jo Bryson
Perth, Western Australia

Acknowledgements

This book builds upon a rich source of ideas that have accumulated from over 25 years' experience in information-related work in the public and private sectors and academic institutions. This experience has been gained at senior, mid-level and line management levels, and as a lecturer. I have learnt a great deal from my interactions with my team members, managers, peers, students, colleagues and friends over the years. Some of this has been what not to do, as well as what to do. I am grateful for the opportunity to have shared a working life with them all.

Ideas have also come from general management and information management books and journals that I have read over the years. I appreciate the time that others have spent in documenting their wisdom and knowledge so that individuals like myself could share it.

Finally, I wish to thank my husband, Vic Fazakerley, for his support and constructive feedback on the book's contents.

I have written the book to give something back to the people working in information services, so that they may continue their excellent contributions to organizational success.

JB

Part 1

Understanding the role of manager

Managers have traditionally performed five management functions. They plan, organize, command, co-ordinate and control. In today's changing and competitive environment, the manager's role is much more complex. He or she is inspirational; building and sharing a vision for the future of the information service. This does not just mean having an idea about what the future services may look like and sharing this with others. It means building a total commitment so that everyone can personally identify with, and own, the vision and work together to achieve it. In creating the common identity amongst individuals, managers will use communicating, networking, motivating and leadership skills.

The vision cannot be achieved just by focusing upon individuals and the internal or corporate environment. The manager must also focus upon the relativity of the information service to its existing and potential competitors in the external environment. This requires skills in competitive positioning, image-building and politics.

Survival in a competitive environment also relies upon profitability and productivity. This is achieved through the effective management of information, people, finances and technology resources. In addition to these tangible items, risk, quality, and the customer and stakeholder interface have also to be managed.

Chapter 1 explains some of the roles of management in a non-traditional manner, the levels of management and the managerial skills used by managers (see Figure P1.1).

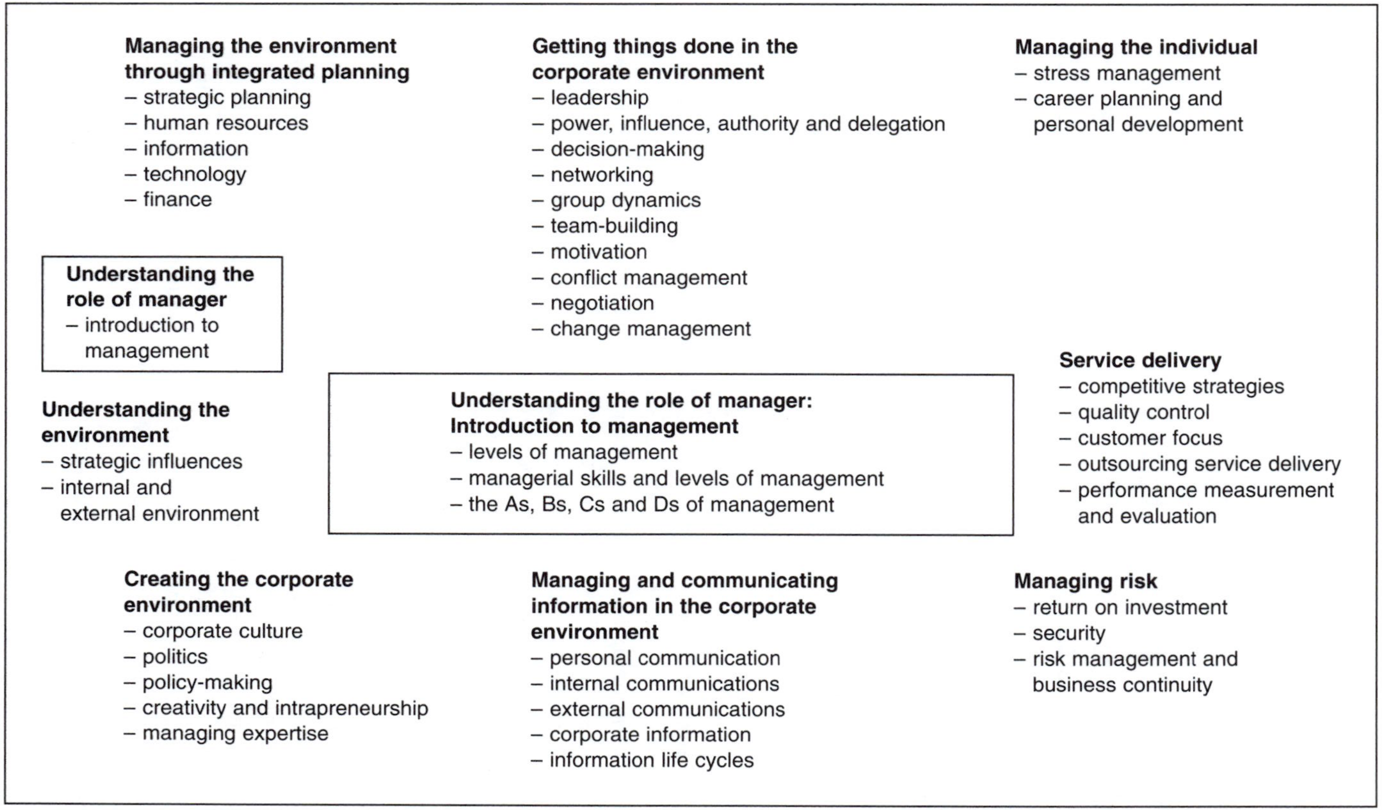

Managing the environment through integrated planning
– strategic planning
– human resources
– information
– technology
– finance

Understanding the role of manager
– introduction to management

Understanding the environment
– strategic influences
– internal and external environment

Creating the corporate environment
– corporate culture
– politics
– policy-making
– creativity and intrapreneurship
– managing expertise

Getting things done in the corporate environment
– leadership
– power, influence, authority and delegation
– decision-making
– networking
– group dynamics
– team-building
– motivation
– conflict management
– negotiation
– change management

Understanding the role of manager: Introduction to management
– levels of management
– managerial skills and levels of management
– the As, Bs, Cs and Ds of management

Managing and communicating information in the corporate environment
– personal communication
– internal communications
– external communications
– corporate information
– information life cycles

Managing the individual
– stress management
– career planning and personal development

Service delivery
– competitive strategies
– quality control
– customer focus
– outsourcing service delivery
– performance measurement and evaluation

Managing risk
– return on investment
– security
– risk management and business continuity

Figure P1.1   Understanding the role of manager

1 Introduction to management

Introduction

Three levels of management are found in organizations. These are known as senior management, mid-level management and line management. Each of these levels has a different role and uses different skills. It is necessary to understand the requirements of the different levels of management in order to ensure that each management level is performing its proper functions.

Managers can also use the As, Bs, Cs and Ds of management to understand their roles and to develop better skills that enable them to achieve the organization's goals.

Levels of management

Managers operate at different levels in an organization. Their activities and skills differ according to their level. The number of people at each level decreases towards the top, so that there is finally only one Chief Executive position. However, the traditional triangle shape is being distorted as the mid-level management stratum is disappearing through organizational downsizing (see Figure 1.1).

The information service is usually part of a larger entity, the parent organization. The information services manager may be the executive management position for the information service, but he or she will be part of the senior management team within the parent organization.

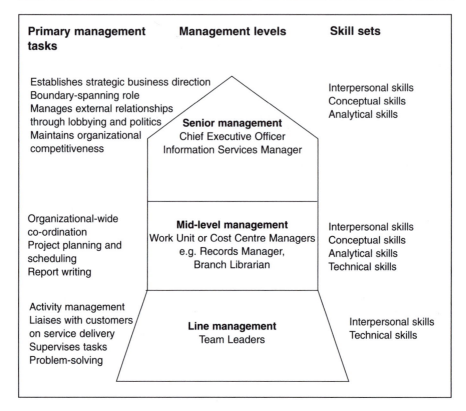

Primary management tasks | **Management levels** | **Skill sets**

Establishes strategic business direction
Boundary-spanning role
Manages external relationships through lobbying and politics
Maintains organizational competitiveness

Senior management
Chief Executive Officer
Information Services Manager

Interpersonal skills
Conceptual skills
Analytical skills

Organizational-wide co-ordination
Project planning and scheduling
Report writing

Mid-level management
Work Unit or Cost Centre Managers
e.g. Records Manager,
Branch Librarian

Interpersonal skills
Conceptual skills
Analytical skills
Technical skills

Activity management
Liaises with customers on service delivery
Supervises tasks
Problem-solving

Line management
Team Leaders

Interpersonal skills
Technical skills

Figure 1.1   Levels of management and their associated tasks

Senior management

The senior management or executive team reports directly to the Chief Executive. It includes the most senior members of the organization. The information services manager will be part of the senior management team. Senior management is responsible for strategic planning and for scanning the environment for changes that may affect the organization's competitiveness. Theirs is a boundary-spanning role. They are the interface between the organization and main stakeholders. They interact with external organizations by lobbying and negotiating on issues that have an impact on the organization's business strategies, and they spend time troubleshooting and managing the political environment.

Managers at this level spend a considerable amount of time with their peers and stakeholders, and to a lesser extent their employees. Most of their work is verbal and is often reactive. They receive short snatches of information that they have to piece together to manage customers, competition and change.

Mid-level management

Mid-level managers receive broad overall strategies and policies from senior management and translate these into specific action programmes that can be implemented by line management. They analyse issues such as the emerging trends in technology and their impacts on service delivery and future customer requirements, and summarize these in reports for senior management. Managers who have responsibility for work units such as records management, branch libraries or computing services are regarded as mid-level managers.

Mid-level managers perform a co-ordinating role between the various parts of the organization. They have an in-depth knowledge of their area, and how this interacts with other sections or divisions within the organizational structure.

In acting as the buffer between senior management and line management, mid-level managers spend most of their time using high-level communication skills in telephone conversations, sending and receiving electronic mail messages, attending meetings and preparing reports.

Line management

Line managers are directly responsible for service delivery by their work units and the administration of resources to meet the parent organization's short-term objectives. They are often the team leaders. Theirs is primarily a supervisory and grievance-handling role that requires strong technical and interpersonal skills. Grievances may come from, for example, their staff regarding rosters and other work-related issues, or from their customers on service delivery issues such as delays in the supply of equipment or information. Line managers spend little time with senior management or managers from other organizations, but deal mainly with their own staff and customers. Their jobs are hectic with continued interruptions, and they often communicate on a one-to-one basis to solve problems and maintain quality standards.

Managerial skills and levels of management

A skill is the ability to translate knowledge into an action that results in an outcome at the desired level of performance. Managers use technical, interpersonal, conceptual and analytical skills. Not all of these skills are used in equal proportion.

Managers at different levels in the organization use different skills. As managers progress through the management hierarchy they use less technical skills and more conceptual and analytical skills. Interpersonal skills are used at all levels of management but for different purposes.

Technical skills

Technical skills comprise the skills needed to accomplish service delivery tasks. These include expertise in using equipment such as personal computers or servers, and knowledge of sources of information, software and information systems. People develop their technical skills on the job or through formal education and training programmes.

Technical skills are used most by line managers who are responsible for training and supervising the use of equipment and knowledge sources to deliver information products and services to customers. In order to troubleshoot, answer questions and maintain credibility amongst their staff and peers, line managers must be competent in the use of technical skills.

Interpersonal skills

Interpersonal skills are used by all levels of managers in interacting with people internal and external to the organization. They are used to inspire others and to maintain the network of contacts and relationships through which the organization's objectives are achieved.

Senior managers utilize their interpersonal skills in networking to obtain competitive and other information relating to the external environment, to communicate their vision for the organization both internally and externally, in negotiating, lobbying and in using political acumen with stakeholders.

Mid-level managers use interpersonal skills in liaising between senior and first-line management, in discussing needs and delegating, and in translating policies into actions.

Line managers use their interpersonal skills in working with, understanding and motivating others, both individually and in groups. They create an environment in which tasks are effectively and happily accomplished.

Conceptual skills

Conceptual skills are used in understanding the relationships of individual parts to the whole, and the whole itself by breaking it into parts. The skills require an understanding of cause and effect relationships external to and within the organization. Mid-level managers, and senior managers to a lesser degree, use their conceptual skills to understand how different sections or divisions interact with each other to achieve outcomes that meet the organization's objectives. Senior managers use their conceptual skills to maintain a strategic view of the organization and its future direction, and to respond to changes in the external environment that may positively or adversely impact the organization.

Analytical skills

Analytical skills provide the ability to acquire, analyse and interpret information to determine the cause of change, and to suggest corrective action or ways in which to take advantage of the change. They provide the means to identify the key variables in a situation, to determine how they interrelate and to decide the ones that need attention.

Senior managers use their analytical skills in obtaining and using competitive intelligence that can be used for their own areas and for the organization as a whole. Mid-level managers use analytical skills in the preparation and writing of reports on issues within the organization.

The As, Bs, Cs and Ds of management

Achievement, activities and the allocation of resources

Managers allocate resources, make decisions and oversee the activities of others to achieve the information service's and its parent organization's business objectives. They are also held accountable for the use of these resources.

To achieve outcomes that meet the objectives, managers plan and develop an overall strategy that takes into account both the internal and external environments. This requires an understanding of the strategic influences that impact upon the information service and its parent organization and the availability of resources.

Allocation of resources depends upon managers' ability to identify, select and deploy the available human, information, technical and financial resources within the information service in a cost-effective manner.

Managers get things done through people. In overseeing the activities of others, managers use leadership skills to influence people to deliver outcomes, such as timely service delivery, that will best meet the organization's objectives. They actively seek input and participation, and provide continuous and timely feedback on performance.

Many activities involve teams or groups, the members of which could have a diversity of skills and backgrounds. Achieving outcomes through group activities requires a different set of management and leadership skills than dealing with individuals, as group behaviours differ from individual behaviours. Individuals also behave differently in groups than they do by themselves. Good managers recognize this and manage group activities accordingly.

The ability to get things done in the organization also depends upon managers' attitudes to their use of power, persuasion, politics, policy-making and personal communication. Good managers provide clear instructions and expectations of what is required, and allocate responsibility to others.

Bargaining, business re-engineering and burn-out

Bargaining (or negotiation) is a key management skill in the resolution of conflict and in the implementation of decisions in the information service. It can also be used in industrial relations such as negotiating an award agreement, contract management, acquiring resources, policy development and implementation. Effective bargaining requires experience, confidence and the possession of high-level communication skills.

Business re-engineering is the latest management recipe for the survival of organizations in changing and competitive environments. Business re-engineering is a high-risk business and functional strategy that supports the fundamental questioning of the organization's activities. The scope is broad and cross-functional. The change is quick and far-reaching, realigning operations and relationships both internally and externally.

Managers who consider business re-engineering as a strategic tool in information services must have a very detailed knowledge of how the parent organization thinks and works, and a very clear vision of the future position of the parent organization amongst its competitors.

The avoidance of burn-out is a stress management issue affecting both managers and their staff. Burn-out is most likely to affect the best, the brightest and the most highly motivated. People who are susceptible to burn-out are those who set high personal goals and achievements. Burn-out can be minimized or avoided through stress management strategies at organizational and individual levels.

Customers, competition and change

A common theme of this book is the three 'Cs', which is how Hammer and Champy (1983) describe the new business reality:

Three forces, separately and in combination, are driving today's companies deeper and deeper into territory that most of their executives and managers find frighteningly unfamiliar. We call these forces of change the three Cs: Customers, Competition and Change. Their names are hardly new, but the characteristics of the three Cs are remarkably different from what they were in the past.

It is no longer good enough to be very good at what a manager does. If organizations are to survive they must achieve three concurrent goals: customer satisfaction, market domination and increased profitability. If a manager is to survive, he or she must be prepared to constructively use his or her power and political skills to create a vision, interpret what is happening in the internal and external environments, inspire and drive change.

As a champion of change, the manager promotes ideas, builds support and implements new ideas. Mistakes are celebrated to encourage risk-taking with no penalties, for it is only with taking risks that change can occur.

Good managers use their skills to obtain competitive advantage in the market-place. They increase profitability and productivity, undertake niche marketing, provide quality information products and services, and provide customers with specialized services tailored to their expectations and needs.

An important role for management is to obtain and use intelligence about:

- their competitors' objectives, strengths and weaknesses, performance and strategies;
- changes in the market-place, including emerging technology directions; and
- their customers' objectives and strategies.

Whilst some of this information comes from published and unpublished sources, the more strategic information is obtained through building personal networks with customers, distributors, suppliers, past and present employees, consultants and business contacts.

Inspirational managers clarify the direction of the parent organization, the information service and work units so that individuals know the part that they play and in what direction the organization is going. They continuously extend and develop individuals, coaching them to greater achievements in attaining the vision as well as responding to their aspirations.

Disseminator, decision-maker and disturbance handler

A key role of management is to act as a disseminator of information. Managers communicate information received from outsiders or from within the organization to others. Some of this information is factual, whilst other information involves interpretation and the integration of diverse opinions from peers and senior management within and external to the organization.

Depending on their position within the organizational structure, managers must be comfortable making decisions:

- in different time horizons (past trends, the present and future);
- relating to different problems (strategic, planning and operational);
- with different degrees of problem structure and detail (high, low and mixed); and
- with different degrees of problem variability (unique, *ad hoc* and recurring).

Good managers are decisive, their decisions are fair. Decision-making involves discussion to allow the cross-fertilization of ideas and better solutions.

As a disturbance handler, the manager takes corrective action when the organization faces important and unexpected disturbances either in the internal or external environment. Senior managers put corrective actions in place at a strategic level, for example changing the focus of the organization to meet new competitive challenges. Line managers undertake a disturbance handler role in resolving grievances with their staff or with customers.

The roles, activities and skills of managers are continually changing in response to the changing environment. New management roles have been added and their activities are now more proactive. Their area of responsibility is spread over human, financial, technology and information resources, requiring new skills to assist them to manage these diverse resources.

References

Hammer, M. and Champy, J. (1993), *Reengineering the Corporation: A Manifesto for Business Revolution*, New York: Harper Collins.

Part 2

Understanding the environment

The environment in which information services operate is undergoing continuous change. Chapter 2 introduces the reader to some of the forces of change in the external environment and the necessary leadership skills and competences that will be required to position the information service to deliver appropriate services in changing times.

Chapter 3 provides an understanding of the external environmental domains that impact upon information services and their parent organizations. In addition, the chapter addresses complexity in the environment and provides a description of the internal environmental characteristics that are most likely to be found in organizations that are able to remain competitive in complex and changing environments.

This chapter allows the reader to step through various processes and methodologies that create an understanding of the internal and external environments in information services. These include the strategic audit, critical success factors, SWOT (strengths, weaknesses, opportunities and threats) analysis and capability profile (see Figure P2.1).

An understanding of the internal and external environments and the correct assessment of the performance of the information service within these environments is a necessary prerequisite for the next stage of the integrated management approach, the strategic planning process.

Managing the environment through integrated planning
- strategic planning
- human resources
- information
- technology
- finance

Understanding the role of manager
- introduction to management

Understanding the environment
- strategic influences
- internal and external environment

Creating the corporate environment
- corporate culture
- politics
- policy-making
- creativity and intrapreneurship
- managing expertise

Getting things done in the corporate environment
- leadership
- power, influence, authority and delegation
- decision-making
- networking
- group dynamics
- team-building
- motivation
- conflict management
- negotiation
- change management

Understanding the environment

Strategic influences
- forces of change
- leading for tomorrow

Understanding the environment
- the external environment
- the internal environment
- strategic audit
- critical success factors
- SWOT analysis
- capability profile

Managing and communicating information in the corporate environment
- personal communication
- internal communications
- external communications
- corporate information
- information life cycles

Managing the individual
- stress management
- career planning and personal development

Service delivery
- competitive strategies
- quality control
- customer focus
- outsourcing service delivery
- performance measurement and evaluation

Managing risk
- return on investment
- security
- risk management and business continuity

Figure P2.1   Understanding the environment

2 Strategic influences on information services

Introduction

Consideration of the strategic influences on information services over the next decade requires an analysis of the factors that will most likely create the need for change or impact upon people and organizations during this period. Such a consideration is necessary in order to determine the likely management scenario for the future to ensure the appropriate delivery of services and, ultimately, the information service's and its parent organization's survival. Whilst it is difficult to accurately predict the future, the likelihood of being able to forecast certain scenarios can be increased by analysing trends and strategic influences, and applying 'what if' scenarios to potential change factors.

The ability to survive in a turbulent environment will centre upon cost-effective strategies that make appropriate information available to customers thereby enabling them to make decisions. Information users and the decisions that they must make are the primary reasons for the provision of information services. However, other stakeholders, such as suppliers of goods and services or members of governing bodies such as local authorities, are also important to the information service for it could not survive without their co-operation and knowledge. Customers and suppliers, managers and organizational decision-makers, employees and members of the governing bodies are some of the people that benefit from the symbiotic provision of information services.

The purpose of information services, be they libraries, corporate records, global information networks or information systems, is intricately linked to facilitating access or disseminating information to assist people and organizations predict the future and facilitate decision-making.

The following section presents an analysis of the main forces of change that are likely to strategically influence the management of information services during the next decade together with an overview of the new leadership skills necessary to manage such influences.

The forces of change

Speed

Of all the factors affecting organizations in the future, the most consistent will be change. However, it will be both the speed and the extent of change that will have the most strategic influence upon the management of organizations and the information services that support their business needs. The successful organizations of the future will be those which are able to move quickly and change quickly. Even bureaucracies, which traditionally consist of unchangeable procedures, are having to become flexible and adaptable.

The need for intelligent organizations

In addition to being able to manage change, the successful organization of the future will need to be intelligent. An intelligent organization is one that utilizes information and its supporting technologies for competitive advantage. The contribution that information services such as libraries can make to the accumulation of intelligence within organizations should not be underestimated.

Quality drivers

Information and knowledge are also the tools that drive quality and improved performance. Quality is just not concerned with product or service outputs; quality procedures eliminate costly time, energy and waste in the production cycle. Appropriate information enables management and employees to make decisions in order to provide an environment in which quality is embraced and valued in products and services. This type of information underlines the basis upon which performance is measured and strategies for improvement are decided.

Impact of the global economy

Global competitiveness will be a factor in competition and in the delivery of services. Organizations will increasingly be competing in a global economy.

This will either be in developing offshore markets or in protecting domestic markets against foreign penetration. Significantly, a larger proportion of information sources will be from the vast array of electronic resources available world-wide, having potential impacts upon sovereignty and the longer-term ability to sustain a uniqueness in national cultures. For example, global information networks will be used to market services and products and to obtain information for research.

Supporting technologies will also be an economic and business necessity to overcome distance and different time zones allowing all employees immediate access to corporate information. The virtual organization that uses technology in this way will become the necessary reality rather than the exception.

Those individuals having access to computers and modems either in their home or in outlets such as libraries will be empowered through their access to information from an increasing diverse and international source. However, physical access to the information will not be enough. Skills in information retrieval, navigation and the ability to synthesize and validate the information provided through the global information networks will be necessary. Such skills may be learnt by the individuals or they may use the services of information specialists to obtain the information for them.

Competitive strategies

The economic necessities of financial stringency and lower profit margins required to offset strong competitive forces will necessitate the delivery of traditional services with fewer resources. However, financial savings will not be enough to remain competitive. The most successful organizations will be those that apply innovation and creativity to the use of information and information technologies, delivering information in new and different ways.

Customer focus

The emphasis will be on tailoring information services to meet clearly defined and individual customer needs, no matter whether it is in the context of operating in a multinational organization or in delivering public library services in a small community. Information will be packaged in terms of content, method of delivery, format and timing specifically targeted at the end user or customer.

Service delivery

Changing environments will also affect the way in which the general community will access information. More information will be in electronic form, accessible from the home through networks of information and interactive services. The skills of librarians and information workers in describing, linking and organizing the print media traditionally found in libraries will be readily transferable to the electronic media. However, the mode of delivery of the services offered may be different.

Drive for flexibility

In order to respond to change, employing organizations require flexibility in the types of services offered and, consequently, the skills and competency profiles and numbers of employees. The drive for flexibility will require a different employee mix than that previously employed. Contract employment and outsourcing of services will be two methods by which organizations will achieve this flexibility. The impact on the individual may be that he or she will have a series of part-time jobs or contracts, rather than working long term for a single employer.

The need for flexibility and the desire to provide services to customers will require considerable autonomy within organizations. This will be reflected by loose autonomous organizational structures and autonomous individuals working together co-operatively. Leadership styles that support collaborative individualism will be favoured.

Leading for tomorrow

New leadership skills and competences will be required to position information services so as to ensure that they meet the information needs of the organization or community in the new information environment.

Sharing the vision

Employees are more comfortable with change if they have confidence that strategies are in place to manage the future. One way of doing this is for managers to share a vision of the future – what the organization will look like in five years' time, the services or information products it will provide and the types of markets that it will operate in. A shared vision will enable all employees to work together to achieve the same goal. The shared vision can be supplemented through the manager leading by example with regard to the organizational values that support the vision.

Managing rapid change

The effect of rapid change in the business environment, be it public or private sector, is that management must now seize opportunities quickly, rapidly redesigning information products and services to meet changing customer needs and finding new ways of doing things cost-effectively. Speed is a deciding factor and nothing is exempt from change. In identifying new end uses for services, resolving problems that enhance quality of output and reduce waste or in making organizational changes to better cope with the environment and optimize scarce resources, managers will continually have to lead in turbulent environments.

Customer needs focus

An important factor for survival in any organization is to be in tune with customer needs and what they value in terms of service. This requires the ability to listen to customers to identify their requirements and to suggest improvements for current information products and services. It is also important to maintain a total service focus in meeting the needs of the customer as this can be important in creating a win-win situation. The total service focus makes it easier and more efficient for the customer as they have to deal with fewer organizations; it also lessens the interface between competitive entities and the customer, resulting in a significant business advantage to the service provider.

Contract administration

The trend, adopted by market-oriented governments and large corporate entities, towards the outsourcing of all but their core business activities can significantly impact upon the way in which managers manage the provision of services and utilize their human resources. In an outsourced or market-testing environment, the manager's role is no longer that of managing a workforce that delivers the services. Rather the manager's role changes to one of a purchaser of services. This involves contract administration and performance review to ensure that the outsourced or contracted out service meets the specified service levels and customer needs.

Participative management

The skills typified in rigid management styles have had to give way to more flexible and participative management skills and structures that lead and empower all employees. The ability of an organization to develop and successfully manage growth in a turbulent environment rests on the participation of all of its members. Whilst change may be senior management driven, all employees will be constantly called upon to make improvements. Managers will be required to develop corporate cultures which value participation throughout the whole enterprise.

Making information accessible

An empowered workforce or community is one that has access to information. An important task for the information services manager is to ensure that information is made available when and where it is required. Information is needed at the desktop in order to make decisions related to work, to allocate resources and to provide better services to customers. Information is also needed for psychological and motivational reasons. If people can share the vision of the organization and are kept informed of changes, particularly in turbulent environments they feel more secure in the knowledge that they know what is happening. As a consequence they are more willing to participate in the changes and make suggestions. This also lessens the amount of time spent on speculating what may happen. Information has traditionally meant power to those having it, so managers may need strong persuasive and negotiation skills to ensure that everyone within the organization has access to it.

Information is also required for people to make everyday decisions within the community. As in the corporate environment, this form of empowerment is very influential. It is also the root of the democratic society.

Balancing incongruent goals

Constant attention will need to be paid to customer needs. Staff will need to be motivated so that excellence in customer service and quality products can be achieved in a corporate environment where long-term employment may not be guaranteed. This will require the ability to balance the seemingly incongruent goals of encouraging amongst employees a sense of belonging, self-control over quality, energy and enthusiasm in organizational environments where organizational change and rapid downsizing may occur.

Meeting demands with fewer resources

When greater emphasis is placed on contracting out the delivery of all but core services, some difficult decisions may be required about the funding, structuring and delivery of information services. External funding and sponsorship may need to be attracted for some services. This may require lobbying, negotiation and marketing skills in order to ensure that the integrity and impartiality of services are not compromised.

In an effort to curtail expenditure it may not be easy to abandon services or levy charges. There may be enormous exit barriers to some services both socially and economically. There is also a risk of being locked into certain services which in the long term consume more resources than can realistically be afforded. A low coverage of too large a customer market is inferior to a good quality service for a focused market. Services offered by other entities should not be duplicated.

Exploiting information and technology

The strategic influences covered in this chapter present new opportunities for the information services manager, particularly because information and information technologies lie at the very heart of many of the changes taking place.

Information and its supporting communications technologies can help steer the organization through the change processes. For example, an organization that has immediate access to reliable and up-to-date information about their competitors' strategies, customers' and other stakeholders' needs, external environment and current performance levels is in a much better decision-making position about the future than one that does not. Similarly, information technologies and telecommunications can be used to strategic advantage by providing customers with specialized services tailored to suit their individual needs, for example in shortening the time taken to make a decision so that approvals for services can be provided on the spot rather than being referred elsewhere.

Fostering creativity and innovation

Creativity and innovation exploit change and provide organizations with the means to deal with the unstructured problems arising out of changing environments. The challenge for the leader is to generate an environment in which change is perceived as an opportunity rather than a threat. This enables employees to put forward suggestions without ridicule or judgement, and risks to be willingly assessed and decisions taken, allowing staff to make mistakes as part of the learning process. The leader should espouse encouragement and support for creative ideas in their conversation and action.

Managing cross-cultural issues

The global information market and the growing diversity in the cultural make-up of the community increase the exposure of information services to cross-cultural issues. The impact of this is that information content can be obtained or disseminated instantly to most parts of the globe. This may necessitate the management of issues such as national sovereignty and transborder data flows. Secondly, the greater cultural diversity will be represented in both employees and customers of the information service. Changing religious and racial compositions in the community have implications for management style and service delivery. Cross-cultural issues will have an increasing influence on organizational behaviour. The differing cultural values and attitudes of individuals to their own individuality, ambition, job satisfaction, authority and time orientation will need to be recognized and respected.

3 Strategies for understanding the environment

Introduction

Information services operate in the context of two environments – internal and external. Both of these affect the way in which information services are planned and managed to deliver services to their customers. Unless management and staff have a clear understanding of these environments and how they impact upon their operations, they will be working in a vacuum.

The external environment comprises the surrounding conditions in which the information service and its parent organization operates. Most organizations operate in complex and changing environments that continuously create new challenges that must be managed to ensure survival and success. The most consistent feature being that once one set of challenges has been mastered, a new set will take their place.

The internal environment of an organization requires an equal amount of management attention. The internal environment relates to the internal factors that shape the organization and its operating environment. Factors such as structure, culture, management styles, values, communication and use of technology make up the internal environment. Internal environment factors are influenced by the external environment.

A key management task is to continually assess how the information service is performing and adapting to changes in the internal and external environments. This can be achieved through a number of processes. Initially information on the external and internal environments must be gathered, assimilated and evaluated. Some of the evaluation processes that can be used include a SWOT analysis, the identification of critical success factors and a capability profile.

A common fault of management is to ignore or omit the need to continuously audit the performance of the organization against the external and internal environments. Often the excuse is that this practice is too time-consuming. Unfortunately those who take this stance fail to see the advantages in terms of reducing the risk factor in decision-making and in providing the opportunity of capitalizing on the information service's strengths and opportunities whilst minimizing the threats and weaknesses. Planning is made more effective through the use of such processes.

This chapter aims to take the reader through a step-by-step guide to create an understanding of the two operating environments and to assess the performance of the information services within these environments.

Understanding the external environment

The need to understand the external environment in which information services operate is fundamental to positioning the services to take advantage of technological change, obtaining the necessary resources in a contracting environment and delivering appropriate services to customers. The external environment is dynamic and needs to be constantly scanned to identify new realities, challenges and uncertainties.

The assessment of the external environment is one of the first inputs into the situation audit stage of the strategic planning process. It allows managers to identify changes, trends, issues, opportunities and threats, and provides an information base for the conduct of other assessments such as the capability profile.

Complexity of the environment

In scanning the number and nature of the domains of the external environment, the information services manager determines whether their services, and those of the parent organization, are operating in a simple or complex, stable or unstable environment. The complexity and stability of the environment affects the structure, management style and corporate culture of the internal environment. The complexity of the environment relates to the number of domains that impact on or influence the organization. A simple environment is one where only four or five domains impact upon the organization. A complex environment exists when over ten domains readily impact on the organization. The stability factor is related to the degree and frequency of change within the domains. If domains continually change in the intensity of their impact and, as a result, services change moderately or continually, the environment may be considered to be unstable. Turbulence does not always strike organizations in the same way or at the same time.

Environmental domains

The environmental domains that may impact on information services and their parent organizations are:

- economic conditions;
- availability of financial resources;
- geographical situation;
- degree of technological integration and innovation;
- the historical development and parentage of the information centre and its parent organization;
- customers and markets;
- demographic patterns;
- labour market and industrial relations;
- availability of resources;
- industry strata;
- cultural-social conditions; and
- the political climate.

Economic conditions

Economic conditions reflect the general economic health of the country and sector in which information services operate. Economic conditions can influence both demand and customer usage of services, and the supply and demand of resources. For example, in times of high unemployment the demand for free information services such as those operating out of public libraries increases. High unemployment may also lead to a much larger labour market from which staff may be selected. The information service's purchasing power in terms of equipment, electronic information services or book stock may be affected by changes in international exchange rates, inflation rates or shortages of supplies in equipment.

The demand for services may have an inverse relationship to the ability to supply services. For example, the budgets (appropriations) and purchasing power of libraries and information services have generally fallen over the past years whilst their customers have demanded more and different types of services.

The changing characteristics of the economy in terms of inflation, employment, money market and exchange rates should be monitored. As the information market is now a global one, the economies of the main international (electronic and traditional) publishing countries need to be monitored in order to predict trends in future pricing structures.

The information market is itself dynamic, influenced by international takeover bids of information suppliers and service providers. The potential to globalize ownership of the electronic and traditional media giants and publishing houses, telecommunications service providers and software suppliers will also have a significant impact on competition and pricing policies.

Information relating to economic conditions can most readily be obtained from the business and financial pages on the Internet or in newspapers, and by scanning other professional information outlets for information on economic conditions in the main publishing countries and their effects on information services.

Availability of financial resources

The days of tying the availability of funds for information services to the previous year's annual appropriation plus an allowance for inflation (with separate provision being made for any large capital cost) have long disappeared. In place of this is a trend towards the provision of core services only and costs in service provision being passed directly to the consumer. As a result, the information services manager needs to be more accountable, market oriented and entrepreneurial.

Modern accrual and other accounting techniques also assign 'total costs' to operating facilities, with provision needing to be made for depreciation on assets, interest and loan repayments.

Entrepreneurial and marketing activities require information about different sources of income and the customers' maximum thresholds in their willingness to pay for services. Alternative sources of income to fund discrete services may be available through employment-generating schemes, grants or sponsorships, or the provision of certain value-added services that can subsidize other services.

Geographical situation

The geographical environment involves both the level of reach involved in servicing customers as well as the geographical spread of operations of the parent organization. Both of these elements can either facilitate or hinder the service levels of the information service. As more services are delivered in an electronic environment the distance factor is lessened, however, issues such as transborder data flows and national sovereignty can arise if the information services are operating in international environments.

Information services need to be geographically positioned to best service their customers. This no longer means a single physical location to which customers must go for information. Rather it incorporates the geographical proximity to the appropriate telecommunications bandwidth and equipment through which services are delivered. For example, customers in work environments requiring access to multimedia from the desktop need to have access to broader telecommunications bandwidth than those who require only text data. Special libraries or information centres serving employees may still need a physical proximity close to an area of heavy use in which to house the specialized journal and printed material collection, whilst also being able to deliver electronic information services direct to the desktop.

Public libraries, kiosk or other public access services should be located in or near shopping centres within easy reach of car parks and public transport stops. Barriers such as highways or territorial boundaries such as political borders or campus sites may also determine the extent of service provision to customers.

Degree of technological innovation and integration

Technology may be defined as the available knowledge and techniques to produce goods and services. The complexity of the technology influences the skills and competences required by the information service's employees and customers. It may also enhance or inhibit the service's ability to quickly adapt to change.

Competitive advantage can be obtained in either being the first to market or having the ability to maintain the leading edge in a unique application of technology to deliver specialized information services to customers. The information service can also provide other services that can strategically position the parent organization in the competitive market-place. However, if the complexity of the technology is so great that it inhibits flexibility then the inability to respond to change will itself become a burden for the organization.

The level to which the technology is integrated into the business practices of the parent organization and there is seamless communication with customers will influence the ability of the (parent) organization to position itself ahead of its competitors, an example being the strategic advantage given to a publisher that can offer online ordering and other unique services ahead of its competitors. Likewise those information services that can tailor services to meet individual customer needs through the use of technology will develop a stronger customer base than those who are unable to do so.

Changes in technology occur in such quantum leaps that what is new technology today is old technology tomorrow. Market-driven technology obsolescence can be costly to an organization in terms of capital costs and a loss of customers. The focus should not just be on keeping up to date with new developments in technology, but also in discovering new business applications for existing technology or new combinations of technologies in order to deliver more appropriate services or increased productivity.

Historical development and parentage of the organization

The present and the future is always shaped by the past. In order to predict the future, it is necessary to consider past trends. Whilst the future is never certain, the likelihood of recurrent past trends being repeated when the same conditions apply tends to make the exercise of predicting the future more successful.

The historical development and current policies of the parent organization, amalgamations and takeovers will all impact on the values and culture of the organization, the allocation of resources and the way in which services can be delivered.

Customers and markets

In order to deliver effective services, information services managers must be aware of their market – that is, their present and potential customers, and their status. The type and level of service provision should be influenced by market expectations and demands which should be continually analysed in order to gauge the most appropriate service levels.

The needs of potential customers should also be considered as the information service may not be reaching its full market potential. This may mean that some less used services may have to be reduced or deleted in order to diversify into an area of increased demand. Market changes can occur from either a changed market base or changing needs of an existing market.

Market research may be carried out by using surveys and questionnaires, group interviews and discussions with customers and non-users, and by analysing information about the make-up of existing customers.

Demographic patterns

Market research can be further assisted by analysing the demographic make-up of the customer and potential customer base. Language, culture, income and purchasing power, age of the population and population distribution and mobility are some of the demographic factors that influence the provision of information services. Specialized information services delivering services within an organization may also find employee and organizational profiles that provide details of areas of expertise, positions and nature of responsibilities to be a useful planning and market research tool.

Labour market and industrial relations

Industrial relations and award conditions may affect the ability of the information service to attract key people as employees. These conditions will also impact on budgets, rosters, the make-up and classification of staff, as well as conditions of employment. Government legislation, such as equal opportunity or affirmative action, may influence human resource selection procedures.

Information services, like all organizations, rely on a knowledgeable workforce. Without an adequate supply of appropriately trained and skilled personnel, the ability to provide quality information services may be inhibited. The quality and quantity of the supply of labour is reliant upon the level and number of courses in universities and training institutions. Input should be given to the designers of university and training courses so that changes in the market-place can be reflected in the requirements of the course outcomes.

Availability of resources

Information services require ready access to resources that originate from the external environment. Books, journals, multimedia, workstations, hardware and software, electronic information, mail (paper or electronic) all originate from the external environment. Information services rely on the suppliers of these goods and services in order to perform their own tasks. Changes affecting suppliers' abilities to deliver goods and services on time may also affect the delivery of information services. Examples of changes may be in industrial disputes, cutbacks in production levels, increased labour costs or discontinuities in products or services.

Industry strata

The industry may be defined as those competitors or potential competitors that are in the same type of business. Industries may be further grouped according to the characteristics of ownership, services or markets. Within each industry there are leaders and followers. To ensure a common bond and some measure of quality control within various types of information services, minimum standards have often been developed. Standards may be applicable at international, national or organizational levels. International standards cover situations where information needs to be transported and shared across countries, an example being standards or protocols for telephony or facsimile transmission. National standards may be set for meta data, that is data that describes the qualities of data so that it may be used and shared between organizations. Increasingly meta data standards are becoming more universal in description. Organizational standards may relate to the use of a standard suite and version of software for office automation across the organization.

Cultural–social conditions

The social climate and culture of the environment in which the information service operates will affect its services. Social values will need to be reflected in the content, services and employees' attitudes to work.

Political climate

The political climate has a major influence upon the management of information services, particularly in terms of the organizational environment, how employees and customers are valued, and the types of services delivered. For example, political philosophies that espouse market testing or contracting out can result in considerable change to the role and focus of management, the change being from that of a service provider to one of contract management and purchaser of services.

Stakeholders may also exercise a significant influence upon the making of strategic decisions. Stakeholders do not normally become politically active in 'day to day' routines, but have a considerable influence upon new or strategic initiatives in services.

Understanding the internal environment

The success of an organization in a highly competitive environment is heavily dependent upon the contribution of its people. This is influenced by their perceptions and feelings of well-being towards the organization. People have needs and expectations that are either enhanced or frustrated by aspects of the organization. The interaction of people and structures influence the behavioural processes such as leadership style, planning, communications, conflict management, decision-making processes, problem-solving and other interpersonal behaviours. These behaviour processes influence the work output and level of support for organization.

Characteristics of successful organizations

The following provides a description of the characteristics most likely to be found in organizations that are able to remain competitive in complex and changing external environments.

Structure

The complexity and rapid rate of change in the external environment influences the internal organizational structure. Organizational structures become much flatter, with fewer management tiers, in order to be more responsive to changing environments. The trend is also to smaller organizations with more flexible structures. This allows the organization to adapt more quickly to change.

Culture

For employees to operate effectively in changing environments, lateral rather than vertical communication is required. The emphasis is on the provision of advice and relevant information, rather than instructions and decisions. The culture is often risk-taking and innovative. Support is readily given in an environment of trust.

Management style

The managers who achieve the most success in maintaining their organization's competitiveness in changing conditions are those who have a strong sense of vision. They share this vision with others and create a collaborative and supportive environment. A participative style is used. That is, groups of people are used to provide input and make decisions. Decision-making is delegated down to those in the service area. There is a network structure of control with a high degree of two-way communication. Information is freely available to those required to make the decisions and there is an emphasis on personal expertise and power.

Values

There is mutual respect for people, they are assumed to be interdependent and mature. Individuals are valued and rewarded on performance and innovation rather than on staff functions or length of service. Opportunities for self-development are frequently provided. Importance is attached to expertise, affiliations and ability to network outside the organization. As tasks are continually changing, a greater emphasis is placed on the organizational values such as trust, openness and individual accountability to act as the binding force within the organization.

Communication

Communication is open and free-flowing. Individuals have access to the appropriate information that they require for decision-making. Information is readily shared in a trusting environment within the organization and with stakeholders.

Use of technology

Technology is viewed as the supporting mechanism for increased communication within the organization and with stakeholders. It is used for competitive advantage to encourage customer loyalty through the ability to offer benefits and specific services that others cannot match. The technology also supports open communications and access to information that empowers staff. The trend towards networked services and customer server architecture is indicative of the ethos that communicates and shares information rather than centralizes control in a single database.

Applications are developed as interorganizational and intra-organizational systems focused on service delivery and integration, rather than being designed as information silos or stovepipe systems that perform singular functions such as payroll without reference to other human resource management information or financial information systems.

Strategic audit

The strategic audit provides the information services manager with important background information that can be used in the strategic planning process and for strategic marketing. After scanning and carrying out an analysis of the external and internal environments in which the information service and its parent organization operate, the manager should be able to use the strategic audit to determine the role of the information service in its environment, its influence and image, and the appropriateness of the services that it provides.

The strategic audit should also yield information on existing and potential customers, stakeholders, competitors and other important influencing factors, as well as implementation and evaluation mechanisms. A knowledge of these factors should make the information services manager more aware of the opportunities and threats facing the information service and increase their ability to manage these. If this knowledge is extensive, covering all the relevant domains of the internal and external environments, the element of surprise is reduced. This in turn allows the risk to be managed at the appropriate level. The planning task is also more effective as more of the variables are known. Accident and chance will still play their part in a dynamic environment, bringing with them the need for sudden or unexpected change. However, it is the manager's role to lessen the element of surprise and to respond and adapt to the change as it occurs, in order to ensure the information service's long-term survival.

Strategic audit for information services

A strategic audit can be undertaken for information services by working through the following questions (see Table 3.1). These questions have been adapted from Wheelen and Hunger's (1986) strategic audit. In doing so it is important to consider the situation of the parent organization of the information service as well as the issues that affect the management and use of the information service itself.

Table 3.1 A strategic audit for information services

Future

1 What is the broad future direction for the information services sector and the industry sector to which the parent organization belongs?
2 What are the main trends occurring within the information services sector and the parent organization's sector at the current time?
3 What are the strategic influences that are impacting on the management and use of the information service, and upon the parent organization.
4 Where does the information service and its parent organization aim to be in the future?

Present

5 What are the current vision, mission, objectives, strategies and policies of the information service and its parent organization?
6 Are they clearly articulated and acted upon or merely implied?
7 Are the vision, mission, objectives, strategies and policies of the information service and its parent organization consistent with each other and with the external and internal environments?

Stakeholder influence

8 Who are the main stakeholders?
9 How much influence do the stakeholders have on the operational and policy decision-making of the information service?
10 Do they contribute to or hinder the success of the information service (through their knowledge, skills, influence, networks)?

---

11 Do they actively participate and suggest future directions?
12 How sympathetic are they to the information service?

Management influence

13 What type of leadership style is portrayed by senior management?
14 Do they contribute to or hinder the success of the information service (through their knowledge, skills, influence, networks)?
15 Is there a systematic approach to strategic planning and understanding the external and internal environments?
16 Do they actively participate and suggest future directions for the information service?
17 How sympathetic are they to the information service?

External environment

18 What are the major external environmental factors affecting the information service and its parent organization?
19 Which of these are important at the moment? In the near future?
20 What are the opportunities and threats for the information service and its parent organization according to the external environment?

Internal environment

21 How close are the information service and the parent organization to displaying the characteristics most likely to be found in organizations that are able to remain competitive in complex and changing external environments?
22 Is there a well-defined corporate culture for the information service and its parent organization? Are these consistent?
23 Is the culture consistent with the vision, mission, objectives, strategies and policies of the information service and its parent organization?
24 What is the impact of organizational and external environments upon the information service and its parent organization? Do these hinder or assist processes and decision-making?
25 Are the information service's policies consistent with those of the parent organization?
26 What is the information service's approach to managing its expertise for the good of the whole organization?
27 Is the leadership style of the information service compatible with that required to remain competitive in complex and changing external environments? Is it consistent with the leadership style found within the parent organization?

28 Where is the power base in the information service and the parent organization? Does the power base enhance or detract from the organizational success of the information service?

29 Is the decision-making style of the information service compatible with that required to remain competitive in complex and changing external environments? Is it consistent with the decision-making style found within the parent organization?

30 How is conflict treated within the information service and its parent organization? Are the mechanisms consistent?

31 Is there a high turnover of staff in the information service? If so, why?

32 How well is the information service performing in relation to other information services?

33 How well is the information service performing in terms of improving the fit between the individual employee and the job?

34 Are appropriate techniques being used to evaluate and improve corporate performance? For example, performance review systems or risk assessments.

35 What are the information service's current marketing objectives, strategies?

36 Are these clearly articulated and acted upon or merely implied?

37 What is the information service's approach to quality control in the services that it provides?

38 Has the information service defined its key customers? What mechanisms does it have to obtain customer feedback?

39 Is planning for information and its supporting technology tied to the business needs of the parent organization and the customers' needs for information?

40 What are the information service's current financial objectives? Are these consistent with the financial objectives of the parent organization?

Issues

41 Are the current vision, mission, objectives, strategies and policies of the information service and its parent organization consistent with the broad future direction for the information services sector and the industry sector to which the parent organization belongs?

42 Should they be changed? If so, what is the effect upon the information service?

43 Are alternative strategies required? If so, which ones are feasible?

Implementation

44 What kinds of programmes should be developed to implement the recommended strategies?
45 Who should develop or be responsible for the programmes?
46 Are there sufficient financial, technical, human and information resources to implement the new programmes?

Performance evaluation and review

47 Are appropriate standards and performance measures used?
48 Is the current information system capable of monitoring and providing feedback on standards and performance measures?

Source: Adapted from Wheelen, T. L. and Hunger, J. D. (1986), *Strategic Management and Business Policy*, 2nd edn, Reading, MA: Addison-Wesley, pp. 38–45. Reprinted with permission of the authors.

Critical success factors

Critical success factors can be used to identify the most important ingredients for the information service's success. They focus upon the key determinants of success in the operating environment. Examples of critical success factors are visionary leaders, a motivated and knowledgeable staff, quality and responsive service to customers, and managerial support.

Critical success factors identify certain key components that must be present if the information service is to be successful. Through the use of critical success factors, certain goals can be clarified and levels of performance identified. Employees and stakeholders can also be made aware of the key issues and priorities in operations and service delivery, an example being the response time taken to satisfy customer enquiries. In this example the ability to respond quickly to any enquiry is not only a goal; it is also critical to the success of the information service. Employees are able to identify with the goal and prioritize workloads accordingly. The information service is successful when the goals are met. It quickly builds up a customer base because of its responsiveness. The rate of response can also be used as an indicator to measure the performance of the service.

SWOT analysis

The SWOT (strengths, weaknesses, opportunities and threats) analysis provides an objective assessment as to whether the information service is able to respond to and manage the environmental impacts. The more competent the information service is in dealing with its environmental impacts, the more successful it is likely to be. Strengths and weaknesses deal with factors internal to the organization, whilst opportunities and threats are concerned with its external environment.

A strength is a resource or capability that an organization has in order to effectively achieve its objectives. In an information service, a strength may be its innovative use of technology or depth and coverage in content. It may also be a particularly helpful and creative member of staff who consistently applies innovative ways to tackle problems.

A weakness is a limitation, fault or defect in the organization that keeps it from achieving its objectives. Limited technology capacity or floorspace may prevent an information service from meeting all of its customer needs.

It is often difficult for management to carry out an objective assessment upon the information service's strengths and weaknesses. Usually, only outsiders can remove themselves from the emotional and personal issues involved. Information for the assessment can be gathered through interviews with members of staff, stakeholders, customers and non-users, evaluations of internal reports and other documentation, questionnaires and observation.

An opportunity is any favourable situation in the information service's external environment. It may be a trend or a change that supports the demand for a service that has not previously been identified or filled. An opportunity usually allows the information service to enhance its position, and may be brought about by a technical change. The use of Internet and other online public access systems are recent examples of technology applications that have created opportunities to deliver new customer services direct to the home.

A threat is an unfavourable situation in the information service's external environment that is potentially damaging to it or its strategy. It may be a barrier or a constraint, or anything that may inflict problems on the information service.

The SWOT analysis allows strategies to be planned that can realize the strengths and opportunities and overcome the threats and weaknesses. It is used extensively in marketing processes.

Capability profile

A capability profile is the means of assessing the information service's strengths and weaknesses in dealing with the opportunities and threats in the external environment. Its capability in the fields of leadership, marketing, technology and finance helps to identify the strengths and weaknesses in dealing with variables in the internal and external environments.

Leadership capability can be gauged by considering the extent and use of strategic plans, the image of the information service, its speed of response to changing conditions, communication and control, the information service's ability to attract and retain highly creative people and the prevailing corporate culture.

Marketing capability can be demonstrated by the level of customer loyalty and satisfaction, percentage of customers versus potential customers, quality of service and ability to maintain growth.

The presence of technical skills, sophistication of technology and its applications, utilization of resources and personnel, economies of scale, currency and appropriateness of equipment, level of co-ordination and compatibility, and the integration and effectiveness of service, are some of the factors that may determine the information service's technical capability. Financial capability is determined by access to capital and stability of costs.

To complete the capability profile, a bar chart is prepared detailing the degree of strength or weakness in each category. After completing the chart the relativity of the strengths and weaknesses to each other can be determined. Whilst the capability profile is highly subjective, it is still useful. It provides the means for examining the current strategic position of the information service and highlights areas needing attention.

The mechanisms described in this chapter are tools that can be used to evaluate and understand both the internal and external environments in which the information service operates. This understanding is a necessary precursor to any strategic planning exercise.

Reference

Wheelen, T. L. and Hunger, J. D. (1986), *Strategic Management and Business Policy*, 2nd edn, Reading, MA: Addison-Wesley.

Part 3

Managing the environment through integrated planning

The planning process provides a more systematic approach to managing dynamic environments. Whilst the activities of strategic planning and human, information, technology and financial resource planning are described in separate chapters for convenience, an integrated approach is advocated. Human, financial, information and technology resources should be planned together as part of the strategic planning process (see Figure P3.1).

Chapter 4 addresses roles and responsibilities in strategic planning. It points out that the manager of the information service should be involved in setting the direction for the parent organization. The strategic plan for the parent organization should also set the strategic direction for the information service. Chapter 4 takes the reader through several logical steps in the strategic planning process, from defining the mission, conducting the situation audit and needs analysis to developing objectives and programmes.

Chapters 5 to 8 deal with specific planning strategies for human, information, technology and financial resources. Macro and micro approaches to planning are recurrent themes.

Chapter 5 considers the macro or organizational approach to human resource planning process. This is followed by the micro approach that reflects the interface of individuals with their jobs. It covers the development of the job description and job specification through the job analysis. The

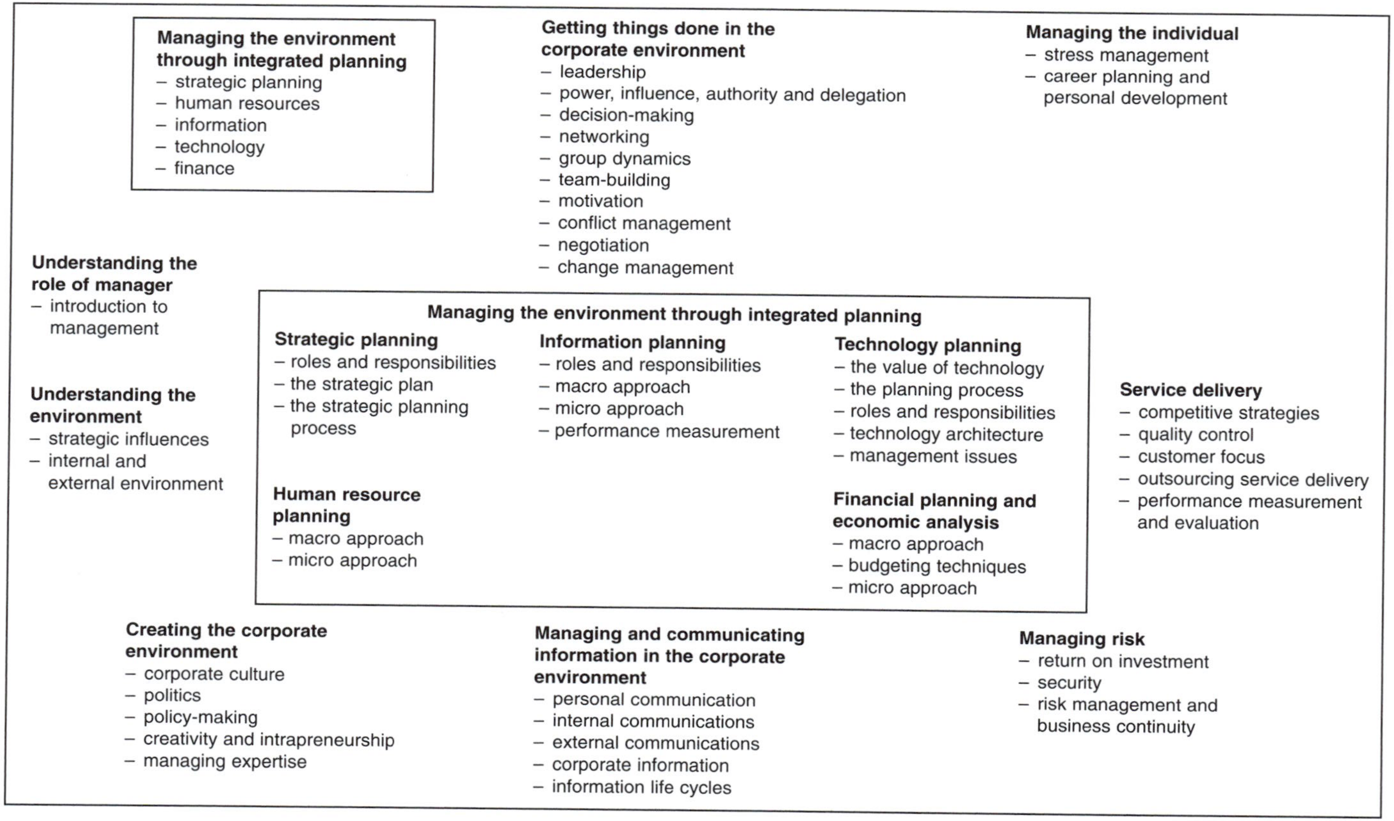

Managing the environment through integrated planning

Managing the environment through integrated planning
- strategic planning
- human resources
- information
- technology
- finance

Understanding the role of manager
- introduction to management

Understanding the environment
- strategic influences
- internal and external environment

Strategic planning
- roles and responsibilities
- the strategic plan
- the strategic planning process

Human resource planning
- macro approach
- micro approach

Getting things done in the corporate environment
- leadership
- power, influence, authority and delegation
- decision-making
- networking
- group dynamics
- team-building
- motivation
- conflict management
- negotiation
- change management

Information planning
- roles and responsibilities
- macro approach
- micro approach
- performance measurement

Technology planning
- the value of technology
- the planning process
- roles and responsibilities
- technology architecture
- management issues

Financial planning and economic analysis
- macro approach
- budgeting techniques
- micro approach

Managing the individual
- stress management
- career planning and personal development

Service delivery
- competitive strategies
- quality control
- customer focus
- outsourcing service delivery
- performance measurement and evaluation

Managing risk
- return on investment
- security
- risk management and business continuity

Creating the corporate environment
- corporate culture
- politics
- policy-making
- creativity and intrapreneurship
- managing expertise

Managing and communicating information in the corporate environment
- personal communication
- internal communications
- external communications
- corporate information
- information life cycles

Figure P3.1 Managing the environment through integrated planning

various mechanisms for recruitment are considered, as are processes for selection and induction. Finally, staff turnover and separation are addressed.

Chapter 6 covers information planning. Information is the 'content' of the technology systems. The chapter advocates a strong consultation process in planning and managing information at the micro and macro levels. Senior management must also action and champion the macro level planning process that includes an environmental analysis, the development of an information architecture and a gap analysis. The micro approach incorporates strategies for the management of information as a shared corporate resource. These include mechanisms for data classification, information standards, information definitions and information directories. The desired outcomes of these strategies are listed at the end of the chapter in an organizational context.

Technology planning is covered in Chapter 7. As information-related technology is susceptible to radical change, the chapter has not covered the micro approach in detail. Neither has it included descriptions of various information-related technologies. Instead emphasis is placed on obtaining business rather than technology solutions. Chapter 7 identifies how the technology presents opportunities for the information service and its parent organization to successfully compete in the market-place. The technology planning process is described at the macro level; role and responsibilities for the planning process are defined and the components of the technology architecture are summarized. The management issues associated with developing the technology to support the business strategy and with implementing the technology strategy are discussed.

Chapter 8 considers financial planning and economic analysis. The macro level deals with the budget process. The relationships between the budget cycle and the strategic planning cycle are explored. The activities associated with preparing and controlling the budget are described, as are different budgeting techniques. The micro approach covers different costing mechanisms. It describes capital costs, distinguishes between cost accounting and activity-based costing, and explains mechanisms for costing such as fixed and variable costs, unit costs, productivity curves, the law of diminishing returns, variable and total costs per unit.

4 Strategic planning

Introduction

Strategic planning is a continuous and proactive process. It enables information services to influence external forces in accordance with their chosen strategies and initiate new activities conducive to their market needs rather than adjust or respond to those imposed upon them. The strategic planning process introduces a more systematic approach to managing dynamic environments and enables the information service and its parent organization to respond effectively to new situations.

The strategic planning process recognizes that organizations cannot achieve everything they would like to do. Instead, it allows for the allocation of resources and planning of strategies on a priority basis to best achieve the organization's mission within the resource constraints and dynamics of the external environment.

The activities associated with collectively planning for the future, articulating the organization's objectives and creating an understanding of its purpose and values are useful in themselves. They serve to generate a greater knowledge and understanding of the organization and, ultimately, increase the level of commitment, communication and cohesiveness across the organization. This in turn leads to individual feelings of empowerment and strengthens the effectiveness of individuals.

This chapter considers the various stages of the strategic planning process and the roles and responsibilities for strategic planning within the information service and its parent organization. The hierarchy of objectives is also explored in terms of time-scale, management responsibility and relationships to the organizational structure.

Roles and responsibilities

Prior to embarking on the strategic planning process the roles and responsibilities of all of the stakeholders should be defined. All stakeholders who have the potential to be affected should be involved. This includes customers and suppliers, members of the governing body and funding allocators.

To be effective strategic planning requires the commitment and involvement of senior management. There has to be a clear understanding throughout the organization of its purpose and value, and of the process. The process will fail if inadequate time or resources are spent on it, or if there is a lack of commitment to the process. There should also be good communication channels throughout the organization.

Whilst senior management will not produce the plan alone, their personal commitment and involvement are crucial to its long-term effectiveness. Their roles are to be the initiators of the process, to encourage support and to oversee the process. An important responsibility of senior management is to create the necessary environment to dispel fears and encourage the enthusiasm that allows other employees and stakeholders to have input into the strategic planning process.

Planning must not only be wanted, it should be seen to be wanted. All too often it is associated with negative connotations: it is viewed either as a mechanism for organizational reorganization that has the capacity to engender a loss of power or position, or as a waste of time and resources. The enthusiasm for strategic planning can be enhanced by discussing the successes in organizations where it has been used; by explaining how other information services have benefited from strategic planning, and in revealing how proper strategic planning benefits both the communications and decision-making processes within organizations.

The initial introduction and handling of the management issues associated with the strategic planning process will greatly influence employees' perceptions of it and their long-term enthusiasm for its implementation. The process may threaten individuals or require attitude changes amongst the staff. Their reason for existence, control or power over information may be threatened. Careful handling of the process may pay dividends at the time when the planning process is implemented. If all staff are involved from the beginning in the planning process of their own particular areas and are allowed to participate in some decision-making, they will identify more readily with the strategic plan and actively support its implementation.

The strategic planning process should be an integrated and two-way process involving the managers of all the corporate resources. The manager of the information service should be involved in setting the direction for the parent organization. The strategic plan for the organization should set the strategic direction for the information service. The strategic direction for the information service should also be aligned with those of the human, financial and technology resources.

Line management must be motivated to value and spend time on the proactive planning process. The allocation of such time will be in competition with shortages in personal time to manage the other issues of the day. In order to allocate the necessary priority to the strategic planning process a formalized system should be used that allocates time and resources to the task. Line management is responsible for championing the value and importance of the strategic planning process within the organization, and also to use the process to strengthen their delivery of services to the whole community. The manager's contribution to the strategic planning process should be assessed as part of their individual performance appraisal.

The strategic plan

The documented output of the strategic planning process is 'the strategic plan'. This is the written record of the organization's vision, mission statement, its objectives and the mechanisms to achieve them. The plan should be objectives-driven as it is primarily concerned with outcomes. It should also present a clear rationale for the specific objectives, give a clear impression of the relative priorities, provide a choice of strategies and provide the justification for all projects, activities and resources. The planning process may be tailored to suit the needs of the organization.

The objectives should be developed at two levels: strategic and operational. The strategic objectives should be geared to increasing the organization's flexibility, ability to adjust to change and capacity for creativity. They should lead to the definition of operational objectives, policies and standards.

The strategic objectives are operationalized into operational plans and objectives. These provide the details of the services to be delivered to meet the strategic objectives, together with an estimation of the resources required. A set of results and outcomes, qualified by performance measures and a timetable for their achievement should be provided for each service or project. The operational plan should also identify how the human, financial, information and technical resources are to be acquired and used to achieve the strategic objectives.

The plan should be flexible, enabling smooth and quick adjustments where necessary. However, it should not need extensive modification and ought to be abandoned if this is the case. When the plan has outlived its usefulness, it should be replaced by another as part of a continuous planning cycle. The replacement plan should not be an extrapolation of the old. It requires the rethinking of the future in the light of the existing environment and prospective changes. The plans should be kept simple and straightforward as complex plans are difficult to understand, implement and monitor.

The strategic planning process

Vision and mission

The first task of the strategic planning process (see Figure 4.1) is to determine the desired future position, or vision, in terms of outcomes. The vision statement should articulate the desired state of being. From this, a mission statement is created. If a separate mission statement is to be developed for the information service, it should reflect the mission statement of the parent organization. It should clearly identify the core business and purpose of the information service in contributing to the wider organizational mission statement. The mission statement also identifies those critical factors that distinguish the service from its competitors. It may be a declaration of attitude or value that establishes the organizational climate, or a quality statement about customer service delivery.

These statements serves as the focal point for individuals to identify with the organization's purpose and direction. They provide information about the future direction of the organization and its customer base. In order to be readily understood and remembered by all stakeholders, the wording should be simple and explicit.

The mission statement should avoid being too prescriptive. It should be written in such a manner that avoids:

- a narrow perspective of the information service's role;
- the assumption that the information service will be the sole deliverer of specific services;
- locking the information service into outdated technology or service provision; and
- consideration of options in service delivery.

Situation audit

The next stage of the strategic planning process is to conduct the situation audit. This involves:

Vision and mission statements *Strategic plan*
Determine future position and desired state of being
Define mission in terms of core business and distinguish service from others

Situation audit *Environments*
Assess internal and external environmental factors
Evaluate current resources and performance
Identify desired future outcomes
Develop broad policy statements

Needs assessment
Define stakeholders' needs
Identify gap between current and desired service levels
Forecast future needs

Objectives
Develop strategic objectives in terms of results or outcomes
Determine operational objectives in line with opportunities
and constraints

Programmes
Establish programmes and implement through activities and tasks
Link organizational structure to programme structure

Programme review
Monitor programmes and evaluate progress towards achieving objectives
Revise objectives and programmes where appropriate

Figure 4.1   The strategic planning process

- the identification of the internal and external environmental factors that impact upon the information service and its parent organization;
- a strategic audit of the organizational issues;
- the analysis of critical success factors, SWOT analysis, and capability profile;
- an outline of the present level of resources and organizational performance;
- statements of policy and managerial philosophies;
- the formal and informal mandates imposed on the information service;
- a statement of the desired future in terms of major results and outcomes; and
- a statement of organization-wide objectives that represent the philosophical basis for the information service's operations and articulate the desired future conditions to be achieved.

Needs assessment

The needs assessment provides additional environmental information for the development of the plan. It enables the information service to:

- identify the gap between the current provision and desired level of service;
- forecast future needs;
- plan provision to meet such needs in good time; and
- ensure that the operational policies are effective in meeting real needs.

The needs assessment should not just relate to customers of the information service. All stakeholders, including potential customers, should be involved. Many sources of information can be used to provide input to the needs assessment. For example, previous customer surveys, community analyses, census figures and organizational reports.

The needs analysis should not be solely reliant upon the staff's professional judgement or indicators such as (lack of) volume of complaints, comments or suggestions by customers and other stakeholders. To do so may provide a bias that could lead to an inaccurate assessment of service needs. Underestimation and overestimation are two other pitfalls. Underestimation may arise when the needs of non-vocal sectors of the community are overlooked. Overestimation of needs can occur by not being aware that a large sector of the customer base is satisfied with the existing provision of service.

The preliminary stage of clarifying what is meant by a need in a particular programme area can be useful in that it forces management and customers to examine their real objectives and definition of needs. The concept of need implies a normative judgement: a particular level of need is arbitrary and depends upon attitude. Ideas of what constitutes need can change over time and circumstances in the same way that motivational needs change. 'Wants' and 'needs' should be distinguished; for example, you may *want* to drive a Mercedes or Porsche to work, yet you may only *need* a bicycle.

Surveys of both customers and potential customers can be important mechanisms for the collection of information about customer needs. They can be comparatively expensive to conduct and require careful planning to provide valid and meaningful results. If such surveys are not properly planned, incorrect information may be obtained that could result in the implementation of a programme totally unsuited to the real needs of the community. This could eventually be more costly to the information service in financial, political and social terms than the original costs in conducting the survey.

Implemented correctly, surveys can be a valuable planning tool. However they should not be relied upon as a 'proven management technique' at the expense of other methods. The manager's 'gut feeling' that arises from a close involvement and working knowledge of the situation should also be considered.

Having determined the future stakeholder needs, and using information obtained from the situation audit relating to the present level of service delivery and existing resources, the objectives can be developed.

Objectives

Hierarchy of objectives

Objectives may be distinguished according to their level in the hierarchy (see Figure 4.2). There is a relationship between level, scope and impact on the organization and the time frame for implementation. The highest level objectives – the strategic objectives – relate to the organization in its entirety and are usually long term. The objectives become more specific at the lower levels in terms of application within the organization. They are also shorter in time frame.

The hierarchy continues in terms of programmes, projects or activities, and tasks. Activities and tasks are directly related to subsets of the objectives and programmes. They are usually short term or repetitive, easily measurable and relate to groups or individuals.

The hierarchy is generally shaped like a pyramid. The broader and more future-oriented objectives are fewer in number and appear at the pinnacle of the pyramid. The immediate or short-term objectives are to be found in greater numbers. They are more precise in definition and quantification.

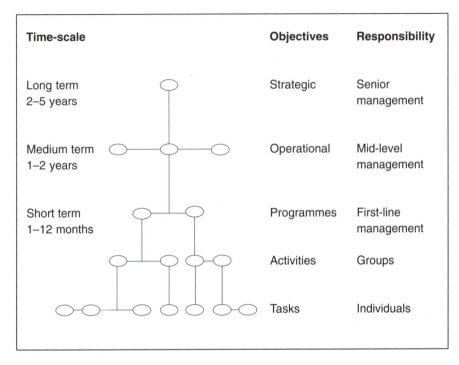

Time-scale		Objectives	Responsibility
Long term 2–5 years		Strategic	Senior management
Medium term 1–2 years		Operational	Mid-level management
Short term 1–12 months		Programmes	First-line management
		Activities	Groups
		Tasks	Individuals

Figure 4.2   The hierarchy of objectives

Developing objectives

The strategic objectives should be long term in nature and allow for improvement and co-ordination of corporate operations. Operational objectives are mid- and short-term focused, and are translated in turn into programmes and activities. These are framed with inputs, outputs and constraints in mind. Resources for these are allocated through established functions such as the budget process.

Objectives should be developed within the context of the situation audit and the needs assessment. Opportunities for better service delivery or internal productivity gains should be considered as well as the impact of any known constraints on resources. The parent organization's management philosophies or political ideologies may also shape the development of objectives for the information service.

Effectively formulated objectives should result in concrete outcomes desired by the organization. The formulation of meaningful objectives takes careful thought and analysis. The intention of the objective should be clear and its focus well understood. It should stimulate the action as well as specify it. The objectives must be challenging yet capable of achievement. They should be written so that they can be analysed and reviewed.

Objectives should be defined in terms of results or conditions to be achieved rather than in terms of the activities to be performed, as it is against the objectives that performance will be measured. They should be stated in positive terms, that is, in terms of what is to be achieved rather than in terms of what is to be avoided. Above all the objectives should be quantifiable, since the more concrete the information, the more likely will be the achievement of real meaning. An example of a hierarchy of objective within an information service is shown in Figure 4.3.

The quality of results is just as important as the type or kind of results. Time limits or delays in service provision, percentages, workload volumes and frequency rates are measurable points that can be incorporated into information service objectives. Quantifiable objectives and outcomes define and clarify the expectations and results better than verbal descriptions. They provide a built-in measure of effectiveness.

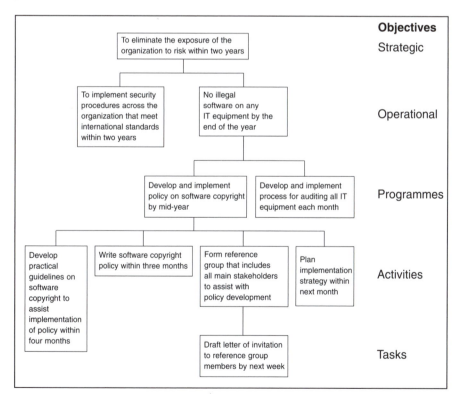

Figure 4.3　An example of hierarchy of objectives in an information service

Programmes

The development of programmes takes place after consideration of the alternative strategies whereby the objectives can be achieved. It should be a creative and innovative process, with only the best possible alternative selected. The programmes selected should represent the best possible use of resources when considered against all other possible uses. Each programme selected should lead to improved organizational performance or service delivery and derive the greatest possible benefit for the least cost. The evaluation of programme alternatives should assess not only the financial and economic costs and benefits, but also the social and political costs and benefits. Outcomes (quality and quantity) should be measured against inputs.

Programmes are implemented by organizing activities and allocating tasks. Implementation of the plan at this level is often a difficult task as it invariably means organizational and personal change. The programmes are often linked to the organizational structure. Consequently any significant change in programme structure may involve an internal reorganization. Strategies for dealing with the required change should be considered prior to the introduction of the new programmes. Responsibilities should be assigned, and monitoring and control processes devised, to measure progress towards the attainment of goals.

In addition to linking organizational structure into programme structure, successful planning processes tie implementation strategies into action plans. For example, personnel should be recruited with skills and outlooks that reinforce the strategies. Personnel performance review systems should be also linked into the achievement of programmes and activities.

In implementing programmes, the emphasis should be on the outcomes of the decisions rather than the techniques by which the decisions are made. Successful implementations are those that improve the quality of service delivery through employee motivation and an increased commitment to the organization's goals. Positive results should be highlighted and reinforced. Short-term improvements can be made permanent through positive reinforcement, monitoring and review.

Information-sharing is paramount. All staff are entitled to be fully informed. The need for staff to contribute and be involved in operational decision-making is important. This collaborative approach anticipates that all employees have a commitment to the achievement of organizational goals. It shares the onus of high performance amongst all members of the organization. Mutual discussion regarding the implementation of programmes includes agreement upon resources and assistance necessary to achieve stated objectives. This leads to more effective co-ordination and co-operation throughout the organization. Improvements in management–

employee relationships may be expected due to the increased communication and participation in the objective-setting process and feedback at the performance review stage.

Critical to the success of the implementation of the planning process is the need to determine the proper sequencing and relationships of the activities. Appropriate starting and completion dates must be set in order to avoid plans being implemented before the strategies for dealing with the resultant changes are considered. Appropriate financial, human, information and technical resources must be made available at the right time and in the right place.

Programme review

The success of the strategic planning process can be recognized in the achievement of the organization's goals. Often the planning process is considered to be complete upon the implementation of the programme. This is not so. The last and most significant part is the evaluation of the process and the measurement of the success of the selected programmes. Evaluation through monitoring and review processes is the accountability aspect of planning. It determines whether the objectives are being achieved. It also provides important feedback to fine tune the delivery of services to meet customer needs. More detail on this issue can be found in Chapter 38, 'Performance measurement and evaluation'.

5   Human resource planning

Introduction

People are an organization's most valuable resource, yet salaries and associated overheads such as superannuation are often the most expensive component of the budget. Managed appropriately, an organization's workforce is its lifeblood. Managed inappropriately, the workforce becomes an expensive commitment that leads to few rewards but many problems.

Successful planning and management of human resources are critical for overall organizational effectiveness. The organization's skills, knowledge and experience requirements should relate to its objectives and programmes. Human resource management involves more than developing procedures for annual review, and equal opportunity. It is a complex process that ensures that people are given the opportunity to develop both their personal and professional competencies and so maximize their output and contribution to the organization's effectiveness.

Every manager has to be aware of the relationships between the management of human resources and other resources, as well as the need to plan for the more effective and efficient use of their staff. Motivation, training and personal development are recognized techniques for improving personal performance and efficiency. The emphasis is on the need to 'marry' the job, the person and the situation.

Effective human resource management is planned and executed at a macro (strategic) and micro (operational) level. Macro human resource management planning and forecasting activities relate to the overall organizational objectives. They are dependent upon the organization's strategic plans for its future (e.g. projections for growth or diversification). Micro human resource management activities relate to personnel processes that affect individuals.

An integrated approach

Like all planning, human resource planning should be a continuous and proactive process. It should take into account external and internal environmental influences in both the information service and its parent organization. Personnel programmes and activities should be related to the organizational objectives. There should also be mechanisms for review and feedback (see Figure 5.1). As part of the integrated planning approach, the human resource planning process for the information service will be influenced by the parent organization's other resource planning strategies and its human resource policies.

The two external factors that are most likely to affect human resource planning and employment practices are industrial relations legislation and systems, and the supply and demand for labour. Unions may also be influential in classifying positions or work practices. Awards and workplace agreements often govern conditions of employment. The supply of labour is affected by economic conditions, changes in academic requirements and the organization's ability to attract and keep appropriately skilled people.

Internally, the size, structure, culture and type of organization affect human resource planning. Its degree of specialization, personnel configurations, professionalism, formalization, and its technology and financial capacity have the potential to attract different types of people.

Once the organization's skills, knowledge and experience requirements have been identified through the strategic planning process, management then has to determine how these requirements can be met. The job analysis process identifies the necessary characteristics and skills to properly fulfil the responsibilities of the job as described by the job description and job specification. Once the position requirements have been adequately described the position can be filled. This may be through identifying existing staff who have the required expertise, recruiting new people with the required skills and expertise, or developing and retraining existing staff. Appropriate selection processes should be developed to ensure that the required skills, knowledge and experience are obtained. The input stage is completed through the placement of the right employee in the right position.

A number of management processes can be used to effectively develop individuals so that their performance contributes to the objectives of the information service. Proper orientation and induction allow the employee to become conversant with the job and how this relates to the information service's programmes and activities. If the employee is new to the organization, the induction process should also provide them with insight into the information service and its parent organization's culture and objectives. The induction programme is the first stage of a number of activities that enhance the development and performance of both the person and the job.

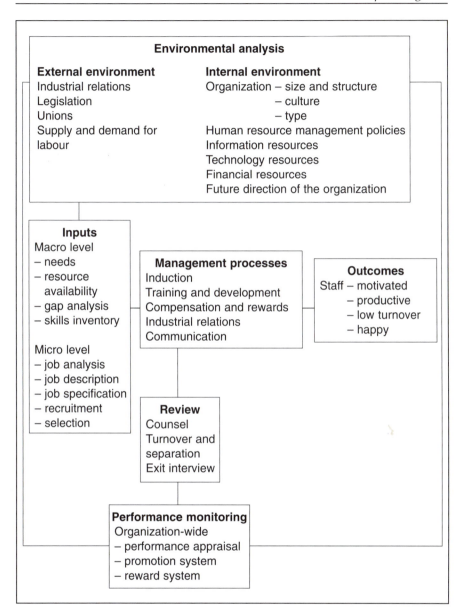

Figure 5.1   The integrated approach to human resource planning

Further training and development should take place on a regular basis. This should be a balance between the individual's personal training and development needs that have been identified as part of a performance appraisal system, and those that are tied to the organization's and work group's programmes and activities. Training and development may take the form of on-the-job training, attendance at conferences and seminars, management placement programmes, targeted management or professional courses or further study.

An appropriate compensation and reward system is required as well as a system for managing industrial relations. The latter provides for arbitration and appropriate grievance procedures. Finally, good communication is the basis to human resource management.

The development of a performance monitoring and appraisal system across the whole of the organization should be tied to the organizational objectives. Opportunities for internal promotion should also be developed and a reward system put in place to encourage productivity and innovation. These opportunities are also important in creating a highly motivated staff and maintaining morale levels.

Monitoring and review processes can be in the form of counselling and disciplinary action where negative activities are identified, with organizational-wide rewards, recognition and promotional opportunities being available to reinforce positive ideas and output. Transfer and separation are other activities associated with review. Feedback mechanisms can also be found at the macro level in the organization-wide performance appraisal.

The aim of all these processes is to create a highly motivated staff who are creative, productive and happy. A further aim is to ensure that the turnover rate is low as any change is disruptive in terms of organizational efficiency and effectiveness.

Macro approach

The macro approach to human resource planning can be broken down into various stages (see Figure 5.2). Stage one consists of the determination of requirements based upon the environmental analysis. It looks at what the organization is trying to achieve and how well structured it is to do the job. It also takes into account the productivity, growth, developmental stage of the information service and its parent organization, together with any other influencing factors and trends. This is followed by a projection of the skills, knowledge and expertise required for the planning period (needs), as compared with the existing inventory (availability).

The next stage requires the identification of gaps between projected

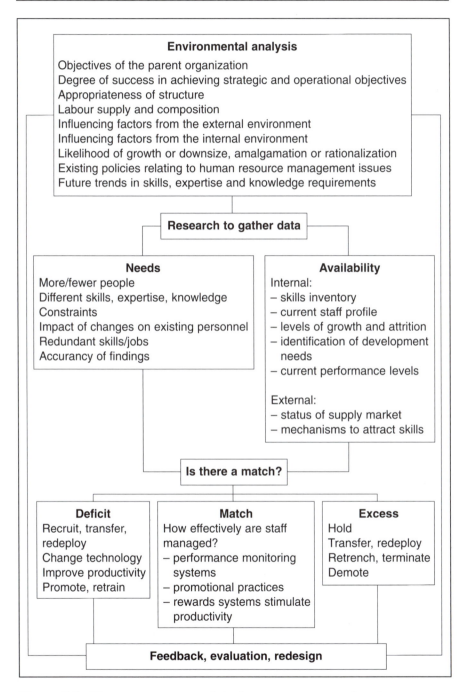

Environmental analysis
Objectives of the parent organization
Degree of success in achieving strategic and operational objectives
Appropriateness of structure
Labour supply and composition
Influencing factors from the external environment
Influencing factors from the internal environment
Likelihood of growth or downsize, amalgamation or rationalization
Existing policies relating to human resource management issues
Future trends in skills, expertise and knowledge requirements

Research to gather data

Needs
More/fewer people
Different skills, expertise, knowledge
Constraints
Impact of changes on existing personnel
Redundant skills/jobs
Accurancy of findings

Availability
Internal:
– skills inventory
– current staff profile
– levels of growth and attrition
– identification of development
  needs
– current performance levels

External:
– status of supply market
– mechanisms to attract skills

Is there a match?

Deficit
Recruit, transfer,
redeploy
Change technology
Improve productivity
Promote, retrain

Match
How effectively are staff
managed?
– performance monitoring
  systems
– promotional practices
– rewards systems stimulate
  productivity

Excess
Hold
Transfer, redeploy
Retrench, terminate
Demote

Feedback, evaluation, redesign

Figure 5.2 The macro approach to human resource planning

requirements and the current status, expressed either as a match, excess or deficit of personnel and skills. This may relate to specific skills, occupations or levels of staff and may not be consistent across the organization. Programmes may differ in their types of activities and require different skills and numbers of staff.

Alternative actions are considered to overcome anticipated gaps. These may involve recruitment, redeployment and/or termination of personnel, changing the technology, the redesign of jobs or reorganization of work processes to improve productivity, changing the skill and competency requirements for prospective employees, or developing skill-training programmes. Once an appropriate match has been achieved, the attention should turn to effectively managing the staff at the micro level.

Revision and alteration of the programme and/or objectives may be necessary, depending on the feedback. This stage of monitoring, feedback and revision ensures that the human resource planning process is continual and dynamic rather than periodic and formal.

The macro approach to human resource planning encourages organizations to plan for their future skills, expertise and staffing structures and to take into account changes in services and technology. Exercised properly, and on a continuing basis, it should eliminate problems of over-supply or under-supply of particular skills and expertise within the information service. It also aids in the determining of training needs in relation to required skills.

Skills inventory

A skills inventory is a management information system that describes the organization's workforce. Skills inventories may be designed for several purposes. For example, they may be used to strategically monitor workforce capabilities and performance, or to assist in the identification of employees for promotion, transfer and/or training. The usefulness of any skills inventory depends upon the appropriateness, accessibility and current validity of the data. A simple file system may be adequate for a small, relatively stable organization, whilst a computerized data system, updated daily, may be required for a large, more dynamic organization.

Micro approach

The micro approach to human resource planning reflects the interface of individuals with their jobs. As part of operational planning it covers personnel selection and placement, training, appraisal and staff development. The micro approach is systematic. It begins with a job analysis and ends with the exit interview. This interview takes place at the time of separation between the employee and the organization (see Figure 5.3).

Job analysis

Job analysis is the process of studying and collecting information relating to the operations and responsibilities of a specific job. It is fundamental to the preparation of the job specification and job description.

The process of collecting data usually consists of interviews (individual or group), observation, questionnaires, filming activities, the keeping of daily diaries or timesheets, and written descriptions. Observation is a particularly useful method of data collection if the job is simple and repetitive. If this is coupled with an interview, it may result in the provision of information that is not readily observable. The interview will also allow verbal verification of information already obtained from observing job practices. A sincere, attentive and assuring attitude on behalf of the interviewer is required to ensure accurate and complete information, since job analysts are often viewed with suspicion.

Questionnaires and written descriptions rely upon the ability of the job holder to provide an organized and complete report of the job. These skills are not always forthcoming at lower levels in the organization hierarchy where report writing and analytical skills may not be required. In such cases, daily diaries or timesheets provide a more structured approach to analysing tasks.

The job analysis provides details on a quantitative as well as a qualitative basis. Quantitative statements refer to such factors as the size of the work group and the number of times a task is performed per hour, day or week. Qualitative statements refer to working conditions, and personnel requirements. Often the job is broken down into elementary units or tasks; the focus being on the work activity itself. This is called the task-oriented approach.

A second approach to analysing jobs is the person-oriented job approach. This approach analyses the generalized human behaviours required to do the work. Similarities and differences are described in terms of processes that are common to all jobs, not idiosyncratic to one particular job. The third approach is to analyse the underlying competencies and abilities required to perform the work.

A variety of information is collected. This includes a description of the work activities performed, for example, scanning copies of all correspondence received or applying a bibliographic description to an item. The purpose of the work, the procedures used and the frequency of the procedures are noted. Work-oriented behaviours are listed. These include details of equipment used, for example, a fax machine, word-processing

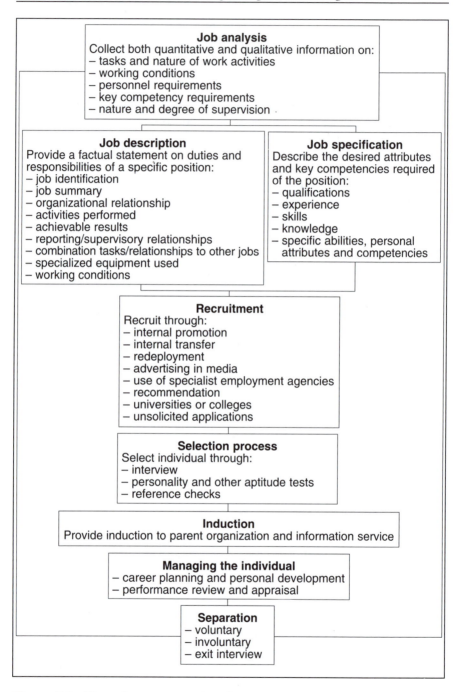

Figure 5.3   The micro approach to human resource planning

facilities or geographic information system. The proportions of time spent sitting, standing, moving about and the amount of time devoted to, or the importance of, communication or decision-making skills may also be noted. Individual demands such as aptitude, personality or physical characteristics are also included in work-orientated behaviours.

The job analysis should also collect information on accountability, that is, the reporting mechanisms and levels of responsibility. The nature of the supervision, for example, clerical, administrative, technical or professional together with its extent (as in continuous or close supervision) should also be noted.

Job description

The first and immediate product of the job analysis is the job description. This is a descriptive, factual statement of the activities and responsibilities of a specific job. The following information is usually provided:

1 *Job identification*: Includes such information as job title, alternative title, department, division and code number for the job.
2 *Organizational relationships*: Identifies the position within the organizational structure. It usually provides details of the hierarchy of positions in terms of the immediate manager of the position, the other positions that also report to the immediate manager and the employee positions reporting immediately to the position.
3 *Job summary*: Provides a short definition of the job itself, which is useful as additional identification when the job title is not sufficient. It also serves as a summary to orient the reader towards an understanding of the detailed information that follows.
4 *Activities performed*: This is the heart of the job description. It describes what is to be done, how it is to be done and the purpose behind each activity. If possible, activities should be arranged in chronological or some other systematic order. An estimation of the approximate percentage of time devoted to each major activity is helpful as is the degree of supervision received.
5 *Achievable results*: Provides some measure of performance or standards that describes what the position is to achieve and the minimal acceptable employee performance of the specified activities.
6 *Reporting–supervising functions*: Identifies the immediate reporting positions and the degree of supervision received and given.
7 *Combination tasks and relationship to other jobs*: Identifies the vertical and horizontal relationships of workflow and procedures, and the positions within the organization with which co-ordination is required.
8 *Specialist equipment*: Lists and defines each main type of technology,

knowledge and equipment used; where possible trade names should be identified.

9   *Working conditions*: Checklists are often used to indicate working conditions, using such alternatives as hot, cold, dry, dusty, noisy, etc. Hazardous conditions should be noted.

Definitions of technical terms and other comments that clarify the above can be included.

Job descriptions form the basis for human resource planning, recruitment and position management. They can be used to provide intending applicants and new appointees with details of the idiosyncrasies of the position. Job descriptions are also useful in settling industrial disputes. Results-oriented job descriptions provide for some measure of performance and the beginning of a description of the outcomes required for the position. They also serve as a useful basis for staff appraisal.

Job descriptions need to be continuously updated if they are to be effective. Otherwise they become irrelevant and ignored. Unfortunately it is often the case that a job description is only updated when a position becomes vacant and a new staff member is to be appointed. An ideal opportunity to update the job description is at the time of the annual performance appraisal interview. As information service positions usually centre around rapidly changing technology, environmental changes in such technologies make the updating of job descriptions an important task. For this reason it is also helpful to write job descriptions in dynamic terms.

Job descriptions need to leave some scope for initiative and innovation on the part of the incumbent. If they are too specific and detailed, they can allow the incumbent merely to continue the practices of his or her predecessor, thereby stifling initiative and creativity and failing to lead to any improvement in productivity or service delivery.

The value of job descriptions depends very much on how they are used and updated in the information service. At best their value extends beyond the recruitment stage. They should be referred to at times of staff appraisal and when considering staff development and manpower planning. To be of true value, they should be results orientated and written in dynamic terms to allow for changing work environments.

Job specification

Whereas the job description describes the job, the job specification describes the desired attributes of the person doing the job. It is a statement of the minimum acceptable human competencies and qualities required to perform a job properly. Such requirements are usually established for individual jobs on the basis of judgements (such as those of the job analyst), but in some instances they are based upon statistical validation procedures.

The job specification can include the following aspects:

1 *Information inputs to the position*: Interpretations of perceptions, verbal or auditory interpretation, environmental awareness, visual input from materials – for example, visual appraisal of condition of stock in a library.
2 *Mental processes*: Decision-making, information processing, use of job-related knowledge.
3 *Education*: The level of education and specific qualifications.
4 *Physical output*: Manual or control activities, physical co-ordination required, skills and technical abilities, use of equipment, technology.
5 *Supervisory skills*: Supervising of staff activities, public contact, communication of instructions, directions or other related job information, interpersonal communication skills.
6 *Job context*: Potentially stressful/unpleasant environment, potentially hazardous job situations, personally demanding situations.
7 *Other job characteristics*: Attention-demanding activities, vigilant/discriminating activities, structured/unstructured activities, continuity of workload.

Work experience may also be included.

The job specification should be used as a guideline to the knowledge, skills and competencies required to perform a specific job. It should not be allowed to dictate the recruitment process to the extent that, all other things being equal, an applicant who is qualified and capable but deficient in some aspect fails to be appointed.

The main qualifications or qualities required for a job are easy to analyse, as there are fairly acceptable standards of education recognized by all. However, the degree to which each is required to fill the job is harder to ascertain. The degree of training is usually defined in specific terms, for example, the completion of a specific programme. Alternatively it may be defined quantitatively such as the ability to undertake word-processing at so many words per minute. The ability to read, write or count and, in the case of positions attracting non-English-speaking migrants, the ability to understand a minimum of English may be a job qualification. The degree of experience required is best defined in actual job experience, either in the job itself or in a related job. A time measure of experience is sometimes specified, for instance, 'a minimum of three years experience in systems analysis'.

Aptitude, intelligence and personality requirements are usually expressed in such terms as possession of an outgoing personality, clerical aptitude, or the ability to relate to people from differing backgrounds.

As it is used in the recruitment of personnel, the job specification can be condensed and form part of the original advertisement. It should be given to prospective applicants along with the job description so that they are fully informed of the position for which they are applying.

The job specification should form the basis upon which applications are initially screened. It should be used as a comparison between the qualifications of the applicants and the main qualifications required for the job. At the time of the interview, the interviewer should formulate questions to evaluate the interviewee in terms of the qualities and qualifications outlined in the job specification.

The recruitment process

Applicants may be recruited from two sources – internal sources or sources external to the organization. Filling a position internally has the advantage of increasing the general level of morale by providing an example of career path development within the information service. It is a reward mechanism for good work, and may stimulate others to greater achievement. The process of recruiting internally may be more predictable in its outcome as some information relating to the applicant's history of work performance within the organization will be known. Whilst there is a risk that it may contain some subjective observations, the internal information may generally be more reliable than the curriculum vitae or external references furnished by external applicants.

Internal promotion is not always in the organization's best interest. External sources may provide more highly skilled applicants than those on the existing staff, or the organization may need some 'new blood' injected into it.

A number of external sources for recruiting information service personnel are available. These include recruitment advertising, employment agencies, recommendations by present employees, educational institutions, unsolicited or casual applicants or networking.

Advertisements

Advertisements may be placed in the local or national press, trade journals or professional media. The choice of media will depend upon the level of the position to be advertised. Information relating to the organization, job description and specification should be included in the advertisement to assist in self-screening. The advertisement should include the name of the organization, the name of a contact person and telephone number or e-mail address for further details, closing date, person or place to whom applications should be sent and application details required.

The advertisement layout, design and copy should reflect an accurate image of the information service. It should reflect the organization's size and whether the organization is conservative or progressive, centralized or decentralized, dynamic or static. High-quality design can boost the immediate response as well as the organization's image. Advertisements are governed by media deadlines. In general, the more frequent the publication, the shorter will be the deadline, for example a local newspaper will have a shorter deadline than a professional or trade journal.

Employment agencies

Employment agencies can be used to screen potential applicants. Employment agencies want to keep their customers happy by working towards the customer's goal, and they do this by effective advertisement design and placement of staff. Both public and private employment agencies can be used. Often government employment agencies have a professional division for the recruitment of qualified personnel. One concern of using employment agencies, particularly private ones, is the commission that they charge and the cost of their artwork and typesetting. However, some of these costs would also be incurred by the information service in its own placement of advertisements and in time spent sifting through letters of application and the advising and conducting of interviews.

Recommendations

Current employees may suggest prospective candidates for job vacancies. In considering this alternative, it is presumed that the employee knows both the organization and the acquaintance, and would therefore want to please both. The hiring of relatives is an inevitable component of recruitment programmes. Some organizations have policies that prevent this practice. Such a policy does not necessarily coincide with hiring on the basis of merit, but interest and loyalty to the enterprise can be offsetting advantages.

Education institutions

As in the above alternative, staff in education institutions are often in positions to advise on outstanding candidates or suitable newly qualified professionals. Some institutions maintain a job register or have bulletin boards where advertisements can be displayed.

Unsolicited applications

Unsolicited applications, both in person or by mail, provide a source of recruitment. Policies differ between organizations as to how such applications are handled. Some keep all applications for future reference, whilst others note only outstanding ones. Others refuse to take such applications, advising applicants to apply again when formal advertisements appear in the media.

Selection processes

Interviewing

The most widely used method of selecting individuals for jobs is the interview. The aim of the interview is threefold: to collect information about the applicant; to give information to the applicant; and to begin the induction process for the successful applicant. Interviews are useful in assessing an applicant's intelligence, level of motivation and interpersonal skills.

Interviewers are similar to fortune-tellers in that they are in the business of predicting which of the applicants best fit the future direction of the information service. The interviewer has various roles:

- initiating and conducting the interview as they think fit;
- communicating with the others present;
- acting as an observer noting behaviour, speech and other non-verbal communications;
- analysing, listening and watching actions;
- evaluating and correctly interpreting;
- drawing conclusions to what has been seen and heard;
- mind-reading and putting aside what has been said in exchange for what has not been said but is in the mind;
- making objective judgements at the *end* of the interview;
- listening for meaning in order to determine the context correctly; and
- to counsel and to identify emotions, relating these to their cause.

Interviewers must be able to perform two basic functions: to acquire only relevant information and to interpret data correctly, once it has been acquired. To carry out these functions the interviewer needs to have the following qualities: a warm and engaging manner and an ability to quickly establish rapport; a sensitivity to social situations; a quickness in perceiving implications in the remarks of others; a sensitivity to vocal intonation and hesitation; a mental level as high as or higher than that of applicants, enabling them to take control of the situation; and an analytical mind with the ability to make critical judgements, enabling correct evaluation of all factors. Interviewers should also have an open mind and be adaptable, and should also possess a mature personality, showing evidence of sound practical judgement.

The interviewers should show concern for the applicant's feelings while maintaining control over the interview. They should convey a feeling of interest in the applicant by reacting appropriately to the applicant's comments, questions and non-verbal behaviours. An atmosphere of warmth and trust should be created. Interviews should make use of encouragement and praise in order to put the applicant at ease.

A considerable amount of planning is required for employment interviews. The interview questions should be directly related to the activities of the position and the skills, expertise and knowledge requirements that are critical to the performance within the job. There should be an interview committee so that answers are rated by more than one person. It is preferable that both males and females are selected for the interviewing committee, and that there is a balance of management and personnel skills between them.

If the interview is used by itself, it is most important that both equity and equality prevail in the process. Without a proper structure and process, a certain amount of subjectivity could occur. This may occur through a lack of knowledge in the person(s) conducting the interview; or, the 'halo effect' which causes the interviewer(s) to read into discussions an intent that was not intended.

All procedures should be consistently followed to ensure that each applicant has exactly the same chance. The committee should determine in advance a set of questions that can be consistently applied to each applicant, and the same questions should be asked in the same order by the same member of the committee. Incomplete answers or problem areas should be probed whilst maintaining an atmosphere of trust. It is useful for the interviewing committee to have determined sample answers to questions in advance so that interviewee responses can then be rated on an explicitly defined scale. Answers to questions should be documented for future reference and in case of legal challenge. Basic information questions given on the application forms should not be repeated.

Interviews are a two-way process. The interviewer should deliver appropriate and accurate information about the information service and its parent organization to the interviewee. The prospective applicant also evaluates the organization and makes decisions as to its suitability as an employing body. The interview is often the first contact with the information service and provides the first impression of its culture and dynamics.

Correct interviewing procedures set realistic job expectations. Applicants should be able to determine through the interview whether the position meets their own needs for personal development. If there is a fit between their personal expectations for the position and the employer's description of the job, their needs will match the job. There will be high job survival, job satisfaction and less likelihood of resignation. The outcomes should result in a motivated, satisfied staff.

If an incorrect decision is taken on the strength of the interview the results can be expensive, not only in financial terms for the organization, but also in terms of morale. If a too high or too low level of expectation has been set for either the applicant or the job, then their subsequent experience in the job could result in a realization that the job does not suit, with a corresponding loss of morale for both the individual and his or her co-workers. Any thoughts of resignation could affect the productivity of the individual and unsettle other members of staff.

Other selection processes

Other selection tests should preferably be administered in conjunction with the interview, since such tests provide a more objective approach to personnel selection. Written tests can be used to test intelligence, aptitude, ability and interest. Performance job simulations such as work-sampling create a miniature replica of a job. Through work sampling, applicants are able to demonstrate the degree to which they can do the job. These processes offer additional dimensions to the selection process.

Induction

The induction process is a very important facet of management as it establishes what is required of the new employee. Induction also orientates and introduces the new employee to the organization. It can be provided either formally or informally. The first phase is often conducted by the personnel unit (if one exists). It should provide background information to the organization, employee benefits, salary schedules, safety, probationary period, time recording and absences, holidays, grievance procedures, hours of work, lunch and coffee breaks, and use of facilities.

The second phase is performed by the immediate supervisor. It should provide information relating to the information service's environment and include visits to other departments within the organization, introductions to all senior officers and a complete overview of special programmes or facilities within the organization. It is at this stage that the new employee will begin to be aware of the norms and values of the parent organization's and information service's corporate culture and subcultures. The new employee may need some explanation as to why certain things occur and what values are most prevalent within the organization. A typical induction programme follows the format listed below:

First day

- *Review* employee's work experience, education and training.
- *Greet personally*. When the new employee arrives do not leave them standing or waiting unattended. Make them feel welcome. Greet them by name, and address them by it often. Show friendliness.
- *Put them at ease*. They are likely to feel nervous or uneasy at first. Avoid any impression that they arrived at an awkward time. If you cannot see to them immediately, apologize and arrange for someone else to look after them. Discuss their background and interests.
- *Show interest*. Make them feel that the job genuinely needs them. Ask questions in a friendly tone – do not interrogate. Invite questions from them and act in accordance with the genuineness of the invitation. Enquire if they have any problems.
- *Explain* the work to be done. Do not make it sound too difficult. It is often easier to break it up into tasks. Tell them when, where and how they will be paid and other specific conditions of the position. Have their job description available for discussion.
- *Introduce* the new employee to their staff and other co-workers. Tell them whom they report to, and who reports to him or her.
- *Point out amenities*. Prevent them from feeling awkward; show them the work layout, particularly things that immediately concern them – for example, restroom facilities, canteen, locker-room, car park. Have their desk or office and supplies organized.
- *Show them the work*. Show them where they will be working. Introduce them to nearby workers. Avoid nicknames that could offend. Stay with them for a short time. Explain the work of the department, its relationship to the total organization and other departments. Clarify their position in the department, and the relationship to others in the department.
- *Instruct*. Before instructing them in their jobs, find out what they already know. Explain the task carefully step by step and be patient. Repeat key points until they understand. Indicate safety hazards and alert them to job standards. Do not give detailed instructions until they are at ease and have lost their nervousness.
- *Arrange guidance*. Identify the people to approach to solve work problems. Provide the new employee with a policy and procedures manual. Make sure they are not left alone to fend for themselves – this includes lunch-time and coffee breaks. Ensure that someone explains lunch arrangements and invites them to eat in company.
- *Maintain contact*. Meet them again on the job later in the day. Make sure they know where they are to report the following morning.

Second day

- *Make early contact.* Contact them within the first few hours of work. Check over things from the first day. Answer their questions readily. Look interested in their welfare.
- *Inform.* Explain in more detail how their work fits into overall activities. Provide information on things that affect them personally.
- *Maintain contact.* Make a point of seeing them, even if briefly, once more through the day. Encourage them to talk about problems they have encountered.

Within the first week

- *Give further information.* Contact them at least daily for the rest of the week. Help them to develop a sense of belonging. Ask them if they are interested in such things as social club activities and explain how they may participate.
- *Review.* Show interest in their progress. Help them with problems they have met, but avoid criticism. Be alert for personal problems that could affect the new employee's work performance. Clear up any misunderstanding.

Second week

- *Explain rules, norms and values.* Explain why rules are necessary and point out their application to other employees. Discuss the norms and values of the information service and its parent organization and how these affect employees.
- *Discuss informally.* Informal contact should be made about every second day. Listen for dissatisfaction. Counsel them or tell them what is proposed to resolve issues.

End of first month

- *Maintain regular contact.* Regular contact during the first month should help prevent grievances setting in. Make a point of speaking to them briefly at least three times a week.
- *Check progress.* By this time, if they have stayed, they should have settled down. Check their work. Correct errors by arranging further instruction, not by pointing up the failures. Do not reprimand them in public, relieve their embarrassment by correcting them in private.
- *Praise them.* If they have done a job well, tell them so. Let them know that their efforts are appreciated.

Within first three months

- *Review progress regularly.* If they have trouble settling down, a transfer to other work might be discussed.
- *Comment.* If their performance improves, let them know. Be generous and sincere in your comments.

Staff turnover and separation

Staff turnover can be beneficial or detrimental to the information service, depending on the net consequences. On the positive side it allows the opportunity to recruit people with new skills and outlooks and can increase the level of flexibility in the type and numbers of employees. This is particularly important for information services where technology, external environments and customer expectations rapidly change. There is often some financial gain in a controlled turnover of employees as this can contain the level of incremental salary creep.

The negatives are associated with expense in terms of finance, time and employee morale. Financial costs are incurred in severance pay, advertising and the recruitment of new personnel, and, in their orientation and training. There is often an associated downtime in the use of equipment and lost output and productivity until the new person gains the knowledge and skills of the previous incumbent.

There is an optimum turnover rate. This is the point between having insufficient turnover and having too much. Too slow a turnover rate will result in a staid information service; too high a turnover rate is unsettling and disruptive for those remaining and is often a symptom that there is a problem within the organization.

In information services, different jobs will frequently experience different turnover rates. The economic climate will also influence the turnover rate. There are various reasons why people leave organizations. Some of these are voluntary; such as for promotional reasons, to undertake a different career path, to experience a change in a work environment, or to retire. Individuals may also be transferred out of the information service, but still remain employed in another part of the organization. There are also occasions where the person leaves on an involuntary basis. These include redundancy and dismissal which need to be managed sensitively.

Redundancy

This occurs when employees are released from employment because the organization no longer has a need for their services. Redundancy may be temporary or permanent. It may also be voluntary or involuntary.

Redundancy may mean that the individual is placed elsewhere in the workforce, or it may mean total severance. Redundancy can arise through the introduction of new technologies, through business re-engineering, a takeover, or downsizing the organization's operations. Depending upon the reason for the redundancy and the individual, opportunities for retraining or reskilling may differ. The ability or age of some individuals may detract from their potential to be retrained.

Dismissal

This is probably the most distressing method of separation for both the manager and the individual as it may be the culmination of a difficult or emotional situation in terms of behaviour, performance or attitude.

Dismissal should only occur after attempts to improve or correct the offending aspects have failed. It should be recognized that at some stage, the individual concerned was recruited by the organization for their skills and attributes. Having employed the individual the organization has a responsibility to develop the person according to its needs and values. There is also a responsibility for ensuring that every opportunity is provided for an individual to succeed. This includes the provision of adequate communication, counselling, training and supervision. Managers also have a legal and ethical obligation to ensure that the person's case has been heard objectively and fairly before they are dismissed.

Information services should have formalized grievance procedures that are made known and accessible to management and staff. No employee should be dismissed for a first breach of discipline, and no disciplinary action should be taken unless the case has been carefully investigated.

The exit interview

Many managers overlook the exit interview as an opportunity to obtain feedback about their management style and the organization from an employee's viewpoint. Progressive organizations use the technique of holding an interview with employees at the time that they leave. This allows them to actively seek out suggestions that will enable them to be a better employer.

Whilst there should be mechanisms in place to provide for continuous feedback, the exit interview is sometimes more effective. Employees who are about to leave may feel more at liberty to make comments in the knowledge that their job is not threatened or that retaliative measures cannot be taken. Open communications should allow employees to bring their concerns to the attention of management at all times. However, some employees may only feel able to discuss matters that have been of concern to themselves or others when the bond between the employee, the manager and the organization is broken. The highlighting of both the positive and negative aspects of the organization should, if taken notice of, make the organization a better place to work. For example the exit interview might highlight inappropriate policies or procedures or ineffective communication channels that were previously unknown to management.

6 Information planning

Introduction

Information is an important resource that can be used by organizations to deliver more appropriate products or services to customers, and to enable the organization to be more competitive in the market-place. Quality, relevant and timely information can assist organizations to:

- plan and make appropriate decisions;
- better utilize resources and identify waste or inappropriate use;
- monitor quality and performance;
- meet legislative and regulatory requirements;
- recognize what their competitors are doing; and
- understand the mix of products and services their customers need.

Information needs to be planned for in the same way that human and financial resources are planned. An organization that has well thought out and systematic information planning processes will benefit more than one that does not. Information planning differs from information technology planning. Information planning relates to the content of the technology rather than the technology.

The essential objectives of the information planning process are to ensure that:

- an appropriate range of information is provided to meet the objectives of the organization, and its employees', customers' and stakeholders' information needs;
- all information that is critical to the organization is identified,

documented and kept secured;

- all information is managed and maintained in an integrated manner regardless of its source and format; and
- information content, information flows and delivery mechanisms are compatible with the business processes, decision-making and the information needs of the internal customers, customers of the parent organization and other external stakeholders.

The information needs of the parent organization's employees (the internal customers) should be distinguished from the information needs of the parent organization's external customers in the planning process and in service delivery. Whilst the information service will plan and deliver services to both customer groups, their needs may be very different. For example, the information services of a police service will need to support the police officers and civilian staff (the internal customers) in their operational roles in minimizing crime, maintaining security and presenting evidence relating to alleged offenders. The information needs of the customers of the police service itself (e.g. victims of crime, alleged offenders, the community) will be very different. Their information needs will relate more to their rights and responsibilities. The police service may also have other customers such as insurance companies, universities or crime research bureaux who may want to purchase or have access to statistical information relating to incidences such as break-ins or robbery in the form of information products.

Like human resource planning, information is planned and managed at the macro (strategic) and micro (operational) level (see Figure 6.1). The macro level planning includes the creation of an information architecture to support the mission and objectives of the organization. By analysing the strategies, functions and processes of the organization, an architecture can be planned and developed to support the information flows and underlying information needed for the organization to carry out its business.

The micro level processes concentrate on managing and maintaining the standard and quality of the information so that the information can be easily used. These processes assist in making the information consistent, relevant, accessible, concise and accurate.

The information planning process should be a continuous process that is totally integrated with the business strategy, the information requirements of employees, customers and other stakeholders, the organization's systems, its operations and technology. It should also be organizational-wide. Senior management must be involved and committed to the process. Their participation is key to assisting the organization anticipate its future business information requirements.

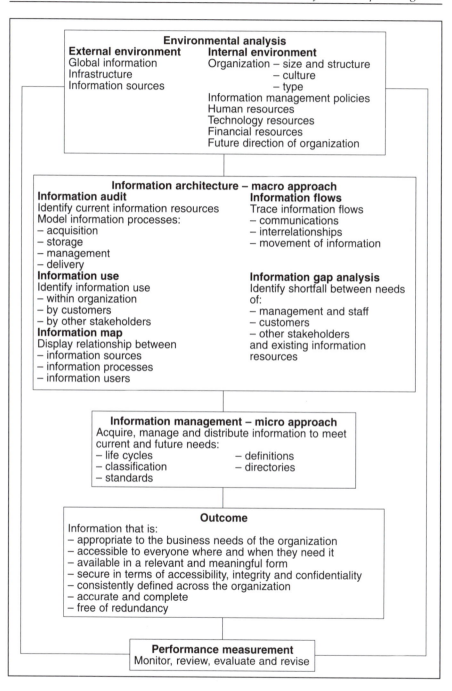

Figure 6.1 The integrated approach to information resource planning

Roles and responsibilities

Senior management should action and champion the information planning process. This is particularly important for the initial stages to ensure that the process is given the required impetus, status and commitment within the organization. Ongoing sponsorship of the management strategies at the macro level may be delegated to a senior manager, but it is imperative that the senior management continues to be seen to be supportive and involved in the process.

If the process is viewed seriously at this level, then others within the organization will be more willing to contribute their time and resources and ensure its success. It is important that the person who takes responsibility for the process has sufficient authority to override differences and resolve conflicting requirements that may arise from different parts of the organization.

As the role of the information service is to ensure that high-quality information is made available to decision-makers at all levels, it will play an intrinsic part in the planning process. Consultation regarding the information planning and management processes should be organization-wide and include other stakeholders who may either contribute to, or need, information. This should be at both the macro and micro level in order to ensure that relevant information can be accessed when and where it is required.

The boundaries should be drawn to include the organization's information flows with its customers, other organizations, suppliers etc. Within the organization, the processes should emphasize the importance of existing and potential intra-organizational interactions. Cross-functional collaboration should be encouraged in the planning process as well as in the outcome. The planning processes must 'fit' with the organization as a whole.

Macro approach

Scope

Information is acquired, managed, used and distributed through many outlets and resources. Library holdings, office automation systems, electronic and paper records and files, inter- and intra-organizational information systems and databases need to be considered in the management and planning processes. These processes are also applicable to all formats, e.g. sound, image (graphic, pictorial, moving), text, data, or multimedia.

Information is supported by information technology applications which capture, store, organize, secure, process, track, retrieve, present, transmit or distribute information. Whilst the processes to be outlined will concentrate on the information planning, they should not take place in isolation from these technology applications and infrastructures.

Environmental analysis

The information planning processes and subsequent information management processes should be designed and implemented to support the organization's objectives and business strategies. The environmental analysis should identify the information needs of management, front-line or service personnel, the (parent) organization's customers and other stakeholders such as members of boards, committees or suppliers.

The organization's corporate culture and future direction should also be considered. The culture has a potent influence on how information is used and valued within organizations. For example, the level of abundance in information flows and the extent of information sharing influence the level of teamwork, trust and confidence in each other. Generally, information will either be protected and jealously guarded, or freely exchanged and available. Conflict and tensions will arise unless the information management strategies are aligned to the culture or, alternatively, the culture changed to match the desired state.

Information architecture

The concept of an information architecture is that it is the blueprint or plan for modelling the global information requirements of an organization. It is used to:

- guide the acquisition and redundancy of information;
- facilitate the integration and sharing of information; and
- provide a proactive basis for the meeting of the organization's, its customers' and other stakeholders' information needs.

In practice, the information architecture:

- models how information is acquired, managed and stored within the organization (information audit);
- graphically displays the relationships between sources, suppliers and users of the information (information map);
- analyses how information is used internally by the employees of the parent organization, (its) customers and other stakeholders (information use);

- looks at communications, interrelationships and movement of information throughout the organization and with customers and other stakeholders (information flows); and
- brings these together with the needs of the organization, customers and other stakeholders to analyse shortfalls (information needs and gap analysis).

Information audit

The first stage of the information audit is to identify all the current information resources and how these are acquired or created. This includes: the paper files that make up the formal and informal records of the organization; information in databases and interorganizational systems such as electronic commerce and data interchange systems; the printed and electronic holdings in the library, divisional and individual collections; information that can be accessed through external databases; multimedia and information in other formats, information held in office automation systems; and, finally, knowledge critical to the business of the organization that is stored in the minds of individuals.

The next stage identifies those people or systems that store, manage or add value to the information. It should identify:

- the cost of the management overheads (including maintenance and storage);
- the information's value and use within the organization;
- the appropriateness of the format and storage devices;
- the technical means of accessing the information;
- the availability of information throughout the organization, to customers and to other external parties who may wish to access and make use of the information;
- whether the management of the technology is appropriate and linked to the management of the information;
- statements of policy or objectives for acquiring or discarding information; and
- appropriateness of procedural manuals or instructions for processing or distributing information.

Information map

The information map identifies those who use the information, mapping the users against those who manage, input, process and store it.

The information map can be applied or developed:

- at the programme level with details of just the main customer groups; or
- in more detail identifying individuals as customers.

It can be used to map different levels of information use with key personnel (the internal customers), customers and other external stakeholders. The level of detail should be chosen according to the organization's objectives and business needs.

Information use

The next stage is to analyse how information is used within the organization, by its customers and the other external stakeholders within the boundary chosen. It should consider what and how information is used in decision-making and also identify what people do with the information. Examples being the use of:

- customer profiles to enhance service delivery or sell new products or services to existing customers;
- financial records to monitor the level of financial expenditure;
- scientific or technical information for research and product development;
- existing information held in libraries or in databases that is combined or made available in a different format to create a value added information product; or
- statistics and other management information to measure productivity or efficiency.

Information flows

The information flow analysis traces the flow of information between people and groups within the organization (the internal customers), and between the organization, its customers and other external stakeholders. The objective is to determine that the correct information is flowing to the right areas and that those who need access to information are able to receive it. The information flow analysis may also highlight opportunities for improved information performance. For example it can expose:

- systems that do not add value to the business strategy;
- activities that are not linked with others in electronic information chains necessitating the rekeying of information;
- activities that create information that is not useful;
- information that could also be used elsewhere for better decision-making or to support others' activities within the organization;

- undocumented decision processes; or
- ill-defined or inconsistent business processes.

Information gap analysis

This exercise identifies the shortfalls between the available information and the critical information that is required for the main decisions related to the management of the organization. The critical information needs of the internal customers, the organization's customers and other external stakeholders should also be matched against information availability. The information gap analysis should consider both current and future needs.

Business Systems Planning can be used for the information gap analysis. This is a two-phase process, the first phase requiring the identification of the business processes, defining information classes, the analysis of systems and getting the executive's, employees', customers' and external stakeholders' perspective. It should be focused on business processes and customer needs. The second phase involves setting priorities for the organization in terms of its future development and identifying the information requirements that will arise from this.

A second methodology that can be used to identify shortfalls in information is Critical Success Factors. This methodology identifies the critical things within an organization that must be done and the information required to do them. These can be defined through a series of interviews within the organization and with stakeholders. Once these have been determined, the findings should also be related to how the information can be used to achieve the organization's objectives, customers' and stakeholders' needs, together with the information needed to monitor performance in the critical areas.

Micro approach

To be totally effective, and depending on its level of confidentiality, information should be managed, maintained and secured as a shared corporate resource for the benefit of the entire organization. The underlying principle of the micro approach is to manage and maintain the information so that it can be cost-effectively used by others for a variety of purposes. The use of classification schemes, standards, definitions and directories will assist in enabling the information to be consistently defined, maintained and used by internal customers across the organization and by its customers and external stakeholders.

Information classification

The classification of information is an important activity in that it defines the parameters of access and use of the organization's information. For example, information may be classified according to its:

- strategic or commercial value to the organization – the extent to which the information is of a commercial-in-confidence nature or critical to the organization's strategic business advantage;
- level of privacy – the extent to which it contains personal information about individuals;
- value in the information market – the extent to which the information can be used to develop value added information products for sale to external customers;
- type and use – the extent to which it can be used in the various activities or levels within the organization;
- subject area – existing records management index or library classification scheme; or
- format or source – the extent to which it is sourced externally or internally, and its format.

Where possible, information classification schemes should be consistent across the organization, regardless of format.

Information standards

To maintain its accuracy and currency, information should be collected once, and then reused to meet the information requirements. The collection or capture point should be as close to the source as possible. In order to ensure that the information can be reused, transferred or integrated with other information, the capture and management of the information should be according to predetermined standards.

The standards should be set by the organization. The choice of standards will depend upon:

- the extent to which the information is to be integrated with external information or used by external stakeholders;
- efficiency and effectiveness.

Standards should be chosen to add value to the use and management of information rather than create an unnecessary level of workload or bureaucracy. Information should not be over-processed for the sake of conforming to national or international standards if this is not warranted by the business case or customers' needs. The purpose of adopting information standards is to maintain the degree of consistency and connectivity that enables information to be shared. For example:

- information used externally by customers or external stakeholders will need to be captured, maintained and transferred according to a national or international standard;
- information used internally across the organization should be captured, maintained and transferred according to an agreed standard within the organization;
- specific information that is captured and maintained to support a single programme or activity may not need to conform to any standard.

Information definitions

Information definitions provide information, or meta data, about the information itself. Their purpose is to increase the understanding about the information and its relevance to a particular use. They may provide information about the quality, rules of use, source, accuracy, currency, projection type or scale, format, coverage in terms of geographical area or time-scale etc. Information definitions may be created as part of a data dictionary in a database administration system.

Information directories

Information directories identify what information exists and where it may be found. Library catalogues, Government Information Locator Services (GILS) or a home page on the Internet that identifies other sources of information are examples of information directories.

Data definitions make up a large proportion of an entry in an information directory. Initially, the information directory can be produced through the information audit and mapping processes as these identify what information is available and its source. To be of long-term use meta data must be continually updated.

Information directories are location tools. Generally they contain information about source, access and use constraints, purpose, availability, point of contact for further information, cross-references and other appropriate information found in the information definition.

To assist users, the information directory should be designed so that it is searchable on a number of fields. It should be easy to use, convenient to access and available in an appropriate format.

Performance measurement

The desired outcomes of the information planning processes are to ensure that:

- appropriate information is provided to meet the business needs of the organization and the information needs of customers and stakeholders;
- information content, information flows and delivery mechanisms ensure that information is made available to the users when and where they need it;
- the people who process and manage the information understand the needs of the people who use it, with the result that information is available to users in a relevant and meaningful form;
- information is secured in terms of accessibility, integrity and confidentiality;
- information is consistently defined across the organization;
- information is accurate and complete; and
- the information is constantly reviewed to avoid redundancy and to evaluate its appropriateness to the organization's business needs.

Efficiency and effectiveness measures should be developed to measure the above and ensure that the planning process is meeting the organization's objectives and the information needs of the internal customers, the organization's customers and stakeholders.

7 Technology planning

Introduction

As a strategic planning activity, the technology planning process is integrated with information planning and the organization's strategic business planning. However, in technology planning, there is a second dimension to integration. The manner in which the technology is used to deliver services and information requires the integration of systems that operate within the parent organization (intra-organizational systems), and, systems that operate between the parent organization and other organizations (interorganizational systems).

Today, technology has moved from the back-room data-processing activities, past the front-line delivery of business services and products to customers to the frontier line of positioning the organization in the competitive environment and supporting new ways of working.

The value of technology

Information and its related technologies can be used to both deliver information and to transform the way in which an organization does its business and competes in the market-place. If the technology strategy is appropriately planned and processes aligned to fit, the organization can build upon its existing strengths and further leverage its technology investment. If the planning is inappropriate to the business needs, the exercise can be extremely costly with ill-fitting and over-priced solutions.

Information-related technology presents opportunities to:

- enhance the delivery of information products and services to customers;
- improve the quality control of products and services and tailor services to meet specific customer needs;
- improve productivity and the way the work units of the organization interact with each other;
- lower costs of production and the need to warehouse both raw materials and the finished products on a 'just in case' basis;
- provide interactive, experiential and 'what if?' scenarios for decision-making;
- broaden the business base, create new service or products and increase market share;
- distinguish or differentiate the way in which the product or service is offered from others, so that the organization no longer has to compete on a price basis;
- improve the way in which services or products are distributed in the market-place;
- increase the exit costs or switching costs of customers to a competitor so that it takes away the bargaining power of customers; and
- shorten the payment cycle and allow better cash management of funds and accounts.

The planning process

Planning for information-related technology involves:

- identifying the strengths and weaknesses in the current contribution of the technology to the delivery of information needs and the success of the parent organization;
- identifying business opportunities presented by new directions in information-related technology and trends in the market-place, and the threats that may come from any competitor's use of technology;
- setting the strategic direction for information-related technology procurement, management, exploitation and use for the critical business areas of the organization;
- prioritizing areas where information-related technologies can add the most value to success of the parent organization and its information needs;
- identifying where the processes and business practices within the organization require re-engineering to maximize the total benefit; and
- measuring and evaluating the value and performance of the technology and its contribution to organizational success.

This approach differs from the reactive and fragmented systems development approach of the past that resulted in information 'silos' and independent systems. It proactively seeks cross-organizational and interorganizational business solutions. This results in a more natural alignment of the technology, the information and the organization, and produces outcomes that are aligned to the organization's business objectives. For example, payroll information and human resource management information that has traditionally resided on separate and quite independent systems is increasingly being integrated with other information such as financial information. Information users are able to link, query and determine 'what if?' scenarios about various relationships such as forward expenditure and pay periods, sick leave and stress-related factors because all of the information is interlinked.

The technology strategy plan

The strategy plan should be written so that it is simple and clear. It should be easily understood by individuals who do not have a technology background. It should be precise, with no room for interpretation. The strategy plan should outline the technical architecture for the present and future uses of information-related technologies, policies and a prioritized list of development projects. Both the technology strategy plan and the technical architecture should be linked to the customer information needs and organizational business needs.

Roles and responsibilities

Technology planning is no longer the sole domain of the information service function. As with information planning, senior management, employees, stakeholders and the parent organization's customers must play an active part in determining their future technology requirements. Senior management should actively be involved in determining and championing the strategic technology opportunities and in the implementation process. Whilst they may not have a technical background, they should assume the same level of responsibility and accountability for technology-based outcomes as they have for other critical activities within the organization.

Stakeholders' (such as suppliers) and customers' input is required to jointly plan interorganizational systems, avoid inappropriate technology solutions or placing too high a demand on their financial or organizational capability to introduce compatible technology.

The information services manager has a responsibility for clearly understanding and promoting ways in which the technology can assist the delivery of information and the organization's business strategy. They should be able to canvass and explain technology alternatives in understandable terms to others. They should also continually evaluate the capabilities and use of the technology in terms of meeting the business requirements and supporting information needs.

Technology architecture

The technology architecture is a general model of the desired structure for the technologies that support information use within an organization (see Figure 7.1). It is the mechanism through which information is located, accessed, stored, manipulated, secured and delivered. In simplistic terms, the main components of the technology architecture are:

Methods, protocols and standards	User interface			Security supporting: confidentiality availability integrity
	graphical user interface			
	Databases			
	distributed, centralized, query languages, database design			
	Applications			
	inter- and intra-agency systems and applications, desktop applications, applications downloaded with information			
	Comp-uting	Operating systems		
		Hardware mainframes, mid-range, work-stations, PCs, notepads etc. storage devices e.g. CD Roms, input and output devices		
	Value Added Network applications e-mail, electronic commerce etc.		Tele-commun-ications	
	Network infrastructure voice, data and image etc. delivered through mobile, satellite and terrestrial services			

Figure 7.1   The technology architecture

- telecommunications
  - network infrastructure – the national and international backbone or infrastructure
  - value added network applications – supporting business and other applications on a global basis;
- computing (hardware and software) – supporting end-users:
  - hardware – the physical components of computing;
  - operating systems – software that controls the computing resources;
- applications – supporting the sharing of common business processes to achieve outcomes;
- databases – collections of data to support the applications;
- user interface – the 'look' and 'feel' appearance to the user.

Supporting the technology architecture are:

- methods, protocols and standards that are used to build the technology architecture;
- security features to ensure accessibility, confidentiality and integrity; and
- tools for building the architecture such as programming languages and software tools.

Aspects of the technology architecture components are converging and it is now more difficult to establish where one component ends and another begins. Two reasons for this are the integration of technology solutions and the market demand for seamless interfaces.

It should be noted that whilst planning for the databases that store data and information (the content) is a technology issue, planning for the information that resides in the databases is not. Information planning requires consideration of a number of different issues and is covered in Chapter 6.

Technology architecture should be used as the enabler not the enforcer of the organization's business strategies. Whilst it can be used as a driver for change in business and process re-engineering, it should not overtake the parent organization's objectives and its business strategy. It is the information needs, objectives and business strategy that should determine its future direction, not the other way round. The key management challenge is to look at the opportunities that the technology can bring and how these can be used to support the business strategy and information needs of management, employees, customers and other stakeholders.

A well-designed technology architecture can deliver information and enhance business opportunities through the use of:

- multimedia to effectively convey and obtain information in easily understood formats. Multimedia utilizes more of the physical senses as it integrates text, sound, moving and visual imagery to provide a multidimensional approach to business information. It supports experiential decision-making based on simulations of real-life experiences and 'what if?' scenarios;

- networking to reduce constraints of distance and time and allow effective information exchange and joint activities. Networking will allow the creation of the virtual organizational structures where people do not physically travel to a place of work, as well as new business opportunities whereby business is conducted and negotiated through telecommunications;
- interactivity that allows individuals to select information that is of importance at times and in the place that they need it. Interactivity also allows individuals to send information to numerous recipients and hear others' reactions to it;
- mobile communications that allow people to transmit and receive information whilst in transit or at sites they are visiting.

The technology architecture should also be structured to avoid duplication, take advantage of economies of scale, support different levels of information use and provide for the security and confidentiality of information.

Management issues in technology planning

Developing the right business strategy for information-related technology is critical in terms of information use, service delivery, productivity, customer retention and return on investment. Information-related technologies can be expensive to acquire in monetary terms, but with either an incorrect choice of strategy or no strategy, the business risks and impact can be even more expensive.

A significant competitive advantage in service delivery and productivity can be gained by exploiting new technologies or new applications of existing technologies ahead of competitors if the correct strategy is chosen. In addition to the business needs, the design of the strategy should take into account the corporate culture, the existing expertise and skills within the information service and the parent organization, customers' and stakeholders' information needs and information competences, the level of commitment to the existing technology platform and the parent organization's financial and resource capacity.

It is anticipated that significant shifts in information-related technologies occur every five years. The technology strategy must look to long-term business solutions that deliver the required return on investment whilst ensuring that the technology does not become obsolete. Examples of how obsolescence can occur include:

- a change in business strategy requiring new technology applications;
- significant changes in customers' technology architectures to the extent that interorganizational systems are no longer compatible;
- changes in the market-place to the extent that maintenance of the technology is no longer supported.

There is an art to keeping the technology strategy finally balanced between seeking business opportunities at the leading edge of technology where the risk may be high, and maintaining cost-effective solutions without being technology-led. The technology strategy often requires a substantial financial investment with a short payback period.

The choice of the technology strategy can commit the organization to a technology direction that will be built upon over a number of years. The information services manager and senior management must have sufficient confidence in the chosen strategy that it will not only bring competitive advantage through the delivery of information, but that it is flexible enough to cope with changes in the environment, mergers and acquisitions, and to sustain the competitive advantage in the long term.

Implementing the strategy

Planning for the technology strategy must take into account the costs of implementation. There may be overheads in terms of process re-engineering and retraining. If it is decided to continue with the existing platform, but to introduce new applications, the full costs of integration, maintenance and support should be included.

The introduction of new technology may require significant changes within the organization. Without the accompanying process re-engineering and changed work practices, the introduction of new technology applications may only result in inefficiencies running faster. The impact of change upon individuals of any re-engineering needs to be taken into consideration. People should be kept informed of any changes. They should also be given training and retraining opportunities. To exploit the full functionality of the technology application, training should include:

- knowledge of the applications and their business potential in terms of expected outcomes to be delivered;
- specialized functions of the system; and
- details as to how the application integrates with other systems and processes within the organization and externally.

Individuals whose positions may no longer exist because of the introduction of the technology should be given opportunities to retrain to meet the requirements of the new technology environment.

The people interface with the technology should be given important consideration. This includes the need to:

- generate a common 'look and feel' or user interface to technology applications;
- ensure that the technology delivers information and services in a transparent manner independent of distance and time;
- ensure that those who will use the technology have adequate training so that they can utilize it to its fullest extent.

Control mechanisms (such as budgeting) for the implementation of the strategy should be placed with line management of the work units. There should be clear lines of responsibility for the implementation and ongoing management of the technology.

Information technology can deliver major benefits to individuals in their ability to access and use information, and to the organization in terms of increased productivity, broadening the business base and improving the delivery of products and services. However it should be properly planned to take into account the information and business needs, the corporate culture, and the financial and resource capacity of the organization.

8 Financial planning and economic analysis

Introduction

Financial planning involves the process of identifying, costing and allocating expenditure and revenue to the resources and activities that allow the objectives of the information service and its parent organization to be achieved. At the macro level this is achieved through the budget process. At the micro level, economic analysis can be used to determine the optimum use of staff and resources in order to effectively cost activities.

This chapter considers the relationship between the budget cycle and the strategic planning cycle, the preparation of budgets and methods of calculating expenditure. Different budget techniques are explored. At the micro level the chapter considers mechanisms for costing information services and activities.

The integrated approach

The planning for financial resources should be integrated into the planning of the other corporate resources (see Figure 8.1).

Macro approach

Budgets

All information service activities are subject to expenditures and revenues that must be accounted for in a budget. The budget is the financial statement that is prepared and approved for a specific period of time and which

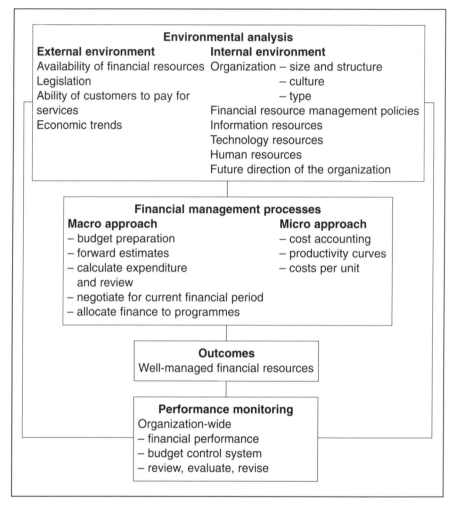

Figure 8.1   The integrated approach to financial planning

provides details of the proposed expenditure and revenues. Usually it is prepared to cover a financial year, but can cover a longer period of time – for example, a triennium. Occasionally, a half-yearly budget is planned.

A budget is prepared prior to expenditure taking place and income being received and constitutes both the means of control as to how monies are spent and a check on what monies should have been received. It earmarks the amounts of expenditure and anticipated income for certain items or services delivered by the information service.

The budget should be related to the strategic planning process in terms of

Strategic planning process	Financial planning process
– revise plan in light of changing environment	– review financial planning process according to changing environment
– main directions set at strategic and operational objectives levels	– forward budget estimates prepared for next three years based on main direction set
– main programmes and projects for next three years established	– forward budget estimates considered by top management and sent to funding body for approval
– review progress and performance of programmes	– review progress and performance of programmes against financial situation
– establish priorities for following financial period based on funding	– negotiate budget for forward estimates for programmes and for following financial period
– revise forward work programmes and activities according to budget allocations and cost increases	– allocate budget for financial period to programmes
– implement programmes and activities	– economic analysis re costings of activities and services
– monitor, review, evaluate and revise programmes and activities	– monitor, review, evaluate and revise expenditure levels

(left margin, vertical: Time frame)

Figure 8.2   Relationship between the activities of the strategic planning process and the financial planning process

timing and content. Figure 8.2 illustrates how the activities of the budget process fit the ongoing activities of the strategic planning process.

Budgets are often broken down by either programmes or activities across an organization. These may be further related to cost centres such as branch libraries, records management office or the geographic information services section. Cost centres may be further broken down to cover specific services.

Preparation of the budget

The preparation of the budget is the responsibility of the information services manager, who is also entrusted with administering the allocated funds within the service's overall programmes and activities. Whilst this responsibility is often delegated to mid-level management, or managers of cost centres, such as the librarian, records manager or information systems manager, the overall co-ordination and accountability rests with the senior management.

Mid-level managers may prepare their own budgets and submit these to the senior management. However, mid-level management is rarely the final arbitrator on the amount of funds to be allocated. This decision is usually made at the executive or ownership level of the parent organization. Therefore it is most important that managers keep the senior management and stakeholders of the parent organization fully informed of their progress and achievements throughout the year.

Whilst discussions about the items on the budget and their justifications will form part of the budget preparation process, justification should not just be limited to this time period. The review and questioning about services and justification for funds should be a continuous exercise. The senior management of the parent organization and other relevant stakeholders such as board members should have their views sought on policy directions and matters for the forthcoming budget well before the presentation of the information service's budget. Senior management and budget committees do not usually view too kindly strange budget proposals for items that have not previously been discussed. Proposals for new services should be introduced in regular or special reports, not in the budget documentation.

Whilst it is important that the proposed budget is fully supported with documentation justifying the proposals and linking these with approved plans, it is not enough. The information services manager should take the time and effort to understand the politics of the budget process within the parent organization. They need to win the budget arguments, not just be part of them. If not already invited, they should ask to be involved in the budget deliberations so that they may learn why, sometimes, their bids are rejected. Networks should be formed with key stakeholders in the treasury or finance department in order to put the information service's point of view forward and gain support for certain proposals.

The lack of a personal opportunity to participate in the final budget deliberations should not prevent the information services manager from obtaining their required budget allocation. Credibility of the budget details and a recognized value of the information service is what matters most. The justification for the information service's budget will already have been made if the arguments for the services have been well presented in detailed and timely reports throughout the year. If the information services manager's personal network has been effective, key members of the budget committee will be supportive of the activities and associated budget.

Calculation of expenditure

The preparation of a budget necessitates the calculation of expenditure, which consists of capital expenditures and operating expenditures. Capital expenditures are one-off items of expenditure such as a new library building, a photocopying machine or new blinds for the windows. Capital expenditures can reoccur, but they are not ongoing costs. They represent long-term investments.

Operating expenditures are current, ongoing costs associated with the day-to-day operations of the information service. These may be divided further into fixed and variable costs:

- fixed costs relate to annual overhead charges such as rent, general insurance or energy costs;
- variable costs vary according to usage and relate to consultancy fees, use of on-line information services or postage and courier costs.

A further explanation of fixed and variable costs is given later in this chapter.

Within the total information service's budget, each cost centre's budget may be broken down into capital and operating costs. A further breakdown according to items is often necessary. This allows for various revenues and expenditures to be categorized. For example, an item on the budget just labelled 'staff' provides very little management information. If this item is broken down into salaries, superannuation on salaries, workers' compensation insurance, training and staff development, conference fees, advertising staff appointments, it is more meaningful.

Some operating expenditure costs will be harder to calculate than others. Some costs will be known at the time of framing the budget. Public utilities such as energy commissions or telecommunications service providers may have already announced their rates or increases in charges for the year and so expenditure in these areas can be calculated quite easily. Cleaning contract costs or maintenance agreements for certain equipment may already be known. Sometimes overheads for buildings are conveniently reduced to a rate per square metre per annum for budget calculations.

Salaries are usually one of the hardest items to calculate. The diversity of employees in records management, information systems or libraries means that few staff are paid on the same salary scale. Some staff receive annual increments in their salaries, whilst others do not. The annual increments may be adjusted according to age or years of experience. As a result, some staff have their salary adjusted on their birth date, whilst others have their salary adjusted according to the date they commenced employment in a particular position. Each position needs to be assessed individually and the appropriate salary figure calculated for the following year.

Inflation rates, international currency exchange rates, salary increases, insurance rates, public utility charges, and so on, are all subject to variations. Some, such as exchange rates, will fluctuate, whilst others will show a gradual increase. These changes must also be taken into account when preparing the budget. Knowledgeable people in the external environment or members of the finance or treasury department may provide assistance in forecasting changes to these rates.

It is important to correctly anticipate revenue patterns and levels. Any income revenue in excess of expenditure at any given time is often invested by the parent organization on the short-term money market to provide additional funds for the organization. Variances in income revenue will disrupt the parent organization's ability to plan its investments wisely. Although some changes in income levels will be unavoidable, any anticipated changes in policies which may affect the income revenue levels should be accounted for in the budget. Examples would be the anticipated increase from a new user pays service or additional income from photocopying fees as the result of additional photocopying machines being installed in the information centre or library.

In planning for the annual budget there is a time-delay process. Planning often commences up to six months prior to the budget being ratified and the necessary funds being available to purchase items. This is particularly the case with such capital expenditure items as new buildings that are costed in preparation for the budget several months before they can be contracted out. Allowances to cover price increases may need to be built-in to the budget.

Budget controls

The budget control process is a continuing one. Generally expenditures and revenues must be made within the framework of the amount allocated against each item. This is part of an accountability process.

Expenditure and revenue is usually documented in either a weekly or monthly budget reports. These reports show the total expenditure and revenue amounts budgeted at the beginning of the financial year, the actual expenditure or income received to date and the committed expenditure to date. Actual expenditure refers to expenditure amounts for goods or services received and for which invoices and/or statements have also been received and paid for. Committed expenditure refers to the outstanding expenditures for goods or services which have been ordered but not yet paid for. The goods or services may or may not have been received by the cost centres in the information service. In calculating total expenditure costs to date, both the actual and committed expenditure amounts should be added together.

Statements of committed and expended funds should be regularly checked and reviewed in order to control the budget. Any anticipated increase in expenditure above that provided by the budget must be offset by a decrease in expenditure activity in that area. Unexpected expenditures such as costly emergency repairs to buildings or mobiles should incur a reallocation of funds from elsewhere. Such a readjustment of funds will usually occur twice or three times per year. The adjustments may need to be authorized by senior management and endorsed by a board if one exists.

In terms of accountability, appropriations for the various items of the budget should be expended for the purposes specified in the budget. However appropriate techniques for making changes and revisions to the budget should be provided to allow for unexpected events or changes in priorities that could not be foreseen when the budget was framed.

Budgeting techniques

Line-item budgets

This is the most traditional approach to budgeting. It divides expenditures into broad categories such as salaries, other operating expenses, equipment expenses, equipment maintenance, materials, capital expenditures and sundries. There are further subdivisions within these categories. Most line budgets are prepared by projecting current expenditures to next year, taking likely cost increases into account.

Whilst they are easy to prepare, very few organizations use line-item budgets today. This is because it is difficult to relate the line-item budget to the organization's objectives, or to the benefits or outcomes that arise from the allocated monies. Line-item budgets provide few incentives for management to question programmes or activities or look for alternative solutions.

Zero-based budgeting

Zero-based budgeting (ZBB) combines strategic planning and decision-making with the budget process. Zero-based budgeting encourages the manager to question priorities and consider alternative methods of service delivery. Activities and programmes are assessed across the whole organization in accordance with the:

● anticipated benefits from the programme;
● desired results;
● advantages of retaining the programme's current activities;
● consequences of not having the programme;
● overall efficiency of the programme; and
● evaluation of the alternative methods of providing the programme.

The required resources and associated costs for the programme are calculated. The programmes are grouped and ranked by management according to a hierarchy based on their cost-benefit and ability to achieve the organization's objectives.

The programmes are progressively funded within the priority hierarchy until the budget is exhausted. At some point in the hierarchy there is a cut-off point. This is the point that allows some programmes to be funded and others not. The cut-off point corresponds to the organization's total budget allocation. Those programmes that are ranked in priority above the funding line are funded; those below it are left unfunded. If further funds become available, those ranked at or immediately below the original funding line are funded.

Budget allocation is based on the priority of the programme in meeting the organization's objectives rather than across the board appropriations. Zero-based budgeting does not allow for incremental growth in budgets. It considers efficiency and the relevancy of programmes to organizational objectives. It exposes all information service activities to the same scrutiny as others within the parent organization, preventing programmes from being approved solely on the basis of tradition. More efficient ways of achieving the corporate objectives are sought by examining different methods of service delivery or activities.

To be effective, zero-based budgeting requires decision-makers to have a thorough knowledge of the organization. The cost centre managers within the information service must be aware of their service's characteristics and objectives, and major customer groups. Activities and programmes must be well conceived. The information service's strengths and weaknesses should be known. Managers and staff should know why they want to spend money, where and what to spend it on and the outcomes that can be achieved if funding is available.

Zero-based budgeting identifies trade-offs among the programmes and objectives. Senior management must decide the level of funding that they are prepared to commit and the programmes and objectives that they are prepared to forgo.

There are some disadvantages to zero-based budgeting: it requires great commitment of time and effort; it involves a great deal of preparation, planning and organization; and it relies upon all participants being more aware of formalized policies and planning priorities. To be effective, it requires extensive training in its techniques and should not be introduced without due consideration of the time and effort involved.

Programme budgeting

Programme budgeting is based upon the provision of programmes rather than individual items or expenditures. It allocates monies to activities or programmes; having previously explored different means to providing services that have been identified as needed by the customers.   Each programme has certain funds allocated for staff, operating expenses, materials and publicity. Programmes may run across a number of cost centres, for example a programme that facilitates the provision of information networks to lecturers within a university may cover a number of cost centres at the faculty level.

Performance budgeting

Performance budgeting bases its expenditure on the performance of activities and services. It is similar to programme budgeting in format but is concerned with efficiency. It uses cost-benefit analysis techniques to measure performance and requires large amounts of data. Performance budgeting has been criticised as it emphasizes economics rather than quality of service.

Planning-programming budgeting systems (PPBS)

PPBS combines the best of programme budgeting and performance budgeting. It combines the functions of planning, programming and budgeting into one.

The information service's objectives are established and short-term objectives are stated in a quantifiable manner. Alternative means (activities) of achieving the objectives are considered and selected on the basis of cost-benefit. These activities are grouped into programmes and funded.

Once the programmes are established they are controlled by comparing them with the stated objectives to see if these are being achieved. The results are evaluated so that corrective actions can be taken. PPBS allows costs to be assigned to programmes so that the benefits can be measured in relation to cost.

PPBS is a time-consuming budgetary procedure. Whilst the approach appears to be simple, it is complex in practice. It is based upon planning steps which may not, in reality, be evaluated during the actual budget preparation. It does not provide an operating tool for line managers or provide the mechanism to evaluate the impact of various funding levels on each programme. Finally, it does not force the continued evaluation of existing programmes and activities.

Micro approach

Capital costs

Capital costs are associated with the use of assets. Two aspects need to be considered:

- the determination of any depreciation costs; and
- the opportunity cost of the capital.

Asset depreciation allows the cost of an asset to be written off over a period of time. Two common methods of determining the depreciation costs are:

- the prime cost or straight line method that allocates the cost of an asset over the number of years of useful life. For example, personal computers are generally written off over a period of three years; and
- the diminishing value method that allocates a higher proportion of the cost of the asset to the earlier years of its life. For example, a motor vehicle may be written off at a higher rate in the first year.

The opportunity cost of capital recognizes that funds invested in assets could have alternative uses and that an allowance should be made for this.

Cost accounting

Cost accounting is a traditional form of assessing cost. It measures what it costs to complete an activity. It can be used in information services to determine the anticipated value of certain activities or for comparative purposes to measure efficiency. Cost accounting is the simple process of breaking down resources to the activity being carried out and then collating the monetary cost to show the cost of the activity. Cost accounting is not an end in itself. It is used to determine if the resources have been used effectively.

Cost accounting falls into two categories: routine costing which is used to provide regular financial and management information; and special exercise costing which deals with specific questions.

Routine cost-output or cost-activity ratios are used on a comparative basis to measure the efficiencies of certain information service functions, cost centres or customer services. By themselves these ratios serve no real purpose. Their value lies in using them to compare cost centres within a system or to make external comparisons between similar types of organizations. Efficient and inefficient services, functions or cost centres can be highlighted using routine costing procedures.

Special costing exercises are concerned with particular activities or groups of activities. They are used to answer specific questions such as the comparison of costs of current operations with the estimated costs of alternative methods. In preparing special costing exercises, it is important to remember that the costs of proposed systems need to be related not only to the existing systems but also to the other benefits that could be achieved. For example, a new system may be approved on the benefits and improvements in service delivery to customers rather than costs savings.

Activity-based costing

Activity-based costing costs the whole process and therefore gives a better picture of the total cost of the service. It takes into account all of the costs involved in supply, process, installation and service delivery. Activity-based costing also records the costs associated with downtime of equipment, such as when the equipment is sitting idle out of hours or is inoperable. It also costs the time waiting for a spare part, the cost of goods sitting in a warehouse or the cost of reworking a piece of programming. Activity-based costing can be used in competitive markets to highlight those activities that are unexpectedly unproductive and those that are yielding the greatest return on investment.

Fixed and variable costs

Fixed costs are those that do not vary with output. Costs which vary with output are called variable costs. Knowledge of both fixed and variable costs is necessary in order to budget effectively. As an example, the total costs of a library's operations will rise if more CD-Roms are purchased. This rise will not apply to all items in the budget or be in proportion, because some library costs will not be affected by the increase in the number of CD-Roms bought. Energy costs for lighting and air conditioning, for example, will remain the same if 3 000 or 6 000 books or CD-Roms are purchased. Energy costs will only increase if more processing time is involved, increasing the amount of time in which the lights and air conditioning are left on. Expenditure on safety equipment or telecommunications will remain unchanged unless the number of staff is increased considerably. Electricity, safety equipment and telecommunications costs will be fixed costs in this example. If an additional staff member is appointed to process the items, the salary component in the budget will be increased. Salaries are therefore a variable cost.

Unit costs

Unit costs are used to measure output. As it is not always easy to compare the rising curve of total costs, economists convert the total cost figures into unit costs. They do this by dividing the total cost of the activity by the number of units, for example, the number of incoming and outgoing pieces of correspondence that are processed by the records management office. This results in a figure for the average cost per unit of output. Unit costs can also be used in time terms. They may be used to measure performance by comparing inputs to outputs.

Unit costs concepts may also be used to allocate a cost to an information product or service. They can also be used to develop a standard for a job in

Expenditure

	£
Salaries – research and content	8,000
– graphics	4,000
Insurance – workers' compensation	500
Superannuation on salary	750
Stationery	1,250
Printing	1,500
TOTAL	16,000

Print run 5,000

Unit cost of production $\dfrac{£16,000}{5,000} = £3.20$

Income

Proposed income from sales 4,900 @ £5.00	£24,500
Profit	£8,500

Figure 8.3   An example of unit costing to determine the price of a printed publication

either time or cost terms. Figure 8.3 outlines how unit costing can be used to determine the price of a printed publication.

Fixed costs per unit

Fixed costs per unit can be used to determine budget allocations and efficiency in information services.

Fixed costs per unit of output fall as output rises. If a kiosk service has fixed costs (energy, telecommunications, rental space in a shopping centre) of £12 000 a year and it undertakes 15 000 transactions (bill paying and enquiries) per year, each transaction will have a fixed cost of £0.80. If output rises to 20 000 transactions, the unit share of fixed costs of a transaction will shrink to £0.60. At 30 000 transactions it would be £0.40 (see Figure 8.4).

With regard to variable costs per unit the situation is more complex. It depends upon marginal productivity and the productivity curve (law of variable proportions).

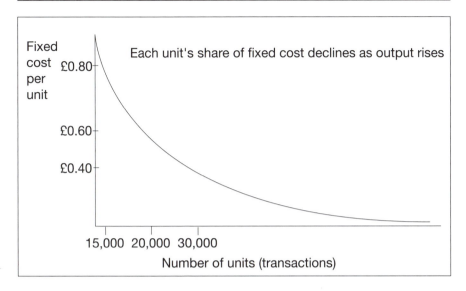

Figure 8.4 Profile of fixed costs per unit

Productivity curves: law of increasing returns

Productivity curves can be used to determine the optimum levels of efficiency in information services.

Physical productivity changes when different amounts of one factor are combined with fixed amounts of others. In a new information centre with a stock of 2 000 items, a certain amount of equipment may be needed. Apart from the librarian or information specialist, there is no need for additional labour. If another person is hired, the information centre has the capacity to process and catalogue more items or provide new services. The capacity increases again when a third person is hired and so on.

The appointment of the second librarian or information specialist will have value as the two can begin to specialize and divide the work. Each will perform the jobs they are better at and save time formerly wasted by moving from one job to the next. As a consequence this division of labour may allow the information centre to catalogue and process a further 5 000 items per year and improve services to more customers. Since the difference in output is 3 000 items, the marginal productivity of labour when the two librarians or information specialists are working is 3 000 items.

The marginal productivity of labour should not be considered in terms of the second person as, by themselves, their efforts would be no more productive than those of the first staff member. If the first staff member left, the second person would still catalogue and process only 2 000 items. What makes the difference is the jump in the combined production of the two librarians once specialization can be introduced. It is regarded as the changing marginal productivity of labour, not the individual.

Increased specialization takes place with the third, fourth, fifth librarian or information specialist so that the addition of another unit of labour as an input in each case brings about an output larger than was realized by the average of all the previous librarians. This does not necessarily mean that each successive person is more efficient and productive. It means that, as units of one factor (librarians or information specialists) are added, the total mix of these units plus the fixed amounts of the other factors form an increasingly efficient technical combination. The range of factor inputs, over which average productivity rises, is called a range of increasing average returns.

Every time a factor is added efficiency rises. The rate of increased efficiency will not be the same, for the initial large marginal leaps in productivity will give way to smaller ones. However, the overall trend whether measured by looking at total output or at average output per person will still be increased. This continues until a point of maximum technical efficiency is reached.

Law of diminishing returns

The law of diminishing returns is used to detect the point of maximum technical efficiency in information services.

Using the previous example of the information centre there is a certain point where the marginal output no longer rises when another person is added to the staff. This is the point of maximum technical efficiency. Total output will still be increasing, but the last person to be employed will have added less output than their colleagues. Labour is now beginning to 'crowd' equipment or the premises. Opportunities for further specialization have become non-existent.

This condition of falling marginal performance is called a condition of decreasing or diminishing returns. The information centre is getting back less and less not only from the 'marginal' librarian or information specialist but from the combined labour of all the staff members.

If labour goes on being added, a point will be reached at which the contribution of the 'marginal' librarian or information specialist will be so small that the average output per person will also fall. Eventually, if even more librarians or information specialists were added, the factor mix would be so disrupted that the total output would actually fall resulting in a condition of negative gains (see Table 8.1).

In the example, the marginal productivity begins to diminish with the fourth librarian or information specialist who catalogues only 3 300 items

Table 8.1 Law of diminishing returns

Number of librarians/ information specialists	Total output (items catalogued)	Marginal productivity (change in output)		Average productivity (total output – number of librarians/ information specialists)	
1	2 000	2 000 ⎫	Increasing	2 000 ⎫	Increasing
2	5 000	3 000 ⎬	marginal	2 500 ⎬	average
3	8 500	3 500 ⎭	productivity	2 853 ⎭	productivity
4	11 800	3 300		2 950	
5	14 800	3 000 ⎫	Decreasing	2 960 ⎫	Decreasing
6	17 300	2 500 ⎬	marginal	2 883 ⎬	average
7	19 500	2 200 ⎭	productivity	2 785 ⎭	productivity

not 3 500 as did the third person. Average productivity continues to rise until the addition of the sixth person, because the fifth librarian or information specialist, although producing less than the fourth, is still more productive than the average output of all four colleagues. Therefore marginal productivity can be falling while average productivity is still rising.

In summary, as successive units of one factor are added to fixed amounts of others, the marginal output of the units of the variable factor will at first rise and then decline. This is called the law of variable proportions or the law of diminishing returns or, the physical productivity curve (see Figure 8.5).

Variable costs per unit

Variable costs per unit can be used to cost increased efficiency in information services. As in the case of the previous example of librarians or information specialists processing and cataloguing the items, the total number of items catalogued (units produced) will rise rapidly at first, then more slowly with the addition of more librarians (see Table 8.2). To convert the schedule of physical productivity into a unit cost figure, the total variable cost for each level of output should be calculated. This should then be divided by the number of units to obtain an average variable cost per unit of output (see Table 8.3).

The average variable costs per unit (items catalogued) declines at first and then rises. This is because the variable cost increases by a set amount (£45 000 per librarian or information specialist). Output, however obeys the law of diminishing returns. The variable cost per unit of output will

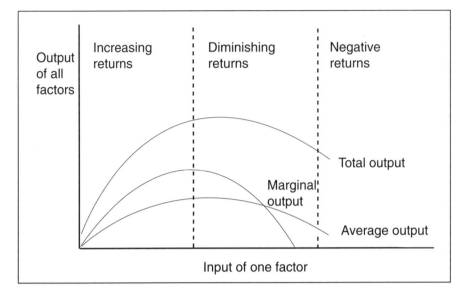

Figure 8.5   Law of variable proportions

therefore fall as long as output is growing faster than costs. It will begin to rise as soon as additions to output start to get smaller.

Total cost per unit

A complete costing schedule can now be established for the combined fixed and variable costs of processing and cataloguing the items in the information centre. This is useful for calculating a processing charge if an item is lost and an account has to be sent for the true value of the item – that is, the cost of

Table 8.2 Schedule of physical productivity

Number of librarians/ information specialists	Total outputs (units)	Marginal productivity
1	2 000	2 000
2	5 000	3 000
3	8 500	3 500
4	11 800	3 300
5	14 800	3 000
6	17 300	2 500
7	19 500	2 200

Table 8.3   Calculating the average variable cost per unit of output

Number of librarians/ information specialists	Total variable costs at £45,000 per librarian/ information specialist (£)	Total output (units)	Average variable cost per unit of output (cost – output) (£)
1	45 000	2 000	22.50
2	90 000	5 000	18.00
3	135 000	8 500	15.88
4	180 000	11 800	15.25
5	225 000	14 800	15.20
6	270 000	17 300	15.60
7	315 000	19 500	16.15

Table 8.4   Calculating the average variable cost per unit of output

	Total costs		Cost per unit of output		
Number of librarians/ information specialists	(£10,000 fixed costs + £45,000 per librarian/ information specialist (£)	Output (units)	Average (total cost – output) (£)	Marginal (changes in cost – changes in output) (£)	
1	55 000	2 000	27.50 ⎫ Falling		Falling
2	100 000	5 000	20.00 ⎬ average 15.00 ⎫	marginal
3	145 000	8 500	17.05 ⎭ cost 12.85 ⎬	cost
4	190 000	11 800	16.10	13.63	
5	235 000	14 800	15.87 ⎫ Rising 15.00 ⎫ Rising
6	280 000	17 300	16.18 ⎬ average 18.00 ⎬ marginal
7	325 000	19 500	16.66 ⎭ cost 20.45 ⎭ cost

the item and the cost of cataloguing and processing it.

Fixed costs (overheads such as electricity, telephones) are added to the variable costs of the salaries of the librarians or information specialists to give the total cost. The total cost is divided by the output to give the average cost per unit of output. The changing marginal cost per unit is calculated by dividing the increase in total costs by the increase in output, each time an extra staff member is appointed (see Table 8.4).

Micro economic analysis can be used to determine the cost of specific information services and activities so as to achieve the optimum use of resources and, if necessary, pass on this cost to the consumer of the information product or service.

Part 4

Creating the corporate environment

This part of the book considers the political and cultural issues that the information services manager needs to address to create and manage an organizational environment that is innovative (see Figure P4.1). It provides some psycho-social guidance to the people interactions within organizations. The reasons for these may not always be explicit.

Chapter 9 considers the values, beliefs, norms and behaviours that create an organization's culture. It explains how corporate cultures evolve and how there can be more than one culture within an organization. Descriptions of different corporate culture types are provided to assist the information services manager to identify and manage the culture type that prevails within their parent organization.

This chapter also describes the activities that take place within organizations as corporate rituals. It provides advice on developing and maintaining a corporate culture within the information service, and addresses the question of ethics and values in information services.

Chapter 10 covers the nature of politics and political behaviour from both an individual and organizational perspective. Not all organizations are equally political and, likewise, not all individuals are as overt as others in their political gamesmanship. Politics is a natural phenomenon arising out of differentiation, competition, and the use of power and influence. The chapter describes a number of political tactics that are commonly used in organizations, and characterizes these as ethical and unethical. Advice is given on the presentation of political arguments on paper and the use of lobby groups.

Managing the environment through integrated planning
– strategic planning
– human resources
– information
– technology
– finance

Understanding the role of manager
– introduction to management

Understanding the environment
– strategic influences
– internal and external environment

Getting things done in the corporate environment
– leadership
– power, influence, authority and delegation
– decision-making
– networking
– group dynamics
– team-building
– motivation
– conflict management
– negotiation
– change management

Creating the corporate environment

Corporate culture
– corporate cultures
– corporate culture types
– values, beliefs, norms and shared meanings
– corporate rituals
– organizational subcultures
– strong and weak corporate cultures
– developing the corporate culture
– ethics and corporate culture

Politics
– individual politics
– political roles of managers
– politics in organizations
– political tactics
– presenting political arguments
– lobbying and lobby groups

Policy-making
– use of policies
– policy development
– policy framework
– policies for information services

Creativity and intrapreneurship
– creating an innovative environment
– roles and functions

Managing expertise
– differentiation in organizations
– developing the common good

Managing and communicating information in the corporate environment
– personal communication
– internal communications
– external communications
– corporate information
– information life cycles

Managing the individual
– stress management
– career planning and personal development

Service delivery
– competitive strategies
– quality control
– customer focus
– outsourcing service delivery
– performance measurement and evaluation

Managing risk
– return on investment
– security
– risk management and business continuity

Creating the corporate environment
– corporate culture
– politics
– policy-making
– creativity and intrapreneurship
– managing expertise

Figure P4.1   Creating the corporate environment

114

Policy-making is addressed in Chapter 11. This chapter provides strategies for developing policy and identifies the type of issues for which policies are appropriate. It emphasizes the need to identify and consult with stakeholders whilst developing the policy. The chapter discusses the policy framework and provides examples of general and specific policy issues that can be found in information services.

Chapter 12 considers creativity and intrapreneurship. The chapter provides strategies to create an innovative environment. It identifies the different roles and functions within organizations that foster a creative environment.

The final chapter in this part, 'Managing expertise', acknowledges that differentiation in expertise can be a source of conflict within organizations. It explains why differentiation occurs and the need to manage expertise for the common good of the organization.

9 Corporate culture

Introduction

All organizations have a corporate culture. Some are more noticeable or stronger than others. A corporate culture is the system of values, beliefs, norms and behaviours that create a certain organizational climate. Tangible factors such as the external environment, technologies, organization size and structure, corporate environment and leadership and management styles also create the corporate culture.

Corporate culture is the product or outcome of behaviour patterns and standards that have been built up by individuals and groups over a number of years. Successful organizations have strong corporate cultures that serve to identify the guiding beliefs and values upon which all policies and actions take place. Effective corporate cultures translate cultural values at the organizational level into behaviours at the individual level.

Information services can have many different corporate culture types. There can also be subcultures. Organizational subcultures arise out of the functional differences between traditional work units such as computing centres, libraries or records management. They are natural, healthy phenomena unless they interfere with or detract from the overall corporate culture.

Effective corporate cultures are developed by managers in their activities and behaviours. They can be reinforced by the selection interview, induction process, training and development processes, performance appraisal interview and reward systems. To be successful, there needs to be an appropriate match between the manager's style and behaviour and the corporate culture of the parent organization.

Corporate cultures

The person who establishes the service creates the initial, and usually the strongest, corporate culture. This is achieved through both conscious and unconscious acts. For example, their values and beliefs will be translated into policies and procedures. They will recruit staff who share the same ideas and values. These values will then be unconsciously manifested into norms and behaviours over a period of time. If the culture is strong and effective, it will remain long after the founding person has left the service.

Where information services have been formed through the bringing together of different work units there may either be a single strong culture or a number of subcultures. In the case of the former, the strong culture will either reflect the person who brought the units together, or it will be representative of the dominant work unit. If there are a number of subcultures these will relate to the cultures of the individual work units. The information services manager will need to promote a single unifying culture and merge the subcultures over time.

In information services where traditions and values are deeply rooted, certain behaviours and customs become deeply ingrained. New employees quickly have to learn how the organization operates in order to 'fit in'. Many of these behaviours are tangible issues, such as whether appointments have to be made with secretaries to see the information services manager, the chief executive officer or other directors or heads of department, or whether employees are encouraged to make suggestions. Others are more intangible, such as an acceptable topic of conversation in the lunchroom (there may be taboos on certain subjects), who goes to lunch first, or whether superiors are addressed formally by title or informally by first name.

Corporate cultures are expressed as languages, symbols, myths, stories and rituals. Information service terminology, corporate logos, myths and stories of heroes and their successes, receptions for important visitors and ceremonies to launch new services are examples of these. They are symbolic devices that serve to identify and reinforce the guiding beliefs and values upon which all policies and actions take place. In fact, the information service's culture may be more influential on employee behaviour than the organization structure because of its subtlety and pervasiveness. Corporate culture translates organizational values such as accuracy or customer focus into behaviours at the individual level. This is achieved when employees share a common management philosophy and set of values, and demonstrate these in their work practices.

Corporate culture types

Information services can have many different corporate culture types. In small operations there should only be one culture. This should reflect the corporate culture of the parent organization. In larger information services, where extensive differentiation occurs, more than one culture may exist.

Handy (1976) and Deal and Kennedy (1982) have identified several different culture types within organizations. These are based upon different organizational influences such as organization structure, the amount of risk associated with decision-making and feedback received from the environment. Whilst none of these culture types have been specifically identified for information services, they are useful to consider. All organizations will display the characteristics of a certain type of corporate culture. It is important to understand the culture type in order to work effectively within and with it. There is no universally correct culture. The culture of the organization should be appropriate for the circumstances and the people involved.

Handy

Handy (1976, pp. 178–85) identifies four cultures relating to organization structure that display unique characteristics (see Table 9.1). These are power culture, role culture, task culture and personal culture:

- *Power culture.* Frequently found in small entrepreneurial organizations, traditionally in the robber-baron companies of nineteenth-century America, occasionally in today's trade unions, and in some property and finance companies.
- *Role culture.* Often stereotyped as bureaucracy.
- *Task culture.* Job- or project-oriented.
- *Person culture.* Not found in many organizations. It exists only for the people in it without any superordinate objective, examples being barristers' chambers, architects' partnerships, hippy communities, social groups, families and some small consultancy firms.

Deal and Kennedy

Deal and Kennedy (1982, pp. 108–23) linked the amount of risk associated with decision-making and the feedback received from the environment to different types of corporate culture (see Table 9.2).

They have identified four cultures based on these factors:

Table 9.1 Descriptors of organizational culture types according to Handy

	Power culture	Role culture	Task culture	Personal culture
External environment	Possible political influence.	Must be stable, organization needs to be able to control environment. Monopoly or oligopoly.	Appropriate to flexible and sensitive environments. Most suited to coping with changes to market or product.	
Goals and values	Strong and proud. Faith in individuals. Judgement by results and tolerant of means. Tough and abrasive.	Role or job description is more important than the person who fills it. Slow to perceive need for change. Offers security and predictability to the individual.	Teamwork obliterates individual objectives and most status and style differences. Culture most in tune with current ideologies of change and adaptation, individual freedom and low status differentials.	Provides a base upon which individuals' careers and interests can be furthered. Allegiance to professional group(s) rather than the organization. Organization is subordinate to the individual.
Technology	Non-continuous, discrete operations, one-off job, unit production. Rapidly changing technology.	Undiversified. Product life is long. High degree of interdependence, systemized co-ordination, standardization. Market stable, predictable, controlled.	Product is important. Rapidly changing technology. Non-continuous, discrete operations, one-off productions. High degree of control over work. Market is competitive, product life is short, speed of reaction is important.	Professions, specialists.

120

Organizational structure	Web connected by functional/specialist strings. Small. Growth achieved by spawning new webs. Few rules and regulations. Little bureaucracy.	Bureaucracy co-ordinated by narrow band of senior management. Controlled by procedures, rules and regulations, authority and job descriptions.	Job/project teams formed, reformed, continued. Matrix structure.	Structure exists only to serve individuals within organization. No formal control measures or management hierarchies.
Corporate environment	Individuals will prosper and be satisfied to the extent that they are power-oriented, politically minded, risk-taking.	Individuals selected for satisfactory performance of role. Role could be filled by a range of individuals. Performance over and above role not required. Could even be disruptive.	Individuals have high degree of control over their work, judgement by results.	Individuals do what they are good at. Specialists.
Leadership and management	Central figures determine whether organization moves in the right direction. Requires resource and personal power at centre in order to survive. Power and influence spread out from central figure.	Use of position power. Expert power tolerated. No influence, organization relies upon rules and procedures.	No presiding deity, right people at the right level and get on with the task. Expert rather than position or personal power. Team-oriented, team leaders will compete for resources if scarce.	Influence is shared. Power base, if necessary, is expert.

Source: Adapted from Handy, C. B. (1976), *Understanding Organisations*, Harmondsworth: Penguin.

Table 9.2 Descriptors of organizational culture types according to Deal and Kennedy

	Tough-guy/macho culture	Work-hard/play-hard culture	Bet-your-company culture	Process culture
External environment	Encourages values of risk-taking. High-risk, quick feedback.	Small-risk, intensive feedback.	High-risk, slow feedback.	Low-risk, slow feedback. Financial stakes are low.
Goals and values	Young culture. Focus on speed not endurance. Tough. Intense pressure, frenetic pace. War games. Individualistic. Outlaw heroes are the norm. Chance plays a major part. Superstitions prevent learning from mistakes.	Activity is everything. Primary values centre upon customers and their needs. 'Find a need and fill it.' Heroes are the supersales people. Worth of their activities measured in volume. Energetic games contests, meetings, promotions, conventions. Short-term perspective, many quick fixes. Language is important in culture.	Primary ritual is the business meeting; people from all levels attend, but seating strictly by rank. Values focus on future and importance of investing in it. Careers, products and profits last a lifetime.	Workers get no feedback. Start to develop artificial ties, small events become important. Values centred on technical perfection. Rituals centred upon work patterns and procedures. Attention paid to titles and formalities.
Technology	High financial stakes.	System full of checks and balances to keep job from being high risk. Volume is important, can displace quality.	High investment – capital goods. High-quality inventions, major scientific breakthroughs, not mass-scale.	Heavy regulated industries. Government agencies.

Organizational structure	Bonding – exclusive and exclusionary. Cabals.	Teams and/or groups produce results.	Large systems.	Formalized work patterns and procedures. Tightly structured hierarchy.
Corporate environment	Immature, point scoring. Temperamental, short-sighted. High turnover.	Active people who thrive on quick, tangible feedback. Young people with stamina.	Self-directed and tough. Need stamina to endure long-term ambiguity with little or no feedback. Cautious and deliberate. Spend long periods evaluating. Share hard-won knowledge. Look to mentors.	No feedback, therefore focus on how they do something rather than what they do. Protective and cautious. System's integrity is protected rather than the individual. Orderly, punctual, attend to detail. Carry out written procedures without querying why.
Leadership and management	Quick decision-maker. Aggressive. Tolerate all or nothing risks because of instant feedback.	Friendly, carousing. Team-group effort. No one individual is more important.	Decision-making is top-down, once all inputs are obtained. Self-directed, tough. Authority and expertise are important. Confident in approach.	Bureaucratic. Emphasis upon procedure.

Source: Adapted from Deal, T. E. and Kennedy, A. A. (1982), *Corporate Cultures: the Rites and Rituals of Corporate Life* (Reading, MA: Addison-Wesley).

- *Tough-guy/macho culture.* A world of individuals who regularly take risks and get quick feedback on whether their actions were right or wrong – for example, television or advertising.
- *Work-hard/play-hard culture.* Fun and action are the rule here, and employees take few risks, all with quick feedback. To succeed, the culture encourages them to maintain a high level of relatively low-risk activity. It is found in sales-dominated industries.
- *Bet-your-company culture.* Cultures with big stakes and decisions, where years pass before employees know whether decisions have paid off. A high-risk, slow feedback environment.
- *Process culture.* A world of little or no feedback where employees find it hard to measure what they do; instead they concentrate on how it is done. This bureaucratic culture is typical of banks and government agencies.

Values, beliefs, norms and shared meanings

Values

An information service's culture can be identified by the values system it ascribes to and the climate it creates. Values comprise those matters most important to an individual, group or organization. They have a moral dimension and influence the beliefs and attitudes of individuals and groups. Examples of such values are honesty, loyalty and ethical performance. Values reflect desired behaviours or states of affairs and can influence a person's or group's perceptions of situations and problems. They are the basis of human activities. Values also influence choices, preferences and decisions.

Values are core to the organizational culture. Information services and their parent organizations may not necessarily share common values. Different work areas may place different emphases on work processes, behaviours and priorities. As a result, different values emerge. These need to be acknowledged and understood.

Corporate values reflect much more than their meaning. They stand for clear, explicit philosophies about the information service's or its parent organization's objectives. Consequently the corporate values should be shared between management and their people.

Beliefs

Beliefs are the acceptance of values or convictions about values. They are to a great extent shaped by the consistencies or inconsistencies between values statements and actions or behaviours of superiors or powerful individuals within the information service or parent organization. If there is consistency then their actions will influence the beliefs that would be expected to evolve from the stated values. Inconsistencies between values statements and actions will result in different beliefs and weaken the organizational culture.

To be successful, corporate beliefs should be visible, known and acted upon by all members of the organization. This can only be the case if they are communicated throughout the organization and reinforced through human resource management processes, recognition and rewards. They then become permanently infused and accepted as the norms by which the organization exists.

Norms

Norms are standards of behaviour. Everyday behaviours based upon rules and systems become norms when they are transmitted unconsciously within organizations.

Shared meanings

Shared meanings are different to social norms as they focus upon message exchange, interpretation and interaction sequencing. Shared meaning assumes that people have similar attitudes, values, views of the world and feelings about situations.

Most positive actions take place on the basis of shared meaning or on an assumption that people in the same situation share common experiences and viewpoints. Shared meaning is consequently the system that allows actions, events, behaviours and emotions to take place.

Corporate rituals

Many activities in organizations are expressions of corporate rituals, the consequences of which go beyond the technical details. Examples include induction, training, organizational development activities, sackings and Christmas parties. Trice and Beyer (1984, pp. 653–69) have identified some organizational rites or activities that have social consequences in organizations and these are described below.

Rites of passage

Rites of passage begin with the induction and basic training processes. These allow employees to part with their past identities and status and take on new roles. They minimize the changes that occur in the transition from old to new and re-establish the equilibrium in ongoing social relations. The induction interview with the Chief Executive Officer, or the refurbishment of an office for a new manager, form part of the incorporation rite. Retirement ceremonies and farewell parties are part of the rites of passage when employees retire or resign.

Rites of degradation

Rites of degradation take place when the Chief Executive or person of high authority is fired and replaced, thereby dissolving his or her social identity and power. Such an action may be interpreted as the organization's public acknowledgment that problems exist. As a consequence, group boundaries may be redefined around the previous close supporters of the executive. These supporters may or may not be incorporated into the newly formed groups. The social importance and value of the role are reaffirmed if the executive is replaced. If the position is not filled, it is an indication that it had no importance in the organization.

Rites of enhancement

Enhanced personal status and the social identification of individuals who have been successful within the corporate or professional environment are provided for by 'rites of enhancement'. Examples of such are the granting of membership to an élite group, or the granting of a fellowship or life membership to a member of a professional association. Such a membership is usually jealously guarded by those who have attained such status. Rites of enhancement spread good news about the organization and by association enable others to share some of the credit for these accomplishments.

Rites of renewal

Rites of renewal are provided in organizational development activities such as strategic planning processes, job redesign, team-building and leadership effectiveness training programmes. These are rites that are intended to refurbish or strengthen the existing social structure and improve its functioning.

The latent consequences of rites of renewal are that members are reassured that something is being done to correct organizational problems. However, they can be used to focus attention away from one problem to another. Many of the activities give rise to certain rituals that legitimize and reinforce the existing systems of power and authority.

Conflict reduction rites

Conflict reduction rites involve collective bargaining or feigned fights of negotiation where parties may become hostile, threaten to boycott or walk out of the negotiating process whilst the other parties speak of compromise, point to areas of co-operation and attempt to overcome the anger in a ritualistic way. These actions may deflect attention away from solving problems.

Other forms of conflict reduction rites are the formation of committees, advisory groups or task forces. Most of these groups serve to re-establish equilibrium in disturbed social relations. Confidence is often renewed when it is known that a committee or advisory group has been formed to investigate or advise on an issue.

Rites of integration

Rites of integration encourage and revive common feelings that bind members together and commit them to a social system. Such rites are found in the parent organization's Christmas party. They permit emotions to be vented and allow the temporary loosening of various norms.

Organizational subcultures

Organizational subcultures arise out of the functional differences between departments in information services. These include the use of different technologies, the identification of different values and interests, the use of different terminologies or languages, the employment of different approaches to problem-solving techniques, and the different aspects of the interactive external environment. Poor organizational performance is sometimes blamed upon the presence of subcultures.

Subcultures can also be based on gender, occupation, status, task, tenure, or ethnic origin of the work group. Socio-economic and educational backgrounds can also lead to subcultures being formed. Where strong cultures exist subcultures do not cause problems as the overall values and beliefs are strong. However, in weak cultural environments they can be very destructive as they may obscure overriding values and result in cultural drifts.

Strong and weak corporate cultures

Successful information services have strong corporate cultures. Strong cultures provide meaning and direction to members' efforts. Everyone knows the information service's objectives; people feel better about what they do and, as a consequence, are likely to work harder. The organization's networks carry the beliefs and values.

Strong cultures come from within and are built by the founders and by individual leaders, not consultants. These are people who care about their employees. No matter how distant the work units are from the organization's head office, all sites are treated equally. This is important in information services, where work unit sites may be geographically dispersed over wide areas.

Strong cultures are created, sustained, transmitted and changed through social interaction. That is, through modelling and imitation, instruction, correction, negotiation, story-telling, gossip and observation. They are communicated and reinforced by organization-wide action. High-performing information services ensure that they have well-conceived human resource programmes that reinforce the culture.

Strong cultural values are important to information services as they provide employees with a sense of what they ought to be doing and a knowledge of how they should behave to be consistent with organizational objectives. Strong cultures represent an emotional feeling of being part of the information service and its parent organization, and lead to greater employee commitment and motivation.

Poorly performing information services may still have a strong culture; although this may not necessarily be an effective or healthy one. In these cases the pervading culture is often dysfunctional; focusing upon internal politics rather than external commitments such as the customers' needs.

Developing the corporate culture

As a service organization, an information service's culture should be the set of norms and values that affect employee behaviour in areas of customer services satisfaction, and a concern for quality and innovation in service delivery. Integrity and ethical behaviour may also be valued, particularly where the information service is dealing with commercially sensitive or personal information. These can be manifested in cultural values such as good customer service, a commitment to quality and productivity improvement, increased employee pride and loyalty, respect for individuals and their privacy.

Values can be reinforced through the values statement. This displays the values of the information service for the customer and reinforces these values in the minds of the employees. Figure 9.1 illustrates a typical values statement.

**Information Service
Values Statement**

We value openness, honesty and integrity in individuals.

We uphold the principles of privacy and confidentiality in our handling of information.

We are committed to meeting our customers' needs for accurate, relevant and meaningful information at their point of decision-making.

We strive for excellence in the delivery of services to customers and seek their input to enable us to meet their needs.

We believe that complaints should be heard and responded to promptly.

We are committed to training our staff to offer leading edge information services.

We actively promote equal opportunity and equity in the workplace.

Figure 9.1 Values statement

Cultural values are also reinforced through the various human resource management processes. The selection interview, induction process, training and development practices, performance appraisal, career development and reward systems all provide opportunities for the cultural values to be reinforced.

Prospective employees can be questioned about their attitudes to certain key values, such as quality of service, during the selection interview. All other things being equal, those who hold similar values and beliefs to the desired culture should be given priority over those who do not.

The induction process provides the ideal situation to communicate the desired cultural values. These should be later reinforced by consistent actions in order to instil beliefs. The information service's philosophies and values and the associated management practices should be discussed with the new employee. This will provide them with reasons why certain norms and behaviours are acceptable and others are not. All training and development programmes should reinforce these foundation values and philosophies.

The performance appraisal interview provides the opportunity for feedback and reinforcement of the required values and philosophies. It may also be used to detect underlying subcultures that may need correction if they contradict the overall culture. Employees should be given the opportunity to discuss their own values and beliefs and how these fit into those of the information service.

The reward system should be structured so as to reward those values that are held in high regard. Incentives should be linked to key values. This serves to reinforce the important values in employees' beliefs and enables them to initiate behaviours leading to good organizational performance.

Corporate cultures in information services are shaped by factors such as organizational clarity, managerial philosophy and orientation towards their staff and customers. These determine whether the culture is progressive, outward looking and service oriented, or traditional and inward looking.

The managers' styles and behaviours must be congruent with the organization's values and behaviours. Employees will look to their managers to shape shared meanings, define and create values and demonstrate corporate beliefs. They can act as agents for change and minimize the conflict between inner and outer directed beliefs. Inner and outer directed beliefs often surface in the conflicts that exist between organizational and professional beliefs. The information services manager should assist their staff come to terms with any conflicting beliefs or values.

Ethics and corporate culture

The corporate culture provides the opportunity to develop an ethical philosophy within the information service. Appropriate and workable ethical principles, values and behaviours can be developed and reinforced through the corporate culture. Ethics define what is right and wrong in terms of the behaviour of individuals towards others. Ethical policies and rules, and the values statement form the basis of a code of ethical conduct that is acceptable to the organization. These are then translated into rights, duties and standards of behaviour.

Ethics are generally based upon three principles. These are:

- utilitarian principles, such as the greatest good for the greatest number and responsible care, and accountability in the use of resources;
- individual rights, or respect and protection of the basic rights of individuals such as the right to privacy, to free speech and to due process; and
- justice, where fair and impartial rules are imposed and enforced on everyone to ensure the equitable distribution of costs and benefits.

Ethics are important to the pursuit of excellence. They are part of the quest for quality management. Societal values, the justice and political systems provide the broad framework within which ethical values operate. However these need to be translated into what is acceptable organizational behaviour. Issues such as honesty, fairness and equity, personal development, respect and integrity, efficiencies and accountability should be addressed from the organization's point of view so that people know what is acceptable. Examples where ethical dilemmas can occur in information services are whether it is wrong to use insider information for personal gain, or, whether an individual should impose their own views in censoring information.

A code of ethics can be used to assist individuals deal with ethical problems and conflicts of interest. The code states the ethical rules and expectations that the organization has of its people. The code is particularly useful in environments where there is financial pressure and intense competition for scarce resources and market opportunities. It sets the boundaries and individual responsibilities for what is considered to be ethical behaviour in situations where personal values systems can differ.

The code of ethics and the values statement are important tools through which the organization can communicate its expectations regarding the behaviours of individuals towards each other. Values such as honesty, respect, fairness, integrity and openness should be reinforced and made part of the corporate culture through management actions, practices and procedures.

References

Deal, T. E. and Kennedy, A. A. (1982), *Corporate Cultures: the Rites and Rituals of Corporate Life*, Reading, MA: Addison-Wesley.

Handy, C. B. (1976), *Understanding Organisations*, Harmondsworth: Penguin.

Trice, H. M. and Beyer, J. M. (1984) 'Studying organizational cultures through rites and ceremonials', *Academy of Management Review*, **9**, October, 653–9.

10 Politics

Introduction

Political behaviour is linked to power, influence and competition and is a natural process within organizations. It is both an individual and organizational phenomena. Organizations are made up of individuals and groups of people with different values and interests. Resources are also limited which leads to competition. Even if everyone's interests are catered for, there is often a perception that some individuals, groups or organizational units have been treated more favourably than others. The basis for this is often politics and the personal interpretation of facts. It is inevitable in a competitive environment that people will personally interpret the facts to support their own, or their organizational unit's needs and objectives.

The activity of organizational politics is evident in the competitive behaviour between groups or individuals. Usually this is to ensure that they achieve a higher level of recognition, resource allocation, power or persuasion than their counterparts. To be successful in a competitive environment it is important that the information services manager is politically astute and able to manage the organizational politics for the benefit of the information service.

It is generally accepted that senior managers have to be good politicians. The incidence of political behaviour is greater at the senior levels of management as they strive to have their goals and values adopted by the organization. Strategic decisions made at senior management level are often politically influenced. At lower levels within the organization, politics are most likely to be used by individuals to further their own ambitions – for example to obtain a promotion or salary increase.

Political behaviour is not usually identified as a formal requirement in a job description. However, it is an important, yet unstated, duty of the information services manager to ensure that they and the information service attract all the advantages of power and influence. To survive, the manager must influence, or attempt to influence the distribution of advantages and disadvantages within the organization for the benefit of the information service.

Most politics and competition are beneficial to organizations as they increase the motivation and output of the various programme units or work groups. However, if unchecked politics or political behaviour is used to further an individual's needs at the expense of others it can be detrimental to all concerned.

Whilst people may perceive political tactics to be unfair, many are quite ethical. In considering whether the tactics should be condoned, the deciding feature should be the ethical impact upon the organization and its members.

Lobby groups are a form of political group that attempt to impose their view or influence others. They may try to influence the information service on some issues, or see it as a vehicle through which their cause may be further supported. Managers will also be involved in lobbying in the course of their duties. For example, they may lobby senior management or other stakeholders before important decisions relating to the information service are made.

Individual politics

Individuals will engage in political behaviour either to further their own ends, to protect themselves from others, to further goals which they believe to be in the organization's best interests, or to acquire and exercise power. Even if individuals themselves perceive politics to be unethical they cannot help but be occasionally involved in political battles and political networks.

Individuals who engage in political behaviour often exhibit certain traits that characterize their political style. Those who are highly competitive and have excessively high self-actualization and power needs are more likely to be involved in political behaviour of a Machiavellian nature. These types of people look for career shortcuts and quick fixes. Other traits include the willingness to manipulate people or situations, a high need for control and the ability to exploit situations for their own self-interest.

A second type of political behaviour is the collaborative style. These types of people get things done through others. They build networks of important people by serving on strategic committees. They keep people informed and build their power based upon knowledge and doing favours for others.

The political roles of managers

Generally, the higher the individual is in the organization, the more political their position will be. This is because senior managers need to go out and across organizational boundaries to achieve successful outcomes. At this level, the organizational environment is often turbulent and very competitive.

The political role of the information services manager is to make things happen. This requires them to create a vision and meaningfully convey this to others. To move the vision forward, they must know how to get things done within the parent organization and constructively use their power to drive the change. This requires them to correctly interpret the political environment, to 'open doors', to identify supporters and sponsors, and to quickly build networks, commitment and support.

Information services managers who are politically astute know what is going on within the parent organization and have control over the rules of the political game. They manage the boundaries of the information service so that it is viewed in a favourable light by those in positions of authority. Skilled political managers understand what the parent organization wants and position their services to provide creative solutions to the important problems facing the organization. They stay focused and do not let distractions or operational tasks deter them.

In their political role, information services managers must speak the language that is understood and valued by the senior decision-makers. They regard everyone within the parent organization as a customer and pay attention to how they project their personal image and that of the information service.

Politics in organizations

Political gamesmanship will occur when resources are scarce, when those in control feel threatened, or where there are competing views, values or agendas. Not all organizations (or groups) are as conspicuous in their political behaviour as others. In some organizations politics are overt and rampant, whilst in others, politics are virtually non-existent. Furthermore, some organizations refuse to admit that political behaviour exists. Preferring to believe that all is well because they are ill equipped to manage the conflict that is often associated with political behaviour.

The extent and type of political behaviour in organizations is influenced by the internal and external environment. Organizations that operate under pressure, have a role ambiguity and a low level of trust amongst employees are more likely to witness an overt and Machiavellian style of political behaviour than those that have clear and objective performance measures, an open and trusting environment and plenty of resources.

In bureaucratic organizations the politics will emphasize standards of control, rules, policies and procedures. The power of particular individuals to control and enforce adherence to these will lead to internal politics. In more open environments there will be less emphasis on these aspects. Here the politics will operate within units, work teams or groups, and stress trust and co-operation.

In diverse organizations where there are different objectives, processes and service delivery mechanisms within units or groups, politics and conflict will often arise through misunderstanding and a lack of knowledge of others' tasks and responsibilities. The diverse structures within information services may create an environment where conflict and political rivalry may occur. For example, help desk people or reader services librarians who are used to dealing with diverse and immediate demands of customers may view technical service personnel as inflexible, bureaucratic or bogged down with unnecessary rules. Technical service personnel may likewise view customer services personnel with suspicion.

In changing and competitive organizational environments, the competition and uncertainty leads to differences of opinions and values, and conflicts over priorities and goals. This is true regardless of the size of the organizational unit. Whilst there will be no internal competition in a cost centre run by one person, the person would still need to compete for resources. Their power, influence and political persuasion must still be used on an organization-wide basis. Competition also leads to the formation of pressure groups, lobbying, cliques and cabals, rivalry, personality clashes and alliances. All of these are evidence of organization politics.

Politics and competition are beneficial to all organizations as they usually result in increased output between the competing groups or individuals. However, unchecked politics can result in the organization losing its sense of direction, or spending too much time resolving the problems at the expense of pursuing its corporate objectives.

Political behaviour that is used to further an individual's own needs may be damaging to others or the organization. An example would be an individual who influences management's perception of a co-worker to the extent that the co-worker was viewed unfavourably for promotion. This is the negative side of political behaviour and should be counteracted.

Political tactics

Whilst organization politics may be viewed ambivalently, most people will regard any political tactics that are used by individuals for their personal gain at the expense of others as being unhealthy and unfair. Political tactics can also be genuine and ethical practices that can be beneficial to the organization.

The information services manager should readily be able to identify and use intra-organizational politics for his or her own benefit and that of the information service. Becoming a 'political animal' takes considerable skill, and necessitates the exercise of caution because, if the tactics are used inappropriately, the exercise will almost certainly backfire. It is necessary, however, for the information services manager to become skilful at identifying political tactics in order to recognize situations where politics are adversely affecting them or their service.

There are several effective political tactics which are commonly used in organizations. Some of these are ethical, others are not (see Table 10.1).

Table 10.1   Ethical and unethical political tactics used in organizations

Clean tactics (ethical)	Dirty tactics (unethical)
1 Establishing an alliance with others who are willing to support the preferred position or action. Others may include peers, subordinates and superiors – but it is important that the right allies are chosen. These should be people who have something to contribute and who can be relied upon. Arising out of such an alliance can be the formation of a power coalition.	1 Attacking or blaming others – creating a scapegoat by falsely attributing blame for negative outcomes to others. Holding others responsible for events they did not produce.
2 Choosing a powerful mentor. Having an influential mentor can be beneficial to one's career. Such a relationship can be an effective tactic to acquiring power as others view associates of powerful people as being powerful themselves – part of the aura is passed on. Powerful mentors can assist in the reaching of important goals by 'opening doors'	2 Withholding or distorting information either restricts the flow of information to others or provides them with misleading 'facts'. Either action will hinder the decision-making process, create frustration and anguish for the individual or groups, and often harm the organization as a whole.

or establishing networks. They can also provide protection and guidance when necessary, a valuable asset in the tough times.

3 Developing a base of support for one's ideas. In effect it enhances the individual's personal power base through the use of reverent power. Once a base of support for one's ideas is gained, the supporters will want to identify with the individual and their idea.

3 Use of hidden agendas. Announcing one agenda for meetings and then following a totally different 'hidden' one, preventing opponents from being adequately prepared.

4 Projecting a favourable image to management and others. People who demonstrate a high level of competence are viewed with having a considerable degree of expert and/or referent power through the 'halo' effect.

4 Spreading false rumours about individuals on a personal or behavioural basis.

5 Establishing control over access to information. As information is a vital commodity, anyone who has control over information flow, or access to information yields considerable power. This 'gatekeeper' function can be determined by organization structure and alliances or networks.

5 Leaking confidential information about the organization to the media.

6 Praising others and ingratiating oneself with powers can create a referent power source. There should be sincerity in the action, otherwise the falsity of the action will be transparent.

7 Neutralizing opponents – co-opting enemies. Often people whose support is required but who currently stand in the way are co-opted into the group. Once they are made part of the group

they become subject to its norms and adopt its values and goals.

In meetings, those known to be opponents of an item on the agenda can be partly neutralized if they are seated next to the individual who is proposing the item.

8 Creating obligations and a basis for reciprocity. IOUs can be scattered by doing favours for others, assisting them with problems or supporting them against their opponents. All these actions will place them in debt. Effective users of these strategies will always get more than they give. The value of a favour may be worth more to the receiver than to the doer, the doers usually find the favours smaller and easy to perform.

In deciding which tactics are ethical or unethical, the impact of the political behaviour upon the rights of others should be addressed. If basic human rights are violated, the political tactics are unethical. The principles of equity and fair play should also be considered, both in terms of individuals and the organization. Often political behaviour is judged according to a utilitarian approach, being the greatest good for the greatest number. Where behaviours are viewed as unethical or illegitimate they should be made to cease immediately.

To survive in competitive organizational environments, it is paramount that the information services manager and their staff identify the political behaviours of others and manage their own. They need also to be aware that, even if their actions are not personally politically motivated, others may assume so.

Several steps can be used by the manager or supervisor to minimize the political behaviour of subordinates where it can be seen to be detrimental to their position or that of the information service. These include bringing disputes or disagreements into the open where they can be solved, and providing challenging situations and feedback to all.

Presenting political arguments

Not all dealings with people can be carried out on a personal basis where the person has the ability to respond to verbal and non-verbal messages in reinforcing their political argument. Similarly, the information services manager may not always be present at meetings to respond to questions, reinforce arguments or apply political persuasion. The political argument may need to be presented in a report that is prepared in advance of the meeting. In this situation, the political argument should be able to stand on its own accord.

In presenting arguments, it is important that each item is properly researched and simply portrayed with the appropriate level of detail and content. Often the audience for the report will have little time. The more explicit and lucid the comments, the more favourably the report is likely to be received.

The contents of the report should anticipate and answer likely questions, and be self-explanatory. Reports should include an executive summary that covers the important issues and recommendations for action. In some situations, senior management or stakeholders may only have the time to read the executive summary in detail. It should articulate the main points that will lead the decision-makers to a favourable outcome.

The full body of the report should be clearly signposted. It should be broken down into headings and subheadings to make it easy to read and find relevant information. It should include an introductory heading, an introduction, current information on the subject of the report, viable alternative courses of action and a recommendation(s). The opening paragraph of the main body of the report should summarize any previous history or background and indicate why the report is necessary. The current situation should be described providing up-to-date, relevant information in as precise and brief a form as possible. The alternative courses of action should be identified. These should discuss the relevant advantages, disadvantages, costings and outcomes. A preferred option should be recommended with reasons where applicable.

Lobbying and lobby groups

Lobbying is an attempt to influence decisions at the ownership level through persuasion and the provision of information. Occasionally the information services manager may lobby as a political strategy. For example, when the survival, stability or growth of the information service is at stake.

Good communication channels between all levels of the organization will enhance the spread of information. At times, it may be necessary to supply additional information which will further the information service's cause. Lobbying occurs when this is provided to higher levels, either verbally or in writing, in an attempt to influence the decisions. Lobbying is a legitimate practice if used positively and with care and thought.

The information services manager may also be the subject of lobbying from lobby groups. Lobby groups that result from organized interest groups are features of modern democratic societies. The information services manager should balance the lobby group's concerns with the overall needs of the customers or community. This should be to ensure that no one sector of the community influences the services to the detriment of others.

Lobby groups often regard government as a pervasive and powerful source, influencing every facet of an individual's life. Most information services are also seen to be influential as information is perceived to be power. Lobby groups may attempt to make the information service an avenue through which their point of view is promulgated to the detriment of the opposing point of view.

Lobby or interest groups can constitute the principal potential avenue of influence outside of official government interaction. They need to be considered but not allowed to impose their requirements upon the organization. If possible, their energies should be channelled in a direction that can help the information service and its parent organization.

Politics is a natural process within organizations, as individuals and work units compete for recognition and scarce resources. Politics is also about the distribution of advantages and disadvantages, and how individuals use their power and influence in this distribution process. Whilst those who lose may perceive politics to be unfair, many are quite ethical. However, unchecked or unethical politics are unfair. They have the capacity to harm the organization as well as its people and should not be tolerated within the organizational culture.

11 Policy-making

Introduction

Policy-making is a complex activity that involves consultation with individuals and groups from within the information service and parent organization and with other external stakeholders. Organizations are made up of individuals and groups of people with different values and interests. Policy-making is one mechanism to ensure that these individual interests are managed for the greater good, and to ensure that individuals within the organization are moving forward in the same direction. Policy-making is also necessary to safeguard individual rights.

The information service and its parent organization may also be subjected to policies and standards that have been established by external parties, such as government bodies.

Policy-making incorporates the development of policies, standards and guidelines. Policy development is an ongoing process that should include continuous consultation with internal and external stakeholders.

Use of policies in organizations

Policies ensure that decisions are in keeping with the organization's philosophies. They can be used to enhance the image that the parent organization is a good corporate citizen. Policies, standards and guidelines are used within organizations to:

- solve a recurrent problem at the organizational level;
- provide guidance for individuals in decision-making;

- ensure consistency in approach across the organization;
- declare an intention or enable a stance to be taken on a contemporary issue;
- clarify organizational values and intentions;
- make a commitment; and
- grant rights or entitlements.

Policies are guides to the decision-making process. Like objectives, policies can either be general or specific. General policies are used throughout the organization, and are usually broad and comprehensive. They affect all work units and levels of staff. General policies address issues such as the use of office equipment for home or personal use; or, security and risk covering access to systems and the need to protect personal information. Some general policies will be influenced by legislation or policies and standards that have been established by external parties. For example, general policies on the protection and use of software may be influenced by copyright legislation or the parent organization's licence conditions with the software vendor.

Specific policies relate to operational issues. They have significance for a particular department or work unit and are more relevant to day-to-day issues or specific activities. Only those individuals who are directly concerned with the activity or work unit will be affected. A policy that relates to the selection process in a children's collection in a public library is an example of a specific policy.

Policy development

Policies are usually carried out by others than those who design them. Good policies are developed with this in mind, for if they cannot be implemented effectively, they will fail. The following provides advice on policy development. For the purposes of brevity, the word 'policy' is used, but the process is equally applicable to the development of standards and guidelines.

The policy-making process should be well planned and thought out in terms of strategic timing, costs, issues at stake, and the values and attitudes of the internal and external stakeholders. All policies imply some form of change, whether at the strategic or operational level. As a result, conflict may arise that may in turn jeopardize the policy.

Policy-making is an ongoing process. It does not start or stop in the form of discrete events. Effective policy-making involves continuous modification, pruning and adjustment. This continuous improvement in the policies should be reflective of any amendments to the corporate objectives or repositioning of the parent organization within the changing competitive environment.

Steps to policy development

Policy development should be undertaken through a series of steps (see Figure 11.1). The first step is to ensure that all environmental factors that could impact upon the policy are taken into consideration. Those developing the policy should be cognizant of the financial, social and political context of the parent organization and how these could shape the available options and strategies. For example, the financial situation of the parent organization may limit the choice of outcome or scale of the policy, and call for a gradual implementation of the policy.

The policy development process should take into account known values of all stakeholders (internal and external). The likely future scenarios for the organization and the environment in which the policy will operate should be identified so that the policy can be designed with the future state in mind. Timing is also an important consideration in policy development, particularly when the policy may have some political impact for the organization.

The next step is to identify the issue and to determine whether this can be solved through a policy or an alternative mechanism. Not all issues can be solved through policies. Likewise, policies should not be created for aggrandizement or self-importance. Policies are useful to resolve common sources of disagreement or provide guidance on an emerging issue that has been identified through the environmental scanning process.

Once it has been determined that the development of a policy may be the best solution to the problem, the objective and desired outcome should be clearly defined. The parameters and priorities for the policy should be set. The internal and external stakeholders should be identified so that they can be included in the consultation process. It is also useful at this stage to identify any champions who may assist in the promotion of the policy at either the development or implementation stage.

The next stage is the research stage. Evidence used in the preparation of the policy and the development of the policy statement should be explicit. The criteria used for the basis of judgement should be transparent. The sources of information that can be used as evidence to support policy development vary widely. They can range from in-depth interviews with stakeholders to literature searches and consideration of like policies produced by similar organizations. Expert knowledge is essential to policy innovation and experts in the field should be consulted.

A cost benefit analysis of the policy options and their impacts as identified to date should be undertaken. Once the background information

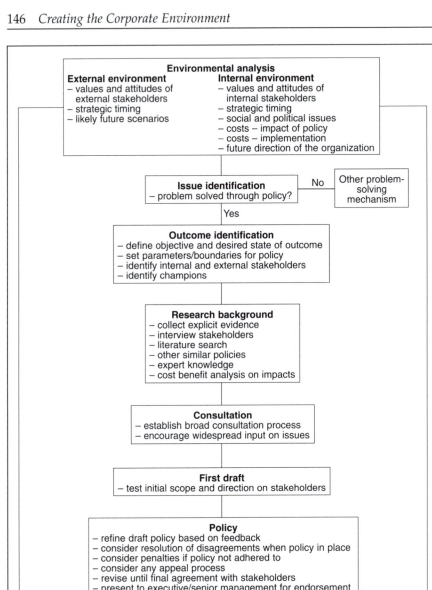

Figure 11.1   The policy development process

has been gathered an impression or judgement of the policy scope and direction can be developed and tested on a number of stakeholders. A draft policy can then be written. This should be further revised after consultation with stakeholders until there is agreement to the policy.

Continuous consultation with both internal and external stakeholders is of particular importance. External stakeholders may include suppliers, the local community, the media, government officials and interest groups. The process of consultation with stakeholders may become a political exercise. The stakeholders may hold vested interests in a particular course of action or in the advancement of their personal power. An objective view should be maintained. Alternative approaches and counter-scenarios should be developed to enable the best possible solution.

The political interests or bias of individual stakeholders cannot be dismissed as the policy will need to be workable for all. The reasons behind the interests must be understood so that these can be considered and accommodated alongside other interests. If these interests are not acknowledged, and the stakeholders are in a position of power such that they can control the activities surrounding the policy, then the result may be that the policy is either ignored or vetoed. Similarly, stakeholders who are known to have opposing interests to the proposed policy should not be ignored. Their views should be canvassed and they should be involved in the decision-making process.

The individual with the task of developing the policy should also ensure that their own values and preferences do not influence the subject-matter. The underlying factor is that policy-making should be free from bias and all points of view should be considered in the formation of the policy.

Policy development should not just take into account the current operative environment. It should be future oriented, anticipating new demands or developments. It does, however, need to be workable and able to address the circumstances that are prevalent at the time. The organization's future ability to fund and operationally implement the policy should also be considered. Impractical solutions create frustration and confusion, and should be discounted. The development of the policy should take into consideration the outcomes that stakeholders regard as being possible. 'Success stories' or 'horror stories' from other policy initiatives should be highlighted and this knowledge built upon.

The policy development process should take into account how issues may be resolved where there is disagreement about the contents of the policy once it is in place. Where appropriate, a disciplinary process and penalties for failing to act within the policy should be developed. Any disciplinary process should be matched by an appeal process.

When all stakeholders have agreed the policy, it should be submitted to senior management for endorsement.

The development of the policy is the first part of the policy process. Once developed, the policy needs to be implemented and its performance monitored. It may need to be refined to take into account changing circumstances.

Inhibitors to effective policy development

Very few policy development processes are fully resourced or provided with sufficient time to investigate and present different options. Often the need for a quick decision limits the level of consultation. There is also the danger that policy development is 'fitted in' to existing workloads and priorities. In these situations, policy solutions can be limited in input, relevant expertise, innovation and strategy.

Policy framework

The policy framework of an information service generally includes policies, standards and guidelines. Standards differ from policies in that they are usually technical in nature. They define levels of conformity and input, and establish performance outputs. Guidelines supplement policies and standards, providing further background information. They are often used to provide advice regarding the implementation of the policy and standards.

Policy statement

The policy statement describes the policy. It is usually brief. The policy statement may be supplemented by statements about:

- the policy objective and scope;
- responsibility for implementation, review and audit;
- background issues; and
- implementation strategies.

Standards

Standards provide for consistency in the use of resources. In information services, standards provide rules about the choice and management of information and its supporting technologies. Standards may be set at the international, national and organizational level. They include protocols, data capture and transfer standards, bibliographic descriptions and standards for record-keeping. Standards may also determine accommodation requirements and service levels. These will be particularly important in identifying customer service levels or in instances where services are contracted out to third parties.

Guidelines

Guidelines provide a more in-depth description about the policies and standards. They are often very practical and address the implementation and operational issues that are associated with the policies and standards.

Policy manual

Policies, standards and guidelines are usually grouped together in a policy manual, although many organizations may also have a set of unwritten policies. The policy manual is a convenient way of communicating the policies, standards and guidelines within an organization. It may be used as one of the induction tools for new members of staff.

The policy manual may not be in paper form; organizations are now recognizing the value of maintaining their policies in electronic form. This allows all personnel to have access to policies independent of distance or time. The electronic reticulation of policies avoids duplication of effort and eliminates the possibility of out-of-date policy material being used in decision-making.

Policies for information services

Effective information service policies solve problems or channel decisions towards achieving the objectives of the service and its parent organization. Once overall policies or standards have been established, they can be effective tools for moving decision-making to the point of service delivery. With an effective policy framework, individuals and groups can take initiatives in making decisions knowing that the outcomes will still be in line with the ultimate achievement of the organization's objectives.

The following provide examples of information service policy issues within an organization:

General policies

- Protection of copyright in the use of software.
- Protection of privacy and commercial confidentiality in information.
- Protection and respect for copyright in electronic and printed media.
- Security.
- Archives.

- Information ownership and accountability.
- Use of office equipment for home or personal use.

Specific policies and standards

- Naming standards for records.
- Charging for information services and products.
- Support for training and education to increase organizational knowledge about the value, management and use of information.
- Data capture and transfer standards.
- Collection selection.

Policies are mechanisms for ensuring that individuals are treated fairly and equitably and that individual interests are managed for the greater good. They are guides to decision-making. Accordingly they should be developed through a consultative process with all stakeholders to ensure that different values and interests are considered in decisions.

12 Creativity and intrapreneurship

Introduction

Creativity and intrapreneurship are necessary ingredients for organizations to survive major changes in the environment. Creativity provides organizations with the means to deal with the unstructured problems arising out of competitive and rapidly changing environments. Creativity and innovation are championed by intrapreneurs.

Creativity requires a culture that supports risk-taking without penalty when mistakes occur. Management should be willing to take risks and allow their staff to make mistakes as part of the learning process. Staff must be receptive to innovation and willing to perceive change as an opportunity rather than a threat. Although conflict is inevitable during the change that innovative processes bring, it needs to be managed to ensure that creativity is not stifled.

The creative environment is one that allows champions of change to set standards, promote ideas, to build support and to implement new ideas. It requires a corporate culture that values flexibility and adaptability; one that is both supportive of open communication as well as being open to ideas. A creative environment is fostered and maintained through management practices, rewards systems and performance reviews that support and actively encourage ideas generation and divergent thoughts in problem-solving.

Successful creativity requires a balanced mix of idea generation, intrapreneurship, project-leading, management, gate-keeping, coaching and operating. These key functions require people with specific skills and personal attributes.

Creating an innovative environment

Intrapreneurs as change agents

Intrapreneurs are the entrepreneurs who champion creativity and change within an organization. They require the cross-specialized talents of entrepreneurship, risk-taking, idea-generation and gate-keeping in order to lead and manage natural love–hate relationships, confrontation and conflict. Interdepartmental rivalries and conflicts need to be resolved with care to ensure that creativity is not stifled, that ineffective compromises are not made and that interdepartmental communication and co-operation are not adversely affected during the period of change.

Creativity produces change that further creates conflict. Creativity can also be used to manage resistance to change and conflict. The conversion of conventional work practices and values into ones that are entrepreneurial and risk-taking takes considerable skill and foresight. A culture needs to be created that not only values better performance, leadership and entrepreneurship, but also sustains that commitment year after year. This means a major shift in the values for some staff, not just a slight increase in awareness of entrepreneurship or the establishment of one or two new programmes or activities for the year. The people leading the change will have to champion their cause, motivate and prepare others to readily accept change.

Staff must be persuaded to accept change, and alter their work tasks and behaviours accordingly. They should be prepared to perceive it as an opportunity rather than a threat. Most people are creatures of habit and resist change, seeing it as threatening their existence. It takes leadership skills to create an environment in which change is accepted as the norm.

Willingness to take risks

There must be a willingness by management to take risks and allow staff to make mistakes. If failure means the loss of a job or not being given the opportunity to try something new again, either on a group or individual basis, creativity and innovation will be discouraged. Furthermore, the corporate culture will hold the belief that if you value your job, it is not worthwhile to attempt anything difficult or challenging.

Risk-taking does not, however, mean short-term orientations, or giving the impression that only winners get promoted. It also does not include proceeding with an action prior to considering all its possible consequences.

Establish direction

There needs to be a clear definition of the mission in order that the intrapreneurs know what the information service is to achieve. The innovative and creative ideas must be congruent with the mission statement and have clearly set directions. The intrapreneurs need to focus upon the real needs of the customers and create a distinctive level of performance that matches those needs.

Creativity and innovation are achieved through long-term outlooks and strategies. It is not achieved through management control systems or short-term efficiencies: the pay-off to innovative practices may not be delivered immediately. This is not to say that short-term efficiencies should not exist. These are still important but are not always linked to creativity and innovation.

Open communication

Creativity and innovation rely upon open communication channels with the external environment. The information services manager must develop reliable networks in the external environment in order to disseminate and obtain information.

Open internal communication of information and advice is also important. Unnecessary bureaucratic procedures or lines of authority should be discontinued as these tend to stifle creativity and innovation. Staff should be allowed to exchange ideas and experiences with people of different levels throughout the organization. They should be encouraged to make suggestions, and all ideas should be evaluated.

Some staff will be more creative than others. Whilst all staff should be encouraged to be creative, divergent thinkers should be particularly motivated. Individuals with talent should be recognized and encouraged to champion their ideas. All staff should be aware that even the most unusual idea will be considered by management.

Creativity and innovation can be stifled if there is lack of support from senior management, lack of necessary time for thought and discussion, and a lack of funds. Managers should believe in and encourage creativity and innovation and communicate these beliefs formally and informally. It is necessary that this is a two-way process, allowing staff the opportunity to provide feedback. Informal, two-way communication of values and beliefs is the most effective method of creating a creative corporate culture.

Impact of organizational structure

Organizational structures can either inhibit or encourage creativity.

Organizations that consist of small teams or groups are more likely to foster creativity as new ideas and fast action can flourish without bureaucratic overheads. Strong lines of authority often prevent initiative and creativity. Organizational structures also influence the behaviours, communication and interactions of people. A structure that facilitates the sharing and testing of ideas is a prerequisite for creativity and innovation. Successful organizations are designed to encourage creativity and change.

Managing the individual

An innovative climate is also created through opportunities being built into policies and practices. Staff should be given the freedom to try new ways of performing tasks. Challenging, yet realistic, goals should be set and immediate and timely feedback on performance given. Participative decision-making and problem-solving should be encouraged. Responsibility should be delegated to allow staff to be self-guiding in their work.

Innovative organizations create a culture in which there is a broad acceptance of responsibility and a commitment to the organization that goes beyond the individual's functional role. Staff view their organization with pride, and, as a leader or role model for others. This in turn reinforces their commitment and dedication to the organization.

Personal development strategies should allow for creative pastimes. The balance of right- and left-brain activities is necessary to assist personal growth and achievement. Creativity can also play a part in making personal career decisions in times of contracting employment opportunities. Individuals who are creative in setting their career goals and proactively seek opportunities to achieve these will be more likely to succeed than those who do not.

Roles and functions in a creative environment

Successful creativity and innovation rely upon a balance of different functions: idea generation; entrepreneurship or championing; project-leading; gate-keeping; and coaching (see Table 12.1). It is also dependent upon routine technical problem-solving, problem definition, idea-nurturing, information transfer, information integration and programme-pushing.

These functions can only be successfully performed by people who have a diversity of skills. The functions require different types of goals, measures and controls.

Routine management units should not necessarily be mixed with

Table 12.1 Critical functions in the creativity process

Critical function	Personal characteristics	Organizational activities
Idea-generating	Expert in one or two fields. Enjoys conceptualization; comfortable with abstractions. Enjoys doing innovative work. Usually is an individual contributor. Often will work alone.	Generates new ideas and tests their feasibility. Good at problem-solving. Sees new and different ways of doing things. Searches for the breakthroughs
Entrepreneuring or championing	Strong application interests. Possesses a wide range of interests. Less propensity to contribute to the basic knowledge of a field. Energetic and determined; puts self on the line.	Sells new ideas to others in the organization. Gets resources. Aggressive in championing his or her 'cause'. Takes risks.
Project-leading	Focus on decision-making, information and questions. Sensitive to the needs of others. Recognizes how to use the organizational structure to get things done. Interested in a broad range of disciplines and in how they fit together (e.g. marketing, finance).	Provides the team leadership and motivation. Plans and organizes the project. Ensures that administrative requirements are met. Provides necessary co-ordination amongst team members. Sees that the project moves forward effectively.

Table 12.1 continued

Project-leading (cont'd)		Balances the project goals with organizational needs.
Gate-keeping	Possesses a high level of technical competence. Is approachable and personable Enjoys the face-to-face contact of helping others.	Keeps informed of related developments that occur outside the organization through journals, conferences, colleagues, other companies. Passes information on to others; finds it easy to talk to colleagues. Serves as an information resource for others in the organization (i.e. authority on who to see or on what has been done). Provides informal co-ordination among personnel.
Sponsoring or coaching	Possesses experience in developing new ideas. Is a good listener and helper. Can be relatively objective. Often is a more senior person who knows the organizational ropes.	Helps develop people's talents. Provides encouragement, guidance, and acts as a sounding-board for the project leader and others. Provides access to a power base within the organization – a senior person.

Table 12.1 continued

Sponsoring or coaching (cont'd)	Buffers the project team from unnecessary organizational constraints.
	Helps the project team to get what it needs from the other parts of the organization.
	Provides legitimacy and organizational confidence in the project.

Source: Reprinted from 'Staffing the innovative technology-based organisation' by Roberts, E. B. and Fusfeld, A. R., *Sloan Management Review*, Spring 1981, p. 25, by permission of publisher. Copyright 1981 by the Sloan Management Review Association. All rights reserved.

entrepreneurial ones. People who excel at organizing, exploiting and optimizing what already exists may not be expert in championing new ideas. Although this should not prevent them from becoming involved. Routine processes and procedures should not be allowed to cut off the generation of good ideas and block their movement through the organization.

Creativity and intrapreneurship require people who:

- know what they are supposed to do;
- want to do it;
- are motivated towards doing it; and
- are supplied with the tools and continuous affirmation that enables them to do it.

A mix of champions, sponsors, innovative leaders and creative, flexible staff achieves this. Champions are people who believe that a new idea is really critical. They will push ahead with their idea, no matter what the roadblocks. Champions are necessary for creative and innovative information services as they get things done, often at considerable personal costs to themselves.

Creative and innovative ideas also need sponsors. Sponsors are people sufficiently high up in the organization to marshal the required resources to support the proposed intrapreneurial activity. Once convinced of the activity's value, sponsors provide the necessary resources – that is, people, information, time and money. Creativity and innovation cannot be achieved without a mix of bright, creative minds and an experienced, flexible staff who are able to convert the ideas into outcomes.

Reference

Roberts, E. B. and Fusfeld, A. R. (1981), 'Staffing the innovative technology-based organization', *Sloan Management Review*, Spring, 19–32.

13 Managing expertise

Introduction

Information services are made up of people whose functions and purposes differ. There are task differentiations of a clerical, professional and administrative nature, people who plan and those who execute, and differentiation according to the subject specialization, media or the technology involved. In addition, most information services belong in organizations where further differentiations of task and perspective occur. These differentiations can often be a source of conflict. An understanding that the true reasons for the conflict are not personal but related to role or specialization can be personally reassuring. The recognition that sources of conflict in organizations are often related to roles rather than individuals can also assist in maintaining good personal relationships between people whose roles are in conflict.

Differentiation is demonstrated in the organization structure and in job descriptions. It is also seen in the social roles of employees, the distribution of power, control and reward systems and the communication process. Differentiation leads to the rise of subcultures and the presence of different values not just between departments, but also between different types of staff. It may also lead to intergroup conflict.

Differences in values occur between specialists and other staff in the organization through varying work emphases, codes of ethics, tasks, work orientations, training standards, identities and sources of motivation. These affect the way individuals view each other and have implications for the management of specialist staff.

Differentiation in organizations

Values

People with different roles and functions will place a different emphasis and value on priorities, time horizons and outlook. Whilst all might have a customer focus and are of equal value to the organization, their own values pertaining to their roles within the organization will differ. For example, differences in values often occur between specialist and administrative personnel, or between people with a strategic focus and those providing technical support. This will often cause each to view the other with suspicion.

Some of the differences occur because people in one work group do not fully understand the roles and functions of other work groups. They are not aware of each others' contribution to the organization. They only see the others' roles in the areas of work that immediately affect them or where the work unit boundaries overlap. Often people with different role functions will be physically separated from each other, which will further reinforce their differences. Their motives for actions will also differ. For example, finance or administrative staff may value their ability to make savings in expenditure for the organization, whilst the front-line or service delivery personnel may wish for more money to increase their opportunities for customer service delivery.

The task environment

Information services staff usually work as a team and have a strong identity with their work unit. This is the result of the task structures within information centres, individuals' dependence upon each other to get things done and, often, the physical separation of each component of the service. For example, computing centres, libraries and records management functions are often housed in purpose-built accommodation and may be separate from each other and from the rest of the organization. As a result, information service staff may be perceived as being 'different' by administrators in the rest of the organization who work to preserve the organization's hierarchy.

Outlook

By their nature, most people working in information services are cosmopolitan people. Their strong sense of specialization in libraries, records management, multimedia or information systems results in the view that they are specialists working for an organization. They often have a low identity with any one particular organization as their career development lies within their area of expertise. In comparison, administrators are local people. They are primarily organization people who just happen to be in the role of an administrator. Often, they are trained internally by the organization and judged accordingly. Their career development lies in promotion up the organization's hierarchy. This often leads to conflicts of goals arising between information services staff and administrators.

Assessment

The standard of training for specialists in information services and their subsequent expertise and competence is often set by the various professional associations. Their professional peers will also judge their ongoing performance. In addition to this, information service personnel have to conform to internal organizational standards. Their annual performance appraisal usually will be based on the achievement of the organizational objectives and standards rather than their professional ones. If the values and norms differ widely between the two, the individual could experience a role conflict situation and this could ultimately affect their motivation.

Organizations and peers frequently recognize and acknowledge a different set of achievements. Peers may recognize achievement through the delivery of papers at conferences, publishing on the Internet or in professional journals. This may not be recognized to the same degree by the employing organization. The recognition of achievement within the organization may be more aligned to the organization's own objectives and values.

Culture

The various specialists that are found in information services have their own culture. They use particular terminologies linked to their specialist areas, display symbols such as their diplomas and degrees, and often hold the norms and values of their professional association. The use of certain terms or phrases may be threatening to others if they are uncertain of their meaning. Likewise, many tasks are specific to their roles. The terminology used to describe the tasks and the reasons for doing them may differ from other parts of the organization. This can lead to a misunderstanding of the reasons for certain tasks and the attitude that some information service personnel are too highly paid.

Motivation

The strong sense of identity within the various specialists in information services leads to other behaviours and attitudes. Motivation is often found in the value of the service rather than in professional gain. Information service personnel will often require a high degree of freedom and autonomy in their areas of work. This is partly due to their physical separation from the rest of the organization and also to the nature of their tasks.

Career development

The difference in outlook between the various specialists in information services has implications for their career development, training and reward systems. The internal career path needs may differ between specialists, and with the rest of the organization. Usually the only avenues of promotion within organizations are to managerial positions. This may be contrary to the needs of the specialist who will find the additional administrative responsibilities unwelcome. Managers need to develop career paths for specialists in information services who wish to continue working in their area of expertise but require more responsibility and recognition and rewards for their achievements.

Reward systems

Reward systems will also differ for the different types of staff employed in information services. Specialist staff can be motivated by improved work conditions, opportunities for professional contact and autonomy in the workplace, rather than by money or status.

The information services manager should be aware of differences in values between specialist staff and staff in other parts of the organization. They may need occasionally to explain these differences in order to minimize conflict. Within their own staff hierarchy, the information services manager should minimize conflict through open communication and the provision of appropriate career development, staff training and reward systems.

Developing the common good

The differentiations in expertise and values within information services and with the parent organization need to be managed so that the competitive elements foster rather than hinder the organization's objectives. The information services manager will need to identify ways to motivate individuals who are specialists in their field, whilst still maintaining the organization's competitiveness. The value of the specialist expertise should be recognized and balanced against the strengths that others can offer, such as their internal knowledge of the history of the organization.

Goals should be set that encourage specialists to look further than their area of expertise. Differences in values, and the reasons for these, should be openly explored and discussed. A greater understanding of the differences in values, attitudes and behaviour will help reduce the barriers of acceptance. Role conflict between specialist groups should be recognized for what it is rather than as a personal issue.

Part 5

Getting things done in the corporate environment

This part of the book addresses the leadership, interpersonal and people management roles needed to get things done through other people in the corporate environment of the information service and its parent organization (see Figure P5.1).

Chapter 14 addresses the issue of leadership. It outlines classical leadership theories and provides tangible mechanisms for measuring the effectiveness of a leader.

Linked to leadership are the behaviour processes of power, influence, authority and delegation. Chapter 15 explores the five bases of power and identifies how individuals often acquire power within organizations. The chapter also considers how influence is used to get things done and how power can be institutionalized in authority. Finally the power–authority continuum is extended to the process of delegation; whereby authority can be distributed throughout the information service so that others may share the work and responsibilities.

Nothing can get done within an organization without decisions being made. Chapter 16 acknowledges that in changing and uncertain environments decisions are sometimes based upon perceptions and intuition. Some managers appear more reluctant to make decisions than others. Some of this is to do with their personal decision-making style. Four decision-making styles are explored. In keeping with the trend to a more participative leadership approach, the advantages and disadvantages of

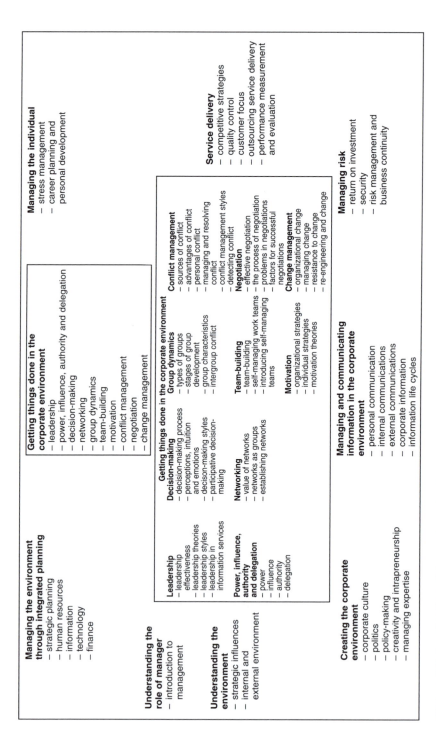

Managing the environment through integrated planning
– strategic planning
– human resources
– information
– technology
– finance

Managing the individual
– stress management
– career planning and personal development

Understanding the role of manager
– introduction to management

Understanding the environment
– strategic influences
– internal and external environment

Getting things done in the corporate environment
– leadership
– power, influence, authority and delegation
– decision-making
– networking
– group dynamics
– team-building
– motivation
– conflict management
– negotiation
– change management

Service delivery
– competitive strategies
– quality control
– customer focus
– outsourcing service delivery
– performance measurement and evaluation

Getting things done in the corporate environment

Leadership
– leadership effectiveness
– leadership theories
– leadership styles
– leadership in information services

Power, influence, authority and delegation
– power
– influence
– authority
– delegation

Decision-making
– decision-making process
– perceptions, intuition and emotions
– decision-making styles
– participative decision-making

Networking
– value of networks
– networks as groups
– establishing networks

Group dynamics
– types of groups
– stages of group development
– group characteristics
– intergroup conflict

Team-building
– team-building
– self-managing work teams
– introducing self-managing teams

Motivation
– organizational strategies
– individual strategies
– motivation theories

Conflict management
– sources of conflict
– advantages of conflict
– personal conflict
– managing and resolving conflict
– conflict management styles
– detecting conflict

Negotiation
– effective negotiation
– the process of negotiation
– problems in negotiations
– factors for successful negotiations

Change management
– organizational change
– managing change
– resistance to change
– re-engineering and change

Managing risk
– return on investment
– security
– risk management and business continuity

Creating the corporate environment
– corporate culture
– politics
– policy-making
– creativity and intrapreneurship
– managing expertise

Managing and communicating information in the corporate environment
– personal communication
– internal communications
– external communications
– corporate information
– information life cycles

Figure P5.1   Getting things done in the corporate environment

166

using participative and group decision-making are also addressed.

Personal networks allow managers to function successfully. They can be used to seek and provide information, for support and to influence outcomes. Chapter 17 explains the value of networks, how a network acts as a group, and provides advice on how to establish networks.

Chapter 18 provides an understanding of group dynamics at the organizational and individual levels. A manager's understanding of group behaviour is as important as understanding individual behaviour. This is because people act differently when they are in a group. In order to achieve outcomes managers have to recognize the roles of different types of groups and their stages of group development. These need different management styles.

Both informal and formal groups can be found in organizations. The presence and leadership of informal groups will often provide an insight into the power, politics and authority within the information service and its parent organization. As groups develop they assume certain characteristics that are associated with group norms, member roles and group cohesiveness. As members of groups, individuals play different roles. These roles can change the way in which people behave in certain situations; they can also create a situation of personal conflict. Chapter 18 explains this and why conflict occurs at the personal level, between members of the group during the development stage and between groups.

A further aspect of group development is team-building. The major difference between a group and a team is that groups generally have one leader. In a team, all the members are leaders. Chapter 19 explores mechanisms to build high-performing teams. Team-building involves all the leadership and facilitation skills that are required to accomplish individual performance, and applies these to a team environment. The chapter also considers a distributed leadership model for self-managing teams. This model can be used to maximize the performance of a self-managing team by enacting different leadership roles at different stages in the development of the team. Finally, advice is provided on the introduction of self-managing teams into the information service environment.

Motivation is a key driver in getting other people to do things to achieve the corporate objectives. Not everyone is motivated by the same thing. Chapter 20 considers strategies to motivate individuals at both the organizational and individual levels. At the organizational level, workforce flexibility, performance-based compensation, job enrichment and job enlargement can be used to motivate people. At the individual level, individual needs must be taken into account. Chapter 20 also explains some of the classical theories of motivation as background to the topic.

Conflict can be a healthy sign of organizational growth and competition. It can also be destructive and inhibit things being done within the information service. Chapter 21 looks at sources of conflict at both the organizational and individual levels. The advantages of conflict are identified. The chapter includes sections on managing and resolving conflict, interpersonal styles for managing conflict and methods for detecting conflict in information services.

Chapter 22 is about negotiating to achieve desired outcomes. It includes sections on effective negotiation, the process of negotiation, problems in negotiations and factors for successful negotiations.

The last chapter in this part addresses the issue of managing change. New technologies, increased competition and complex external environments mean that information services have to change rapidly and radically. Change can be planned, arising from organizational life cycles and other proactive forces, or it can be sudden and discontinuous. The strategies for managing change differ according to whether the change is continuous or discontinuous. Chapter 23 includes strategies for managing both continuous and discontinuous change. It considers resistance to change at both the organizational and individual levels. The chapter also introduces the concepts of business and process re-engineering that are being used by organizations to rethink their mechanisms of operating in complex and competitive environments.

14 Leadership

Introduction

Leadership is the process by which a person or a group tries to influence the tasks or behaviours of others towards a final and required outcome. It is a social influence process within organizations in that it motivates others to do something that is required to achieve corporate objectives. Leadership differs from management in that management directs both human and non-human resources towards a goal, whereas leadership is concerned with creating a vision that people can aspire to.

The skills of leadership can be learnt. They are best developed in a corporate climate that fosters encouragement, co-operation, admiration, trust and loyalty, and where there are role models to provide examples of effective leadership.

Not everyone is a leader. Leaders are people who are able to use their technical, human relations or conceptual skills to influence others' tasks or behaviours. The relative importance of these skills depends upon the leadership situation and the level of management.

Leadership effectiveness in information services can be measured by the extent to which the work units and the information service can achieve their objectives. Effective leadership skills are needed to reconcile the goals of management and individuals with those of the information service and its parent organization.

Leadership theory has developed from the 'Great Man' concept and trait theory to a contingency theory. The 'Great Man' concept assumed that certain people possessed personalities, energy levels and abilities that made them leaders. The contingency theory determines that the environment, group cohesiveness, task structure, material technology, individual attributes, leader–member relations, individual expectations and degree of formalization in the organization's structure all influence the leadership process.

Fiedler's model states that, according to the situation (position power, task structure, leader–member relations), the leader should be task or relationship oriented. On the other hand, House's Path–Goal theory states that the effect of leader behaviour on individual motivation and satisfaction depends upon the leadership situation, nature of the group tasks and work environment. Individual characteristics such as needs, ability to perform tasks and personality traits are also important.

Within information services, leaders are also responsible for creating visions and values, for developing shared meaning between management and their people, and for providing inspiration to achieve the information service' and its parent organization's objectives.

Leadership effectiveness

The most commonly used measure of leadership effectiveness in information services is based upon performance, that is, the extent to which each of the work groups or cost centres within the information service achieves its own objectives. These objectives must, in turn be in unison across the information service and lead to the achievement of the corporate objectives.

Performance is strongly linked to motivational issues. Individuals' goals and sources of information differ according to their level within the organizational hierarchy, and may or may not be congruent with the information service's or its parent organization's objectives. The leader's task is therefore to motivate all individuals and integrate each individual's goals with the organization's objectives.

The personal goals for senior and mid-level management are usually related to the management goals. Their prime motivators are the higher-order needs for achievement, recognition and self-actualization. These needs are to be found in challenging jobs and the creative demands that lead to increased organizational performance.

First-line managers and their people will be more likely to have personal goals that are related to the lower-order needs, such as good working conditions, fringe benefits, friendships at work and good salaries. These goals may not always be congruent with the goals of management or the information service. However, if these needs are not perceived to be met, the performance of the information service may suffer.

Effective leadership is demonstrated through skills that provide challenges and opportunities, secure appropriate resources and working environments, and reconcile the goals of the information service, management and employees. Conflicting goals between management and employees, or inappropriate working environments will lower morale, lessen levels of motivation and, consequently, lower productivity. As a result, the information service may fail to achieve its corporate objectives.

Tangible evidence of performance for information services operating within profit-making organizations is found in the extent to which they contribute to corporate competitiveness, overall profit growth, sales increase and increased return on investment. The measurements of leadership capabilities of the information services manager could include the information service's ability to:

- provide an increased level of services to meet customers' needs;
- improve and extend information systems to match the growth in the corporate demand for information; and
- maintain the competitiveness of the organization through either doing more with less, obtaining strategic information or applying innovative uses to existing technology.

In non-profit-making organizations leadership effectiveness is usually based upon comparative measures such as benchmarking, or subjective evaluations. Comparative measures are often related to budget expenditures such as cost per unit of output, or on market share ratio such as percentage of senior citizens (customers) who utilize the services of a public library.

Objective measures of leadership can be found in the way in which the managerial tasks of planning, objective-setting, problem-solving and co-ordinating are carried out.

Subjective evaluations of leadership can be undertaken by considering the way in which managers carry out their duties and how this is measured by the executive, peers and their staff. The executive may measure the manager's attitudes and initiatives to problem-solving or methods of conflict resolution. Peers may measure their professional capacities and contribution to knowledge, whilst their staff may measure their decision-making style, the extent of their influence on others within the organization, or the way in which the manager expresses his or her appreciation for additional work that has been undertaken.

Effective leaders clarify roles by defining duties and responsibilities. They also set and emphasize performance goals during the annual appraisal interview and monitor these closely throughout the year. Supportive leaders who build individual confidence, share information and structure reward mechanisms to reflect the motivational needs of their staff are usually effective in raising the level of employee performance. However, these attributes are not effective in isolation of other leadership tasks. Effective leaders must also work to eliminate problems in the task environment, minimize conflict, smooth work operations and obtain a satisfactory level of resources to enable the staff to meet the information service's objectives.

Effective leaders act to inspire and stimulate individuals and groups. This leads to increased motivation and a higher level of morale. Through interaction and decision-sharing they develop teamwork and a positive and effective corporate culture. Effective leaders are also successful in improving the quality of management decisions and in increasing the readiness of their people to accept change.

Leadership theories

Fiedler's contingency model

In the 1950s Fred Fiedler began working with some associates on a situational theory of leadership effectiveness. Fiedler (1967) concluded that a group's performance is contingent upon the appropriate matching of the leadership style and the degree of favourableness of the group situation for the leader.

Leadership style, according to Fiedler, was measured by a least-preferred co-worker (LPC) score, obtained by the leader's critical rating of the person with whom he or she least prefers to work. A low-LPC-scoring leader who rates most critically is task motivated, whilst a high-scoring LPC leader shows sensitivity for their relationships with others in their ratings and is people oriented. Criticality is not an overriding feature. In certain situations a task-motivated leader is required.

Task-oriented individuals need to get things done. They gain self-esteem from tangible, measurable evidence of performance and achievement. They are strongly motivated to successfully accomplish any task to which they have committed themselves, even if there are few or no external rewards. Task-motivated leaders feel most comfortable working from clear guidelines and standard operating procedures in situations over which they have little control. When these are missing, they try to develop them by moving in and taking charge early to increase their amount of control in a situation. This may be to the extent where they do not consider people's interpersonal problems or conflicts. When they are in complete control of the situation and do not have to worry so much about getting the job done, task-motivated leaders tend to be considerate and pleasant. They are content to let their group handle the job, but tend to resist interference from those in higher levels of authority.

Task-oriented leaders are out of their element in moderate control situations, especially those with interpersonal conflicts. They are likely to concentrate so heavily on the task that they ignore group members' needs, as well as any conflicts that may exist. Hence the performance of the group may suffer.

Relationship-oriented leaders are concerned with doing a good job, but their primary orientation is towards good interpersonal relationships with others. Their self-esteem is affected by how other people relate to them. They tolerate different viewpoints and are good at dealing with complex problems requiring creative and resourceful thinking. In stressful and challenging low control situations, these relationship-oriented behaviours may become exaggerated. They may become so involved in consultation that they do not pay enough attention to the job. Group support becomes so important that they may be reluctant to put into action necessary job requirements that are known to be annoying to other members.

Fiedler's theory suggests that task-motivated leaders will be most successful in situations of low leadership control. They are likely to be less successful in situations of moderate control. The relationship-oriented leader is at his or her best in moderate control situations where the leader's concern for interpersonal relations is appropriate. Relationship-oriented leaders are not successful in either high or low control situations.

Fiedler's model advocates that the most appropriate leadership style, either task oriented or relationship-oriented, is determined by those factors discussed above. The model also suggests that group performance can be improved by modifying the leader's style or by modifying the group or task situation. It is a situation-type leadership theory as the most appropriate leadership style is chosen according to the situation at hand. Leaders can use either style depending upon the situation to obtain the best results.

House's Path–Goal theory

Robert House (1971, pp. 321–39) developed his Path–Goal theory of leadership to explain how the consideration or initiating structure behaviours of leaders influence the motivation and satisfaction of individuals. In particular, their perceptions of work goals and personal goals.

House's Path–Goal theory links leader behaviour with individual expectations and valences, individual effort and satisfaction, and the characteristics of the task, environment and people. Leader behaviour is described as being either supportive, directive, participative or achievement oriented.

Individual expectations and valences are based upon the 'expectancy theory' in which the motivation of employees is explained through their consideration of the final outcome. Employees will decide upon the amount of effort to devote to a particular task or job depending upon the perceived likelihood of the outcome.

The perceived likelihood is referred to as the worker's 'effort-performance expectancy'. If the employee considers that desirable outcomes are likely to result from successful task completion, the level of motivation will be much higher when completing the task than if undesirable outcomes are foreshadowed. The desirability of each outcome is called its 'valence'.

Individual satisfaction or dissatisfaction is aligned to the intrinsic benefits and costs experienced by employees in performing the tasks. Intrinsic benefits are evident when the work is meaningful, pleasant and interesting. Intrinsic costs refer to psychological stress arising out of boring, tedious, frustrating or dangerous work.

According to House, the role of leader is to increase the rewards for successful task completion and to facilitate the task completion process by clarifying issues, reducing roadblocks and increasing the opportunities for work satisfaction. Leaders should also provide coaching, guidance and performance incentives where they are not provided by the organization.

The leader's behaviour will affect the individual's job satisfaction level and their motivation. It will also affect the individual's satisfaction with the leader.

- Directive leadership behaviour is similar to initiating structure. The leader provides specific guidance, rules, procedures and schedules to employees that are followed to achieve preset goals.
- Supportive leadership behaviour is linked to consideration in that it considers the needs of people and creates a friendly work environment.
- Achievement-oriented leaders set challenging goals for employees. They emphasize performance improvement and display their confidence in their people. Excellence is pursued.
- Participative leadership involves employee participation in management. People are consulted for their opinions as part of the decision-making process.

The nature of the group task and environment are also important in determining the appropriate leadership style. Individuals' needs and their ability to carry out the tasks, the task structure, the material technology involved and the degree of formalization in the organizational structure are variables that will affect the outcome of specific leadership behaviour.

According to Path–Goal theory, directive leadership will increase individual effort and satisfaction when task demands are ambiguous and clarification does not come from elsewhere. In such a situation, leader directives compensate for lack of structure. In clear task situations, directive leadership has the opposite effect and is viewed as a hindrance by people.

Supportive leadership, in situations where tasks are stressful, tedious, boring, dangerous, frustrating or highly repetitive, can make conditions more bearable for people. By showing consideration and displaying other supportive actions the leader will compensate for the unpleasant conditions, increasing both individual effort and satisfaction. However, in a situation where the task is interesting and enjoyable, supportive leadership will have little or no effect on individual effort or satisfaction.

Achievement-oriented leadership will cause people to have more confidence in their ability to achieve challenging goals. Leaders who set challenging goals and show confidence in their people attaining the goals will increase individual effort–performance expectancy in situations where the individuals undertake ambiguous and non-repetitive tasks. In situations where individuals have repetitive, highly structured tasks, achievement-oriented leadership will have little or no effect on their expectancies or effort.

Participative leadership will increase individual effort in a situation where there is an unstructured task. When participating in decision-making, individuals learn more about the tasks and their expected roles. Role clarity will be increased and individuals will have a higher effort–performance expectancy. In a situation where individuals have a highly structured task and a clear understanding of the job, participative leadership will have little or no effect on their effort–performance expectancy.

Hersey and Blanchard's situational leadership theory

Hersey and Blanchard's situational leadership theory considers the two broad categories of leadership behaviour and the maturity of the followers. The two categories of leadership behaviour correspond to the initiating structure and consideration behaviours of the Ohio State Leadership Studies. They have been defined by Hersey and Blanchard (1977, p. 104) as task behaviour and relationship behaviour:

- *Task behaviour*: the extent to which leaders are likely to organize and define the roles of members of their group (followers); to explain what activities each is to do and when, where and how tasks are to be accomplished; characterized by endeavouring to establish well-defined patterns of organizational activities, channels of communication and ways of getting jobs accomplished.
- *Relationship behaviour*: the extent to which leaders are likely to maintain personal relationships between themselves and members of their group (followers) by opening up channels of communication, providing socio-emotional support, 'psychological strokes' and facilitating behaviour.

The maturity of the person is measured only in relation to the performance of a particular task. Maturity is defined by Hersey and Blanchard (1977, p. 161) as: 'The capacity to set high but attainable goals (achievement motivation), willingness to take responsibility, and education and/or experience'. An individual may be quite mature in relation to one task, but very immature in relation to another aspect. For example, an assistant librarian may be very responsible in helping a customer find information, but may be very casual in overseeing and controlling serials and journals.

According to the situational leadership theory, as the level of individual maturity increases, the leader should use more relationship-oriented behaviour and less task-oriented behaviour, up to the point where individuals have a moderate level of maturity.

As individual maturity increases beyond that level, the leader should then decrease the amount of relationship-oriented behaviour, while continuing to decrease the amount of task-oriented behaviour.

Leadership styles

Several descriptions have been used to typify leader behaviours. Generally they can be classified into four groups: the bureaucrat, the democrat, the visionary and the politician.

The bureaucrat

The bureaucrat is generally pleasant and mild mannered. They are slow and cautious in approach, relying upon structure and well-developed management systems. They use working parties to advise and decide upon issues; this slows down decision-making. They focus upon facts, rules and rationale for past decisions. They operate through formal channels of communication, often requiring memos in duplicate. The bureaucrat has a high need for legitimate power and control. They can be authoritarian, their authority being based on position.

The democrat

The democrat operates within the organization as though it is a family. They focus on the people issues, sometimes to the detriment of the strategic issues. They use strong consultation mechanisms that inhibit quick decision-making. They communicate their feelings and seek to understand others' feelings, needs and thoughts. The democrat relies upon their personal characteristics to get things done. Their power is based on referent power.

The visionary

Visionary leaders inspire others through symbols and personal charisma.

They are often very energetic, enthusiastic and creative. They have well-developed interpersonal skills but can lack attention to detail. They act as a facilitator and catalyst by focusing on the vision and values. The visionary influences through persuasion.

The politician

The politician regards the organizational environment as a jungle. They spend much of their time negotiating, focusing on conflict and building coalitions and networks with stakeholders. They will occasionally make contact with the staff asking how they are getting on, but provide little guidance and feedback. Strategic initiatives by staff are well supported, particularly if they are in line with their own objectives. Non-performers are either quickly dispensed with or generally ignored. The politician is an innovator, using a mix of coercive and reward power to achieve outcomes.

Leadership in information services

Effective leadership behaviours lead to a highly motivated staff within the information service. Where leadership, organizational structure, technology and corporate climate are appropriate, motivation is higher. In contrast, an inappropriate leadership style leads to individual dissatisfaction and lowered morale.

Individuals rely upon the leadership skills of their managers to allow them to achieve their needs of motivation, rewards and ability to perform their allocated tasks. House's Path–Goal theory recognizes this as the leader's role in reducing the roadblocks and increasing the opportunities for personal satisfaction during their work-goal attainment.

Leadership actions count for far more than motivation. Leaders are able to articulate and clarify the information service's vision so that others can understand and want to be involved. They often use rational persuasion to act as transformational and change agents. Leaders can change people's awareness of issues and help them to look at problems in new ways.

Executive (leaders') actions involve them in being the creator of symbols, ideologies, visions and other corporate cultural phenomena within the information service. Their attendance and participation at meetings where decisions are made and their involvement in the planning of agendas place them in positions where symbols and language are created, where they shape ideologies and beliefs as part of their work.

True leaders see it as their responsibility to inspire individuals to accept that which they have created, and to provide for shared meaning in terms of the information service's mission and objectives. Leaders create structure, having regard for the tasks, technologies and external environment, which harness the energies of others to achieve the desired result and service levels. Leaders are responsible for the institutionalization of values, motivation, appropriate structure and behaviours within the information service.

References

Fiedler, F. E. (1967), *A Theory of Leadership Effectiveness*, New York: McGraw-Hill.

Hersey, P. and Blanchard, K. H. (1977), *Management of Organisational Behaviour*, 3rd edn, Englewood Cliffs, NJ: Prentice Hall.

House, R. (1971), 'Path–Goal theory of leadership effectiveness', *Administrative Science Quarterly*, **16**, 321–39.

15 Power, influence, authority and delegation

Introduction

Power, influence and authority are behavioural processes that allow managers to achieve their goals through the actions of others. Power is the ability to influence others. It is legitimized in authority. Power may be sought by individuals or groups. The quest for power will inevitably lead to competition which, if healthy and productive, will be beneficial to the information service and its members. However, when such a quest leads to disruptive, selfish or harmful behaviours, the outcomes may not be as beneficial.

Influence is the behavioural response to the use of power. Several forms of influence can be found in information services and their parent organizations.

Authority is institutionalized power. It is based on position, personal characteristics, expertise, knowledge and the situation. Authority can be delegated. The delegation process allows the giving of responsibility and authority to others to execute a job. However, the manager is still accountable for the outcomes. Some managers are reluctant to delegate for a number of reasons. If they fail to delegate, they will become overloaded with work and unable to perform their leadership role. Delegation is also necessary for the development and motivation of people.

Power

Power is the capacity or potential of one unit to influence another in relation to any one or more aspects, such as behaviour or attitude. The power source may never be used. An individual can have power but never use it. The exercise of power may precipitate either willing or unwilling, conscious or unconscious compliance.

The use of the word 'power' often has negative connotations. This is the result of many people associating power with its abuse rather than its ethical use. To avoid its abuse, managers need a good understanding of the various power sources and how to use these effectively to persuade and influence rather than control people and outcomes.

The acquisition and use of power is a natural process within information services. Examples of how the power of an information services manager can be used and measured within the parent organization is the extent to which they can:

- secure good office accommodation and other working conditions for their staff;
- get regular and fast access to the chief executive and members of the governing body;
- influence the future direction of the parent organization; and
- get early information about organizational changes.

Power bases

French and Raven (1959) have defined five sources of power: three are derived from organizational sources whilst the other two are derived from personal sources. Reward, coercive and legitimate powers are the three power bases that are derived from positions within the organization. Expert and referent power sources are personal power sources.

Reward power

Reward power stems from the ability of an individual to provide tangible rewards in return for certain outcomes. People will comply with the requests of others if this will result in a positive benefit. The power base is contingent on the individual perceiving that:

- the person has sufficient authority to be able to offer rewards; and
- the reward is perceived to be a benefit.

The requests should also be perceived to be feasible, proper and ethical, and the incentive sufficiently attractive and at a level that could not be attained by another less costly course of action. For instance, if an assistant records manager asked a staff member to stay late for an hour one night to type a report in exchange for two hours off during the following day, the request would be considered in the light of whether:

- the person had the authority to grant the two hours off, or even to ask the person to stay behind in the first place;
- the staff roster situation and personal workload made it feasible to take two hours off the next day;
- the activities already planned for that night were of more importance; and
- someone else was available and prepared to work late.

Coercive power

Coercive power is the extent to which a manager can deny desired rewards or administer punishments in order to manipulate or control other people. It is a power based upon fear. Effective managers try to avoid coercive power except when it is absolutely necessary. Coercive power is often linked to an autocratic management style. Its use is likely to cause resentment and erode the manager's referent power. Individuals may react to coercion with hostility and aggression.

There are some situations in which coercion is appropriate, such as punishments for the violation of professional ethics. Coercion and punishment are only effective when applied in a small way. There are usually other alternatives to the use of coercive power.

To avoid the necessity to use coercive power, individuals should always be kept fully informed of rules and policies and the penalties for their violation. Work performance should be consistently monitored and corrective action taken before the need to use coercive power. Any warnings should be given in private so as to preserve the self-esteem of the individual.

Legitimate power

Legitimate power is the power based upon position. It is the power most frequently used in formal groups and organizations. Legitimate power is found in authority. An example of the use of legitimate power is in the request of the finance manager for the information services manager to submit their budget papers by the end of the month. Requests using legitimate power should be made politely, confidently and clearly, with their underlying reasons explained.

Expert power

Expert power is based on the possession of knowledge, experience or judgement that the other person does not have, but respects or needs. Most lecturers demonstrate the possession of expert power over their students. However, possession of expertise is not sufficient for managers or lecturers to influence people. It is also necessary for the other person to recognize the manager's or lecturer's expertise and perceive them to be a credible source of information.

Expert power is demonstrated through the display of certificates or awards on office walls; by acting confidently and decisively in a crisis; by keeping informed and informing others of emerging technology issues, by presenting papers at conferences; and by maintaining personal credibility.

Referent power

Referent power is developed out of a person's admiration for another and their desire to model their behaviour on that person's attributes. Role models have referent power as they engender a feeling of personal affection, loyalty and admiration on behalf of the subject.

Referent power is often based upon an individual's personal characteristics. An information services manager is likely to build referent power if they are articulate, show consideration for individual needs and feelings, encourage and develop individuals, and if they exhibit ethical behaviour.

Counter power

Power sources can be neutralized by counter power. Individuals may influence others by exercising a restraint on the use of power. An example of counter power is where employees engage the services of an outside body to negotiate on their behalf their working conditions with management.

Power and counter power sources can be used with management, peers in other sections of the organization, suppliers of resources, customers, stakeholders, competitors, unions and government agencies.

Acquiring power

Individuals often acquire power within organizations through:

- developing a sense of obligation in others;
- building a reputation as an 'expert' in certain matters;
- fostering others' unconscious identification with them or their ideas; and
- maintaining the belief that others are dependent upon them.

Managers who are ethical in acquiring power are sensitive to what others consider to be legitimate behaviour in acquiring and using power. They recognize that power is an essential management tool. They have a good understanding of the various types of power and its effects on different people. They develop all types of power to some degree in order that the correct type can be used in the right circumstances to achieve the information service's and the parent organization's objectives. They exercise restraint and self-control to ensure that power is not abused or used impulsively.

Influence

Influence is an action that creates a behavioural response to the exercise of power. When power sources are activated they can be influential in that they get someone to do something in a required way. There are many uses of influence within organizations.

One of the most common forms of influence is the legitimate request. When an employee requests an officer in the records management section to check the location of a file, the officer will normally comply. The officer sees the employee as having the right to request such an action as it is made within the work-role setting and is viewed as legitimate.

Rational persuasion occurs when a party is convinced of the need to change their mind, or that the suggested behaviour is the best outcome for all. Logical arguments are used to persuade another party that the proposals or decisions are justified and that they will be successful. It is reliant on the party having some knowledge or perception of the issue as the persuader does not have any tangible controls on the outcomes.

Rational faith is based upon expert power. The person's credibility or expertise is sufficient to influence the other party to take a particular course of action. An example of rational faith is where an employee uses a particular database that has been recommended by the librarian or research officer. The employee may not be aware of the contents of the database, but will use it on the recommendation of the librarian.

Indoctrination establishes certain values and beliefs in people that lead to behaviours that support the organizational objectives. The induction process is a form of indoctrination.

Information distortion influences a person's impression and attitudes as it limits or censors the information that they receive. The target person is influenced without being aware of it. Information distortion takes place when reports are edited or when information is withheld from those who need it. A similar form of distortion occurs in situational engineering, where a physical or social situation is manipulated.

Authority

Whilst authority is based upon formal position and legitimacy, its acceptance is governed by factors such as compliance, leadership and expertise. Authority can be gained from position, personal characteristics, expertise and knowledge, and the situation.

Position

This is the part of authority that is conferred upon individuals because they occupy a particular position, such as the Chairperson of the Board of Directors. The position and title are approximately indicative of the relative standing of the position holder's authority compared to other individuals, even though it may not be a specific measure of the exact degree of authority. The true extent of the position holder's authority is measured by the scope and range of their activities within the organization.

Personal characteristics

Personal characteristics such as those exhibited by leaders in getting others to do things are a part of authority. Domination, physical disposition and certain personality traits are forms of authority.

Expertise and knowledge

A person's specialist knowledge can confer on him or her a degree of authority over those not having the same level of knowledge to make a decision or solve a problem. This is known as authority of knowledge. This authority can be independent of level or position. For example, a person's knowledge of a particular information system may provide them with a degree of authority over its future management.

Situation

Finally, authority can exist in a given context, specific as to time and place. The use of authority under such conditions is determined by the elements of the situation. As an example, an individual who, on witnessing a fire in a storage room, rushes to the main area and shouts 'fire', will initiate an activity amongst the people in the room that may not occur given a normal situation. The situation therefore provokes leadership behaviour and the acceptance of responsibility on behalf of an individual who, though not in a position of authority, assumes authority in that particular situation by issuing orders.

Delegation

Delegation is the organizational process by which authority is distributed throughout the information service so that others may share work and responsibilities.

The distribution of authority through the delegation process does not occur automatically; it occurs by deliberate design. Delegation is a three-stage process:

- the individual is given responsibility for a task, such as to write a report or to manage a work unit;
- secondly, they are given the authority to do the job. They may also be given the necessary position power needed to execute the job;
- finally, they are required to be responsible for their actions and outcomes.

Whilst the information services manager may give authority to an individual to achieve certain outcomes, the manager is still in possession of their own authority over the situation. They have neither more nor less authority than they did before they delegated it. The same thing is true of responsibility. No matter how much authority or responsibility the manager delegates, he or she still remains ultimately accountable for the outcomes and results within the information service.

The individual who has been given authority must recognize the fact that they will be judged by their manager on the quality of their performance. They are still responsible and accountable to their manager. By accepting authority, people denote their acceptance of responsibility and accountability.

Benefits of delegation

Delegation improves decision quality and acceptance. It can lessen the load of higher levels of management and allows for quicker responses. Since the delegate is often closer to the point of action and has more specific information than the manager, it allows for a better decision in less time.

It is also a form of job enrichment and an effective method of managerial development and training, providing for internal promotion and career paths within the information service. Individuals' jobs become more meaningful and challenging leading to increased levels of motivation. In situations where organizational levels are being flattened and career paths restricted, delegation serves as one way in which employees can be extended and given further responsibility.

Whilst most people will welcome delegation there may also be some resistance. Some individuals do not wish for any more authority or responsibility, or do not wish to increase their already demanding workload. Others may lack self-confidence or have a low personal need for achievement. Training may also be needed, so that individuals can take on their new responsibilities with the necessary confidence and knowledge to do the job. The amount of delegation that will be acceptable will vary according to the manager, the individual and the situation.

Unfortunately, some managers do not delegate. A failure or reluctance to delegate is caused by a number of reasons. The manager may feel insecure or does not know what to do. They may lack confidence in individuals being able to perform the task. Although it could be argued that this is evidence that their training and staff development programmes are not effective. Their insecurity may be further aggravated by a feeling that their people have the potential to do a better job than themselves. They may also have a desire to maintain absolute control over the operations of the workplace.

Delegation, like other processes, can be learned. The most basic principle to effective delegation is the willingness by managers to give their people real freedom to accomplish their delegated tasks. Managers have to accept that there are several ways of handling a problem and that their own way is not necessarily the one that others would choose.

Individuals may make errors, but they need to be allowed to develop their own solutions and learn from their mistakes. Improved communication and understanding between managers and their people can also overcome barriers to delegation. If managers get to know the strengths, weaknesses and preferences of their people, they can more realistically decide which tasks can be delegated to whom.

The delegation process can be enhanced if the person completely understands their responsibilities and role expectations. They should be given sufficient authority to carry out their tasks. Their responsibilities and limits of discretion should be well defined. Assistance in the forms of psychological support, advice, technical information, should be provided and feedback given at regular intervals. The individual should be willing to accept his or her responsibilities and be encouraged to act on his or her own and make use of this newly acquired authority.

Power, influence and authority are inextricably linked. Power being the ability to influence others, that is legitimized in authority. Delegation allows the giving of responsibility and authority to others. Like politics, power can have negative and positive connotations. It can be abused as well as used effectively to persuade and influence outcomes.

Reference

French, J. R. P. and Raven, B. (1959) 'The bases of social power', in D. Cartwright (ed.), *Studies in Social Power*, Ann Arbor, MI: Institute for Social Research.

16 Decision-making

Introduction

Decision-making is an important management process, particularly when related to the planning function. Without decisions, nothing would ever be planned or accomplished. Some managers seem to make decisions quickly, whilst others always appear more hesitant. Much of this has to do with their personal decision-making style which is linked to their thought systems.

Decisions can be simple and well defined, or complex and ill defined. The latter type is the hardest to make as little structure is provided for the decision-making process. Complex or non-programmable decisions rely to a great extent upon people's perceptions of situations, upon the information that is available to them at the time, and upon past experience.

Modern management techniques encourage the use of participative decision-making, stressing that higher-quality decisions can often result from these practices. Participative decision-making is most successful in an open organization or where individuals possess the knowledge and abilities that enable them to make informed decisions.

The decision-making process

Decision-making is a process of determining a particular course of action after having considered the environment and a range of alternative solutions to a given problem. There are eight basic steps to rational decision-making:

1 The internal and external environment in which the decision is to take place is monitored.

2   The problem, the essential details and who is involved are investigated and defined. The exact nature of the problem is explored and diagnosed with the solution to the problem being seen as the goal.
3   Additional data is gathered.
4   Alternative solutions to the problem are generated. This involves consideration of the means by which the problem may be reduced or solved.
5   These alternatives are evaluated according to anticipated outcomes. The merits of each are assessed according to their probability of success and the relative advantages and disadvantages of each alternative solution are weighed against each other.
6   One solution is chosen.
7   Having chosen the solution it may require authorization before it is implemented.
8   The results are then evaluated through monitoring and reviewing the outcomes. If the results are ineffective, the decision-making process may need to begin again as part of the control process.

The first three steps are problem identification and the remaining ones are problem-solving steps.

Perceptions, intuition and emotions

Decision-makers in information services operate in a complex and sometimes uncertain environment. The result being that decisions are sometimes based upon intuition, or what is perceived to be the facts, as well as factual evidence. Some of the decisions will involve emotions.

An individual's perception of the issues can be based upon discussions with their colleagues both internally and externally to the organization, from accessing information on networks or reading selected reports, and, from personal knowledge and observation. In most situations, it is impossible to obtain every single piece of information relevant to the decision-making process. This is true, regardless of the level of detail that these sources of information provide. Consequently, many decisions are based upon a limited amount of factual information and a certain amount of intuition and perception.

From a management perspective, the need to deal with perceptions is as real as the need to deal with facts. It is important to be aware of the role that perception plays in decision-making as sometimes perceptions can be wrong or misconstrued. For example, a perception or interpretation of an issue can be influenced by past experiences that may not be entirely relevant to the case in hand. People may also be influenced by variables unknown to others.

These may lead to their choice of actions being misconstrued and also affect others' evaluation of the outcome of their decision.

Some variables used in decision-making are based upon intuition rather than fact. Intuition involves abstract thoughts that are not associated with concrete evidence but are based on individual instinct or apprehension. Often the words 'sixth sense' or 'gut feeling' are used. This is the phenomena of adding a further dimension to the five conventional senses that are used by individuals.

It is important for information services managers to be aware that decision-making is an emotional process. Feelings of self-worth, biases and experiences affect the emotional processing of decision-making. Emotions are involved in diagnosing and defining the problem, in selecting acceptable solutions and in the implementation of the solution.

A person's position in the information service may influence the emotional importance attached to decision-making. The value of the decision and its outcome may differ at varying levels within the information service and its parent organization. A decision that is regarded as solving a troublesome issue (such as individual access to a personal computer) at a group or work unit level may appear to be insignificant to the Chief Executive. Alternatively, what may appear to be a small decision taken at one level, may be felt to have great consequences at another.

Decision-making styles

Right- and left-brain hemispheres

Various decision-making styles can be found amongst people. One explanation for the different personal attributes and decision styles of individuals can be found in the way in which they use the human brain.

The human brain can be divided into two halves. Looking down on the top of the exposed brain two hemispheres are present, the left and the right. The left brain controls the right-hand side of the body and the right brain the left side.

The right and left hemispheres have different thinking styles. The left brain in most people is particularly involved in thinking activities that use language, logic, analysis, reason and mathematical ability. It is also associated with awareness of detail, recognition and classification of problems and optimizing results over time. The right hemisphere is more associated with pictorial, image thinking, spatial awareness, creative ability and intuitive thinking. The right, it is argued, is much better at seeing wholes. Problem-solving, writing and planning requires high-level left-side use, whilst the right brain is particularly associated with the ability to make non-logical connections and to see overall patterns or trends. It uses intuition as the basis for decision-making. The knowledge of these two different thinking styles allows individuals to recognize and value the thinking styles involved in the decision-making process.

Four decision-making styles

There are four main decision-making styles; directive, analytical, conceptual and behavioural. Often more than one decision-making style is appropriate, and managers can select the style most appropriate for the situation.

Directive style

According to Rowe (1984, p. 18) managers with a directive style are efficient and logical yet generally have a low tolerance for ambiguity and low cognitive complexity. They are autocratic, have a high need for power and maintain tight control. They focus upon technical decisions, preferring a systematic structure. Decisions are made rapidly, with little information, usually obtained verbally, and few alternatives are considered. Only short-range, internal factors are usually considered.

Analytical style

Analytical managers have a greater tolerance for ambiguity than do directive managers, but require control over decision-making. As their decisions are based on careful analysis, they require more information and consider more alternatives. They are careful but enjoy variety. They are able to adapt to or cope with new situations. Analytical managers are oriented to problem-solving and strive for maximum output.

Conceptual style

Conceptual managers are broad in their outlook, achievement oriented and consider many alternatives. They value commitments and integrity and are creative in finding solutions. They focus on long-range issues, are future oriented and are able to negotiate effectively. They will frequently use participative decision-making techniques.

Behavioural style

The behavioural-style manager is concerned for the organization and development of people. They communicate easily, show empathy and tend to be persuasive. Their focus is short or medium range. They use limited data as their emphasis is on decision-making through people.

Participative decision-making

Participative decision-making is linked to leadership and organizational style. A person-centred (behavioural) leader is more likely to promote participative decision-making than a task-centred (directive) leader. The type of organization in which the information service is operating may also determine whether a participative or authoritative approach is used. An open organization is more likely to encourage participative management than a bureaucratic one.

The degree of individual or group participation in decision-making is limited by such variables as ability, interest, skill of the leader and the area of freedom involved. Knowledge, ability and interest vary among individuals and groups. Organizational constraints may exist in time limits upon decision-making, particularly when the external environment is changing rapidly. There may not be the time to explain the circumstances involved, the background to the decision and other variables necessary for knowledgeable decision-making, or for procedures to take place that allow the group to meet and make the decision. The subject of the decision may also prevent group decision-making. Strategic decisions requiring a detailed knowledge of the external environment may not be able to be made by those at the operational level.

Advantages

Participative decision-making is useful for resolving differences among group members that, if left unattended, may prevent eventual agreement. The sharing of norms and values and the communication processes involved will positively influence the motivation of employees and result in less resistance. Groups are also likely to accept more risk than individual decision-makers, feeling that there is safety in numbers.

If individuals or groups are included in the decision-making process the outcomes will be better. There will be a greater acceptance of the decisions. More practical solutions will result from the inclusion of the people directly affected by the decision-making process. This is because they will possess relevant, practical information relating to day-to-day operations that is unavailable to those who do not perform the same tasks. People will share this level of detail in information if allowed to participate in the decision-making process. Individual input from group members will also provide a wider range of viewpoints in the decision-making process. This leads to greater creativity in finding the solution.

Individuals who have been involved in the decision-making process are more likely to be motivated to ensure that the proposals are carried out. There is a greater feeling of commitment to the decision. This sense of involvement also leads to a greater identification with the information service and its objectives. A further advantage is that individuals will probably develop an increased awareness of the information service's purpose after participating in the decision-making process.

Disadvantages

There are also disadvantages to participative decision-making. It is sometimes used as a substitute by management for making tough decisions. There may be a tendency to stall a decision by taking the problem from one committee to another. Both the failure to make a decision and indecision are ineffective management techniques. The need for the decision still remains and staff will recognize the failure or stalling of the decisions for what it is. Management also remains responsible for the implementation of the decision; it is in everyone's interest that the most sensible decision is made.

Group decision-making can be expensive in terms of staff time. A group decision invariably takes more time than an executive action. In order to estimate the full cost of participative decision-making the decision-making time should be multiplied by the number of people attending the group meeting.

Participative decision-making may sometimes produce lower-quality decisions or a compromise that is not truly effective. It can produce indecision and will occasionally backfire, producing a worse decision than might have been made by an individual.

Participative decision-making can also be dominated. If superiors are present, or if one member has a dominant personality, the decision of the group may in reality not be a group decision. This can have a lowering effect on group morale and act as a negative factor for motivation, giving rise to feelings of frustration and uselessness.

Management emphasis is now placed upon participative management and group decision-making in order to achieve the best possible solution. Depending upon the situation, participative decision-making can result in a more creative or practical solution.

Reference

Rowe, A. J. (1984), *Managerial Decision-Making (Modules in Management)*, Chicago: Science Research Associates.

17 Networking

Introduction

Personal networks allow information services managers to function successfully. They can be used to seek and provide information, for support, and to positively influence outcomes. Networks are a closed-group phenomena. The network group protects its members and has norms and values that are never challenged.

There are four types of networks. These are based on a common purpose of power, ideology, people or profession. Upon joining an organization, an individual needs to quickly establish a personal network in order to obtain information and support.

Value of networks

To enable the information service to function successfully, networks should be established by the information services manager within the parent organization, within the various professions that are represented in the information service, and with external stakeholders such as trade suppliers or politicians. These networks will enable the individual to establish alliances with key people who are likely to support preferred positions or actions, or supply needed resources or services. Networks are particularly important for individuals who work in professional isolation. They provide a source for professional information and advice, and can be useful in sharing resources.

Belonging to the right network will 'open doors'. Many legitimate political tactics rely upon networks. In belonging to others' networks valuable information is often obtained that would not otherwise be forthcoming. This will often lead to improved decision-making or allow corrective or appropriate action to be taken to avoid undesired outcomes. Networks provide support and can influence outcomes. This may be useful at budget time or when important decisions take place about the future role of the information service.

Networking enables the development of formal and informal communication channels throughout the parent organization whereby information can be shared. This is a two-way process where information is freely given as well as obtained. It is important for managers to develop their own personal network of contacts within the organization. These will be a network of trusted people to whom they may also go for advice.

In establishing their own networks, individuals may choose to occupy a central position, through which all information is channelled. This allows them to exert influence over others and provides a power base.

Networks as groups

A network is a natural coalition, that is, a group whose joint interests, viewpoint and preferences need to be protected. Within a network support and advice is freely and positively given.

Networks are a closed group phenomena, with those belonging to the network holding sacred certain unchallengeable values and norms. Intra-organizational networks are often identified by common behaviour modes, certain dress codes and modes of thinking. Like groups, there can be different types of networks.

Practician-oriented networks

These networks are formed for a common purpose that benefits those who belong. They may be practician oriented and comprise individuals who have similar expertise, training or professional interests. These networks provide true intellectual and professional stimuli for new ideas and innovations. In support of their ideals, they may attempt to influence other employees or organizations.

Power networks

Privilege or power networks comprise people who wield substantial influence or wish to be influential. These culture clubs operate through personal power bases. Introductions to the group are either by invitation or through the 'old school tie network'.

Ideological networks

Ideological networks comprise different types of people who wish to pursue particular ideas. Pressure groups are an example of ideological networks in that they are formed to pursue particular social objectives.

People-oriented networks

The most common networks in organizations are the people-oriented networks that exist for the sake of their members. These networks are important as they are valuable sources of information and support.

The gate-keeper

The entrance to the network is facilitated by identifying a gate-keeper, who is an influential member of the group. Personal sponsorship by a gate-keeper is important as this enables the person entering the network to quickly become acquainted with senior network members and enhance his or her channels of communication and success.

Establishing networks

In any new position, individuals should quickly develop their own personal networks inside and outside their organization in order to satisfy their need for information and to establish their power base. This is particularly important in a management role where resources have to be obtained, relationships between organizational units established, and organizational politics managed.

Upon joining any organization, an individual is at first ineffective because they have not established their own internal organizational networks. They do not know whom they can trust, who to go to for accurate information, or who their allies or supporters are likely to be. Whilst it is likely that they will have brought with them networks that were already established with people or organizations from their previous appointments, they will still need support, information and advice from within their new organization in order to deal with everyday internal matters. Until such networks are established, effective communication and decision-making cannot take place.

Personal networks should be established with thought. Members of staff operating in such key areas as the executive, finance and personnel and who are likely to provide support should be identified and personal contact made with them. It is often more favourable for the initial contact to be made on a face-to-face basis. This allows the person to explain who they are and exchange some of their work ideas and values. In the process of the exchange it will become clear whether common values are held, whether support may or may not be forthcoming and whether the individual may be regarded as a useful ally and member of a network.

In making the initial contact, close attention should be paid to the non-verbal communication processes as these will provide valuable information as to the actual support that may be given. This is one of the reasons for making the first contact in person as it could be that support was being offered but may not be forthcoming when needed. It is also seen as being friendly, polite and considerate to make the initial approaches in person.

In areas where vital relationships have to be established, and where initial reactions may not be as favourable as had been hoped, it is useful to continue to interact on a person-to-person basis. The positive side of the work relationship should be emphasized until such time as a firm relationship has been established.

Networks are a vital component of management in that they can be used as a mechanism of influence to achieve outcomes, as well as providing personal support, information and advice.

18 Group dynamics

Introduction

A manager's understanding of group behaviour is as important as their understanding of individual behaviour. This is because people can act differently when they are in a group. Their behaviours will change according to their role in the group. Groups can be formal or informal. Formal groups are defined through the organization's hierarchy or centre on a particular task. Informal groups are based upon individual psychological need, activities and interests.

Groups develop through a four-stage process of forming, storming, norming and performing. As groups develop, they assume certain characteristics of group cohesiveness, group norms and member roles.

Intergroup conflict can increase competition and group productivity. However, like all forms of conflict it may have an adverse effect upon the performance of individuals and the information service. In such a case, steps should be taken to minimize or remove it.

Types of groups in organizations

A group is a collection of people who regularly interact with each other to pursue a common purpose. There are four basic components of a group:

- it needs at least two people to exist;
- the individuals must interact regularly in order to maintain the group;
- all group members must have a common goal or purpose; and
- there should be a stable structure.

Various types of groups can be found in organizations. They perform a number of functions and can be classified into two types: formal and informal. Formal groups such as work groups and task groups will be created within the information service and the parent organization to accomplish the corporate objectives. Upon commencing employment with an information service, a person will usually be allocated to a work group. During the course of their work they may volunteer or be co-opted to serve on a task or project group in the form of an *ad hoc* committee or task force.

Individuals will also join informal groups. The reasons for doing this include interpersonal attraction, an interest in the group's activities, such as sport or chess, or an interest in the group's goals, such as environmental conservation.

Formal groups

Formal groups are created by the information service to accomplish a number of tasks within an indefinite or definite time-scale. They often relate to the organizational structure. Formal groups are created through formal authority for a purpose (see Figure 18.1).

Management groups

In most organizations there will be a management group consisting of senior managers. It may be called the executive management group. This group will meet to consider the strategic issues confronting the parent organization.

Other activities undertaken by the management group are the endorsement of the strategic plan, the ratification of policy and the approval of the overall organizational budget. The information services manager will be a member of this group. As they may also be a member of the various work groups reflecting the work units within the information service, they will form the link between the management group and the work groups.

Managers will be involved in groups in different capacities: as ordinary members or as leaders of a formal group. As leaders they may have the role of a supervisor or a chairperson. They will also be part of an informal group network.

Work groups

Work groups are the most recognized form of formal groups. They are the functional groups that perform a number of functions for purposes specified by the information service. Work groups remain in existence after they achieve their current objectives. They have clearly distinguishable

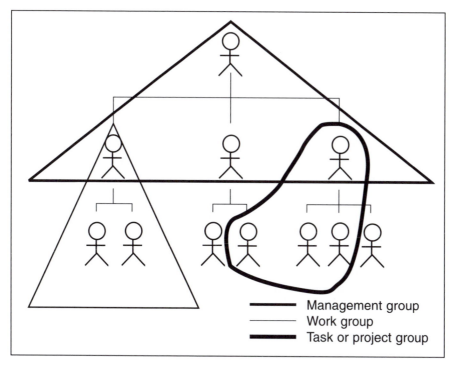

Figure 18.1   The organization as an interlocking network of formal groups

management–employee relationships and are often identified in the formal organization chart as a work unit, department or division. The size and level of the work group will alter according to the size of the parent organization. In some organizations the information service may be regarded as a work group. In others the research centre, branch libraries, records management department, and the information systems unit will be regarded as individual work groups. The senior research officer, branch librarian, records manager or information systems manager being formally designated as the leader of the permanent work group.

The above describes traditional work groups in information services. Depending upon the organizational structure, work groups may also reflect the organization's customers or markets.

Task or project groups

Task or project groups are created for a particular purpose. Usually to accomplish a relatively narrow task within a stated or implied time-scale.

They are temporary formal groups with a 'sunset clause'. *Ad hoc* committees and task forces are examples of task groups.

The group membership is specified by management. They often have a designated chairperson or a formal leader who is accountable for the results. Like the work group manager, the task or project group leader should review progress at regular intervals and provide performance feedback to members of the group. They must have the appropriate interpersonal skills and be prepared to accept responsibility and accountability.

Project groups are often used in a matrix style of management. The individuals forming the project group have two managers: the work group manager and the project group manager. A dual chain of command is established.

Informal groups

Informal groups exist for purposes that may or may not be relevant to the organization. They emerge within organizations without being formally designated by someone in authority for a specific purpose. Each member chooses to participate without being told to do so. The activities of the group may or may not match those of the organization. They will be formed through a common interest.

Informal groups can be a powerful organizational force. The identification of the leaders of the informal groups may provide insight into the politics, power and authority within the information service and its parent organization.

Informal groups can coexist with formal groups in an attempt to overcome bureaucratic tendencies and to foster networks of interpersonal relationships that aid work flows in ways that formal lines of authority fail to provide (see Figure 18.2).

Informal groups can also help individuals satisfy needs that may be left unmet or thwarted by formal group affiliations within the organization. These missing security or affiliation needs may be identified by studying the formation of informal groups and understanding the support mechanisms that they provide.

The formation of a group of this nature is not necessarily an indication that there is anything wrong within the organization. Social or friendship groups are often formed within organizations across formal work group boundaries for the purpose of sharing a common interest.

Stages of group development

After a group has been created, either formally by the organization or by

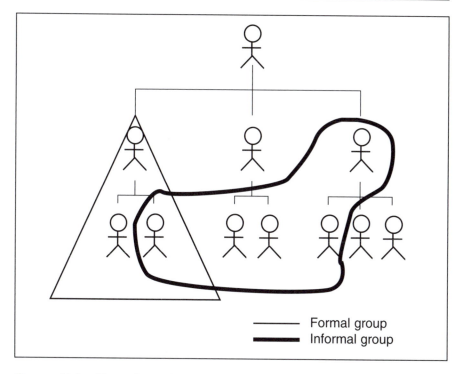

Figure 18.2   Formal and informal groups existing in organizations

group members, it will spend time developing. Group development occurs in four stages: forming, storming, norming and performing. These stages do not occur as discrete steps but are usually quite discernible because of their distinct activities. The passage of time between the stages of group development will differ according to the time-scale set for the outcome.

Forming

The forming stage occurs as individual members of the group become acquainted with each other and begin to test which interpersonal behaviours are acceptable and which are not. Group boundaries and group rules are defined. The real task of the group is clarified.

The forming stage usually takes place at the first meeting of the group. Typically, the different members of a task group describe their background and personal interests in the group's goals at the first meeting. This serves to define a common purpose and shared values. The members of the task group could be drawn from many different work units within the information service, the parent organization or from other organizations. As such, they are often not aware of the potential of the other members and where their expertise and values can be shared. Members may act aloof until they become aware of some shared meanings and each other's needs. As they become aware of each other, they achieve higher levels of interaction and mutual identification in pursuit of the common purpose.

Storming

The second stage (storming) is usually highly emotional involving tension among members and periods of hostility and infighting. Each member wishes to retain their individuality and may resist the structure that is emerging. Interpersonal styles are clarified and negotiations take place in an effort to find ways of accomplishing group goals whilst satisfying individual needs. Gradually a group leader emerges. Attention is paid to items that prevent the group's goals from being met.

In practice, the storming stage is the stage where problems are confronted, criticism is made and discussion becomes more open.

Norming

The third stage (norming) begins the integration process. Each person begins to recognize and accept his or her role and those of others. The group becomes more cohesive, adopting group norms that serve to regulate individual behaviour in order to achieve the group's goals. The group begins to be co-ordinated and teamwork emerges. Harmony is emphasized and minority viewpoints are discouraged.

Performing

Performing is the final stage of group development. The group is totally integrated and is able to focus on the situation at hand. It functions well and can deal with complex tasks through the interaction that occurs. The structure is stable and members work as one unit.

Group characteristics

As groups develop they assume certain characteristics. These can be described as group norms, member roles and group cohesiveness.

Group norms

Group norms are standards of behaviour that the group adopts for its members. These are informal rules that enhance the group's structure and reinforce a certain degree of conformity among group members. Norms differ from organizational rules in that they are not written. They are subtle standards that exist and regulate group behaviour.

Group norms are established during the third stage of group development. They are created through a series of actions by individual members and the others' responses as a group. The ways in which the responses are made provide the basis for the norm. The norms that survive are those that produce the most successful outcomes. The norms are reinforced through their success in positive problem-solving and in integration. Gradually it is assumed that if a norm is followed, success will result. As a result, norms are followed unconsciously.

Norms help groups avoid chaos and influence behaviours. They can be:

- performance related, such as identifying levels of daily work output or appropriate channels of communication;
- social related, such as how to address senior management in public, or acceptable levels of course language;
- behaviour related, such as setting standards of integrity, quality of service and professionalism; and
- appearance related, such as setting standards of dress.

As norms can have either a positive or negative influence on both the group's and the organization's productivity, it is important that positive norms are supported. Positive norms can be supported by rewarding desired behaviours and by monitoring performance and providing feedback regarding the desired behaviours.

Member roles

A role is a typical behaviour that characterizes a person in a social context. As members of a group, people play different roles. Their behaviours will change according to their role in the social structure of the group. One of the communication tasks in life is to understand the role that a person is playing when they exhibit a certain behaviour.

There are several terms that are used to describe the various roles. The expected role is that which the other members of the group expect from an individual. The perceived role is what the individual perceives the role to mean. The enacted role is what the individual actually does in the role. This then further influences the expected role. By rights, these three roles should be congruent. However, this is not always the case.

Role dilemmas

The various roles can present dilemmas for individuals. The following provide examples where role dilemmas that people face cause them to act or exhibit behaviours that are inconsistent with their normal behaviour. Role dilemmas are a normal part of life. However there are limits to which people can cope with role dilemmas. If these limits are reached and left unchecked, they can become sources of internal tension or frustration. They may also result in job disenchantment or dissatisfaction, poor performance and a high staff turnover.

Role ambiguity

Role ambiguity results when there is some uncertainty in the minds of either an individual or members of the group as to precisely what their role is at any given time. If an individual's conception of his or her role is unclear this can lead to role ambiguity even if it is clear to others. The use of job descriptions in information services can help to overcome role ambiguity in an organizational sense.

Role conflict

Role conflict occurs when the appropriate behaviours for enacting a role may be inconsistent with the appropriate behaviours for enacting either another role or other requirements of the same role. The expectations of each role may be quite clear and the expectations be compatible for each role, but the roles themselves may be in conflict.

Role conflict is generally categorized into two varieties. Inter-role conflict is found where there are incompatible demands of two or more different roles being played by the same person. The need for the information services manager to act as service provider and policy-maker may cause an inter-role conflict. The second variety of role conflict may be found in an intra-role conflict. In this case, contradictory demands within a single role are received by an individual. Such an example may occur where the information services manager may have to cancel the annual leave of a staff member whilst recognizing that they have been overloaded with work and need a break.

Person–role conflict occurs where a person is asked to fulfil a requirement that is against their personal values, attitudes or needs. Such an example may be where the librarian must avoid acting as a censor and so is forced to stock material that is in conflict with some very strong personal beliefs.

Role conflicts may sometimes be eased by reducing the importance of one of the roles, or by compartmentalizing the two roles so that they do not overlap. It is important to take steps to reduce the conflict as role conflict is recognized as a source for stress and poor performance.

Role overload

Role overload occurs when expectations for the role exceed the individual's capabilities. Individuals are required to perform more roles than they originally envisaged or have the capacity for. An example may be where a person is required to be a decision-maker in a complex and changing environment, but they have a low tolerance for uncertainty. Role overload should not be confused with work overload.

Role underload

Role underload occurs when an individual feels that they have the capacity to handle a bigger role or greater set of roles than is assigned to them. Role underload may be overcome by assigning additional roles or by delegating tasks and responsibilities.

Both role overload and role underload can be the outcome of a position being filled by someone who was incorrectly advised about the job at the interview. An unrealistic assessment of a position during the interview situation may lead to role overload or role underload and a person's subsequent dissatisfaction with the job.

Group cohesiveness

Group cohesiveness is the extent to which members of the group are attracted to each other and to the group as a whole. Highly cohesive groups are those in which members are attracted to each other, accept the group's goals and help work towards meeting them. Cohesion is likely to be higher in groups where members share similar attitudes, socio-economic backgrounds and needs. Work groups based on a particular expertise are usually cohesive because they share common professional values and attitudes.

Not all cohesive groups are productive for the organization. Some groups can inflict considerable harm if their goals are contrary to those of the parent organization. However, where groups are closely knit and have supportive management, their productivity is increased.

Group cohesiveness can be increased through intergroup competition, through personal attraction amongst those of the group, by rewarding the group rather than the individuals, by frequent interaction and by agreement on the group's goals. Group cohesiveness can be decreased by competition within the group, by the domination of one party, by disagreement on the group's goals and by group size.

As the size of the group increases, the number of possible relationships between its members increases. This leads to the need for increased communication and a co-ordinator amongst the group members. It also leads to the development of subgroups that may be damaging to the group's overall cohesiveness and its associated productivity. Smaller groups enable members to interact more frequently and increases their cohesiveness. The optimum number for a group is five people.

Intergroup conflict

Intergroup conflict occurs when members of a group perceive that they are being prevented from achieving their group goals by the actions of another group. Most intergroup conflict occurs in organizations between work units or departments. This may be linked to differentiation in expertise or cultures. For example, technical support staff may feel that they are prevented from giving a good service to customers because of requirements by the finance or treasury department that all costs and work charge-outs are documented in a very time-consuming fashion.

Conflict may also occur between hierarchical levels over issues of power, authority and control. Proposed takeovers or mergers of work units or departments will lead to conflict on a hierarchical basis and on a horizontal basis for power and control.

Due to the differences in the technologies, values, work tasks and individuals' attributes in work units within large information services, some intergroup conflict or rivalry will be ongoing. Such conflict will be productive by increasing group cohesiveness and output. It is a necessary part of subcultures within organizations. However, when conflicts emerge above the subculture level and become destructive or damaging to performance, managerial action should be taken.

In a serious conflict situation, the cohesiveness of each work unit or department will increase, whilst communication between the conflicting departments will tend to decrease. The group that loses the conflict will find that it will also lose its cohesiveness. It is advantageous that, with any significant conflict involving work units or departments, the issues are resolved quickly and in such a way that each party gain. A win-win situation can be achieved by skilful negotiation and setting a superordinate goal, that is, one that has to be achieved through the co-operation of both groups.

There is an increased focus on group work or teamwork within organizations. Many organizations favour a project group approach when dealing with complex issues that affect a number of work units. Consequently, managers need to be aware of the issues that are associated with group activities in order to maximize group performance.

19 Team-building

Introduction

Organizations comprise individuals who work together. The role of the team-builder is not to manage people as individuals, but to facilitate the group's management of its members. The objective being to obtain a higher level outcome than would be provided by the same number of people working individually. In teams, work and results are shared. Consequently, the team-builder has to improve co-ordination between the team members and get the members of the team to work together to deliver outcomes.

Self-managing work teams consist of highly motivated specialists who do not have a formal hierarchy. They value the ability to operate independently of managers, being given a high degree of self-determination in the management of their work. Instead of having one leader, the leadership capabilities are shared by all team members at different times. Individuals assume leadership in their particular areas of expertise. This distributed form of leadership occurs over a period of time as people assume, through their actions, responsibility for different leadership functions.

Team-building

Team-building involves all of the leadership and facilitation skills that are required in extending individual performance and applies these to the entity called the team. This includes the development of interpersonal relationships within the team so that members share information and collectively set goals and outcomes to be achieved. The team-builder will also need to facilitate mechanisms for:

- managing expertise for the collective good and identifying the roles that each of the team members will play;
- negotiation and resolving conflict within the group;
- identifying customer needs;
- measuring performance and quality control; and
- providing rewards.

The leadership style of developing group cohesiveness and effective communication patterns is appropriate to team-builders. The success of teams rests on there being very high levels of trust and openness between the team members. Team members should be encouraged to discuss their perception of the situation and what is required of them as a team and in their individual roles.

Without the discipline of authority, high-performing teams have conflicts that need to be solved. The team-builder needs to be competent at dealing with this. Negativity should not be allowed to grow as it can weaken the team's cohesiveness. As negativity will grow if attention is paid to it, it is initially best ignored. Attention should be focused upon the positive energies of the team. If the negativity continues to the extent that it has the potential to be destructive, then the source of the negativity should be openly discussed and dealt with.

Teams also develop a culture of self-discipline. They develop group norms and values and work within these to exercise control over individuals without harming their egos. High-performing team members care about the success and growth of others. In this way, teams can be a very supportive mechanism during times of stress and crisis.

Team communications and team-building should encourage employees to review one another's work and suggest alternative ways of doing things. Working properly, teams can be highly creative and innovative in their provision of service and identification of solutions to issues.

Self-managing work teams

Self-managing work teams are given a high degree of self-determination in the management of their work. They usually consist of highly motivated specialists who value the ability to operate independently of managers.

Self-managing work teams do not have a formal hierarchy. Their members have a variety of skills that they collectively use to deliver end products and services. The flexible work structure allows the participants to work efficiently and effectively. The team sets its own controls and quality audits, and collectively determines how the team will go about its work to achieve its goals.

Distributed leadership model for self-managing teams

Barry (1991) has created a distributed leadership model for three generic classes of self-managed teams. These are project teams, problem-solving teams and policy-making teams. All of these classes can be present in information services.

Barry argues that the performance of a self-managed team is optimized when certain basic leadership roles and behaviours are differentially enacted at specific times during the team's life. The self-managed team's performance is maximized by having the right role presented at the right time. The leadership roles and behaviours fall into four broad clusters: envisioning, organizing, spanning and social.

Envisioning involves the facilitation of idea generation and innovation, defining and championing goals, finding conceptual links between systems. Envisioning leaders often have trouble functioning in a group, preferring to invent and create independently. Sometimes they continue to provide new ideas after the group has committed itself to specific actions. The true role of the envisioning leader is to help others to see the vision in order to foster group ownership of the ideas.

The organizing role brings together the disparate elements that exist within the team and its tasks. This person focuses on details, deadlines, time, efficiency and structure. They often work within a few well-chosen solutions. Whilst it is a necessary role in keeping the group from straying off the task, it can be counter-productive when a completely new and innovative direction is needed.

The spanning role includes networking, presentation management, developing and maintaining a strong image with outsiders, intelligence gathering, locating and securing critical resources, bargaining, being sensitive to power distributions and being politically astute. Their natural tendency is to circulate outside the group environment. They can also be self-centred. To compensate for this, the spanning leader should provide the group with a constant source of reality checks, ensuring that the outputs of the team are well received by others in the organization.

The social role focuses on developing and maintaining the team from a social-psychological position. They show concern for individuals and ensure that everyone has their views heard. They are sensitive to the team's energy levels and emotional state. They provide encouragement and reinforcement and are able to mediate conflicts.

Table 19.1 describes the four stages of development of self-managed teams involved in projects, problem solving and policy making activities and indicates the appropriate leadership role for each stage.

Table 19.1   Distributed leadership dynamics in effective self-managed teams

Team phases	Project-based leadership dynamics		Problem-solving leadership dynamics		Policy-making leadership dynamics	
	Team activities	Leadership requirements	Team activities	Leadership requirements	Team activities	Leadership requirements
Phase 1	• getting acquainted • resource discovery • develop goals and vision • assess realism of vision	• social • spanning • envisioning • organizing and spanning	• getting acquainted • resource discovery • finding and assessing problems • locating causes	• social • spanning • organizing and spanning • spanning and envisioning	• getting acquainted • resource discovery • issue-finding	• social • spanning • spanning and organizing
Phase 2	• surfacing of differences; conflict • scheduling • securing outside resources	• social and envisioning • organizing • spanning	• finding solutions • getting ideas from everyone	• envisioning and spanning • social	• developing policy and strategy alternatives • idea clarification	• envisioning and spanning • social

Phase 3					
enactment of the vision	• organizing	assessing costs and benefits	• organizing and spanning	assessing consequences	• organizing and social
establishing control mechanisms	• organizing	summarizing points	• social	tracking team progress	• organizing
presentations to outsiders	• spanning			interlinking ideas	• envisioning and spanning
maintenance of cohesion and commitment	• social				

Phase 4					
project completion	• organizing	solution testing	• organizing	presentations	• spanning and organizing
presentations	• spanning	further search for causes and solutions	• envisioning and spanning	coping with outside resistance	• spanning
getting closure, looking at total effort	• social and envisioning	presentations	• spanning	preparing formal reports	• organizing
team disbanding	• social and envisioning	disbanding	• social	disbanding	• social

Source: 'Managing the bossless team: lessons in distributed leadership' by Barry, David, pp. 31–47. Reprinted by permission of the publisher, from *Organisational Dynamics*, Summer 1991, © 1991. American Management Association, New York. All rights reserved.

213

Introducing self-managing teams

The activities of introducing and building self-managing teams in information services include goal-setting, development of interpersonal relationships between teams, identifying the roles that each of the team members will play, measuring performance and quality control, and providing rewards. Whilst this sounds straightforward, it may not be easy. Most people value their individuality and independence, taking responsibility for their choice of assignment and their own outcomes within the organizational context. They may be content to work in a group but usually expect to be assessed and rewarded on their individual performance.

Teamwork changes this. The team is assessed on its collective outcome. It can even be promoted in this way. Team members jointly decide upon the choice of assignment, how the task will be accomplished, goals and rewards. In the early stage of building teams, the builder has to balance the need to address concerns about individual loss of independence and control whilst building support for team decision-making.

The determination of salaries and rewards, multiskilling and changes to differentiation between professional and non-professional staff are some of the issues to be considered in the initial stages of introducing self-managing work teams into an information service.

Teamwork builds upon the principles of process re-engineering in that the whole of the activity associated with the provision of the service is managed within the team.

Teams can be established to provide specialized information services to specific customer groups. As such all team members are involved in planning and competitive strategies, in customer and supplier liaison. Training is essential to equip all team members with the necessary skills to carry out their cross-functional tasks. Training may also be required in interpersonal skills and conflict management.

Reference

Barry, D. (1991). 'Managing the bossless team: lessons in distributed leadership', *Organisational Dynamics*, Summer, 31–47.

20 Motivation

Introduction

Effective information services managers understand the nature of human motivation and are prepared to use this knowledge to motivate their people to achieve the information service's and parent organization's objectives. Not everyone is motivated by the same thing. The key to successful and effective management is to understand what motivates each individual and to be flexible enough to satisfy these diverse needs. Motivation can be used as a measure of a manager's performance as a leader. The extent to which they motivate others will determine their effectiveness as a leader.

Motivation is linked to management flexibility. Flexible working hours and benefits allow individuals to pursue differing lifestyles whilst increasing their commitment and contribution to the organization. Organizational strategies that promote performance-based compensation, job enrichment and job enlargement can also act as motivators. However, the equity issues need also to be managed.

Motivation is dependent upon the employees perceiving that the outcomes of their behaviours will be beneficial and having an expectancy that their behaviours will actually result in a realization of the outcome. Information services managers can increase the expectancy levels of their staff by tailoring work conditions to meet individual needs, by giving praise and showing confidence in their people, and by providing training and extending the work experience of their staff to allow them to achieve the desired performance levels.

Organizational strategies

Workforce flexibility

Flexible benefits and work arrangements recognize individual differences. They allow individuals to pick and choose from a variety of options that meet the needs of both the organization and the individual. Flexible benefits and work arrangements arise out of an acknowledgement that today's workforce is diverse and no longer fits a stereotype. Not all employees have the same needs, so flexible benefits and work arrangements can be turned into a motivator. The reward factor is that individuals can choose the benefits and work arrangements that best suit their personal needs.

Flexible work arrangements can lead to greater output. Arrangements such as flexitime and job sharing can lessen the level of absenteeism and often utilize the individual at the time of their peak of productivity. Flexible work arrangements can increase individual enthusiasm and make it easier for the information service to recruit new people.

Performance-based compensation

Individuals have traditionally been compensated for the time that they spent on the job. Additional compensation was provided where they spent more time on the job, for example overtime payments or after hours meal allowance. Traditional compensation methods penalized those who were more efficient and productive. They failed to take into account innovation, personal contribution or effectiveness. Individuals received increased compensation linked to years of service rather than to the success or failure of the information service or parent organization.

Performance-based compensation provides incentives for individual or group effort to meet the information service's or parent organization's objectives by rewarding performance. Performance-based compensation can be linked to specific performance measures and provides additional reward mechanisms when certain project milestones or productivity outcomes are reached. Compensation can be in the form of one-off payments, salary loadings, or the sharing of productivity gains. Not all compensation needs to be in the form of a monetary payment. Other mechanisms can be considered, such as the attendance at a conference in addition to that normally considered to be part of training and personal development.

Job enrichment and job enlargement

Variety and challenge in a job can increase job satisfaction and act as motivators. Job enrichment and job enlargement are two different methods to achieve this. Job enlargement occurs when additional responsibilities of a horizontal nature are given to employees. If the additional responsibilities are of a vertical nature, encompassing self-control, the process is called job enrichment.

Information services that are flexible in their approach may resist the strict hierarchical levels of differentiation that can occur between professional and non-professional tasks. Whilst still respecting those individuals who have a professional standing for their knowledge and expertise, they may seek to improve the job satisfaction of those undertaking the more operational tasks through providing variety and challenges in the workplace.

Variety can be produced by adding functions through job enlargement. An additional psychological value may also be derived if job enlargement allows the individual to see the completed process within which he or she works. The identification and performance of the initial and end tasks and/or processes, together with all of the tasks in between, will make the job more meaningful to the employee and provide a sense of achievement and purpose. However, the type of work assigned to provide job enlargement should be carefully considered. There is no point in enlarging a job merely by adding further onerous duties to an individual's existing list of disagreeable tasks, particularly if they are at the same level. If anything, this will have a negative effect on motivation.

Job enrichment is not the allocation of more tasks, but the allocation of autonomy and responsibility to an individual. The level of motivation will increase if the job becomes more meaningful through an increased level of decision making in the information service. By providing a level of responsibility for certain tasks and a knowledge of the operating results, motivation, performance and satisfaction increase in most people.

Responsibility and autonomy can be increased by allowing individuals to set their own work schedules, by varying the workplace, by changing the duties of individuals on a regular basis, by allowing experienced personnel to train less experienced workers, by individuals establishing direct relationships with the customers, and by encouraging staff to make their own quality checks.

Job enrichment will only work when the motivating potential of the job is high. The psychological needs are very important in determining who can, and who cannot, be internally motivated at work. Individuals with high growth needs will eagerly accept the added responsibility. Those people whose growth needs are not so strong may respond less eagerly at first, or react negatively at being 'stretched' or 'pushed' too far.

As with job enlargement, the process has to be instituted selectively and with an acute knowledge of the motivational forces of the individuals. In the worst case, job enrichment can have a negative effect on employee morale if they perceive the information service to be increasing duties and responsibilities without the proportionate increases in compensation. The motivational issues will then be lost in a jungle of pay disputes in which the organization will be viewed only as a 'money-saving' entity with no regard for its employees.

Hackman and Oldham's theory of job enrichment

A fairly specific theory of job enrichment has been developed by psychologists Hackman and Oldham (1976). They suggest that certain core job dimensions have an impact on a number of psychological states, which in turn relate to attitudes and behaviour on the job (see Figure 20.1).

The core job dimensions are found in skill variety, task identity and task significance. Each of these three job dimensions represents an important route to experience meaningfulness in the workplace.

Skill variety is the facility that enables individuals to perform activities that challenge their skills and abilities. The involvement of several skills in performing a job will avoid the monotony of performing the same task

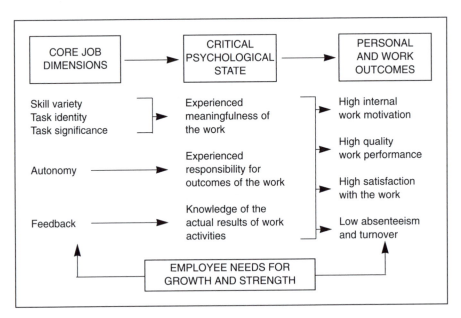

Figure 20.1   Hackman and Oldham's job characteristics model
Source: Hackman, J. R. and Oldham, G. R. (1980), *Work Redesign*, © 1980 by Addison-Wesley Publishing Co., Inc. Reprinted by permission of Addison-Wesley Longman Publishing Company, Inc.

repeatedly. Task identity is achieved when the job requires the completion of a 'whole' or identifiable piece of work. Task significance is found in the job that has a substantial and perceivable impact on the lives of other people, whether in the immediate organization or the world at large.

Increased responsibility for work outcomes is achieved through autonomy, that is, the degree to which the job gives the individual freedom, independence and discretion in scheduling and determining how their work will be carried out.

Feedback is a necessary part of personal development. This can be measured by the degree to which an individual, in carrying out the work activities required by the job, receives information about the effectiveness of their efforts. Feedback is most powerful when it is received directly from the work itself rather than from the supervisor.

Personal and work outcomes are found in high internal work motivation, high-quality work performance, high satisfaction with work, and low absenteeism and turnover.

There are some important implications in this theory. If the changes are confined to only one core job dimension then only one of the critical psychological states will change, and there will be little result. Changing the job will change behaviour only by changing all of the critical psychological states. If the psychological states remain unchanged there will be no behaviour change.

The theory will only work for those who value the higher-order needs of autonomy, growth and responsibility. Individuals who do not find these to be motivators, will respond better to other motivators than those used in this theory.

Individual strategies

Expectations and needs

The traditional theory of motivation is aligned to expectations and needs. Vroom (1964) considered that any attempted managerial influence to motivate an employee would be assessed by the employee according to the anticipated valence or value of the perceived outcome of the prescribed behaviour, and the strength of the expectancy that the behaviour would actually result in a realization of the outcome.

The individual would only be motivated by management where they perceived their effort, combined with their personal ability and environmental factors, would result in a positive outcome and valence. At each step the employee would take into consideration factors that might enhance or hinder the outcomes. Their efforts would increase if they felt that this would lead to high performance and a positive outcome. To do this, the individual must have the required mental or physical skills, knowledge or expertise to perform the task, and the organizational environment must also be conducive to the increased performance. If any of these factors was missing or inhibited, the individual's level of effort would be affected.

Expectations of outcomes would also be reliant upon the employee perceiving a personal capacity to achieve the resultant performance, and making the connection between the desired behaviour and the valued pay-off. If he or she did not associate the rewards as being the outcomes of certain increased efforts or performances there would be no motivation for further increased effort. The individual would weight the outcomes to determine whether any changes in performance would lead to valued outcomes.

Individual needs

Most managers today believe that their employees want to perform well. They try to enhance this performance by tailoring work conditions to meet individual needs, by letting their staff know that they are valued, and by increasing their employees' confidence in their personal capacities to achieve the required level of performance. People who are well trained and allowed to take risks often have a higher estimation of their abilities than individuals who have not been allowed to experiment or vary their tasks.

Individuals have different values and needs in order to be motivated. Whilst one individual may be motivated by the expectation of a pay rise, another may be motivated primarily by recognition. It is important for the information services manager to understand the motivating values and needs of each of his or her staff and to be flexible enough to meet these.

Individual needs are met through two outcomes: the immediate or primary outcomes and secondary outcomes. Immediate outcomes are represented by money, promotion, feelings of achievement, recognition by peers or, negatively, by being shunned by fellow employees. Secondary outcomes arise out of the immediate outcomes. They include the new car that is purchased from the pay rise, the self-esteem that arises out of promotion, or the feeling of loneliness when an employee is shunned by fellow employees.

Rewards that lead to improved performance through increased motivation and effort do not always have to be monetary. Examples are praise, either public or private, status symbols such as employee of the month awards, peer acceptance and approval, consultation and participation in managerial decision-making and promotion to positions with higher responsibility. Many of the activities in information centres can be at the leading edge of technology. The ability to shape or influence the future through the development of new applications of information and its supporting technologies can be a primary motivator in highly creative people.

Individuals translate their needs into behaviour in different ways. Some may express their wants and desires, whilst others' needs may be latent. Likewise, individuals' actions may not always be consistent, nor the needs that motivate them. At various stages of their careers, peoples' circumstances will differ and they will be motivated by different needs. Finally, individuals may react in different ways when they fail to fulfil their needs. Some may become withdrawn whilst others may become aggressive. Some may even increase their performance levels.

Motivators and demotivators in information services

Table 20.1 identifies some motivators and demotivators within information services. Demotivators include inadequate physical working conditions such as bad lighting, lack of air conditioning and heating, long hours or lack of physical security. Low pay and lack of benefits in comparison with other services may also act as demotivators. These demotivators increase in situations where there is also lack of job security, such as when an organization is downsizing.

Motivators include an organizational climate that supports innovativeness, encourages people to learn new skills and respects the needs of individuals to have flexible work arrangements.

Motivation theories

Maslow's hierarchy of needs

Maslow's (1943) hierarchy of needs provides one explanation as to why the needs of individuals are not always consistent. He proposed that people have a complex set of needs that are arranged in a hierarchy of importance (see Figure 20.2).

There are four basic assumptions in the hierarchy:

1   A satisfied need is not a motivator. When a need is satisfied, another need emerges to take its place, so people are always striving to satisfy some need.
2   The need network for most people is very complex, with a number of needs affecting the behaviour of each person at any one time.
3   In general, lower-level needs must be satisfied before higher-level needs are activated sufficiently to drive behaviour.
4   There are many more ways to satisfy higher-order needs than there are for lower-order needs.

Table 20.1   Motivators and demotivators within information services

Motivators	Demotivators
Job security	Poor working conditions
Promotion	Feeling of being overlooked
Pay and benefits	Dissatisfaction with pay and benefits
Quality output is valued	Organizational tolerance of poor performance and low quality standards
Sense of achievement	Being forced to do poor quality work
Feeling of belonging	Being taken for granted
Learning new skills	Poor induction and training
Individuals and teams are set challenging goals	Capacity under-utilization
Sense of usefulness	Unattainable targets
Status	Over control
Power	Unproductive rivalry
Respect	Management by threat
Encouragement of initiative	Personal initiative is stifled
Good working conditions and work practices	Poorly designed work
Managers take the time to encourage and acknowledge good performance	Management invisibility
Able to take risks	Unnecessary rules
Ethical values and work practices	Tolerance of dishonesty, hypocrisy, unfairness and criticism in workplace
Open communication, reasons for change and decisions made known	Poor communication, information withheld
Organizational and individual goals and directions are clear and complementary	Unclear expectations
Opportunities for personal growth	Discouragement of responses

The basic need in all humans is the physiological need. This is the need that relates to the biological maintenance of oneself – for example, the need for food and water. In a working situation basic needs relate to basic salaries and base line working conditions.

The second lower-order need is that of safety. Safety incorporates the need

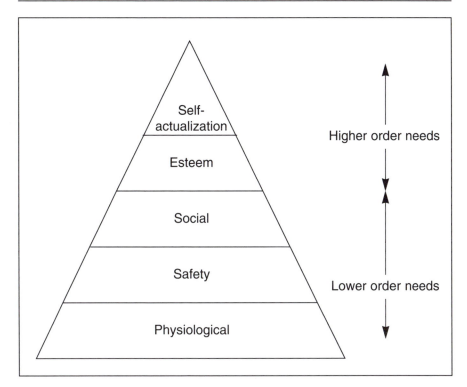

Figure 20.2   Maslow's hierarchy of needs

for security and protection, and, stability in the physical and interpersonal events of day-to-day life. Examples of these second order needs are safe working conditions, an assigned work area such as a personal directory in an office automation system or a physical workspace either at home or in the office.

The third lower-order need is a social need. Individuals need love and affection and a sense of 'belongingness' with their peers. Social needs are found in compatible work groups, friendships at work and an approachable and relationship-oriented boss.

Esteem is a higher-order need. Individuals who have the lower-order needs satisfied will need the esteem of others. This can be demonstrated by respect, prestige and recognition. They will also need to have self-esteem and a personal sense of competency. These needs can be satisfied by being given responsibility, a creative or important job or high-status job title.

The highest order need is that of self-actualization. This is a need to fulfil oneself and to grow and use personal abilities to the fullest and most creative extent. Self-actualization is demonstrated in challenging jobs, creative task demands, advancement opportunities and achievement in the profession or the parent organization. According to Maslow's theory, self-actualization will only be desired in the areas where the individual is capable of achievement. It has a low priority on the needs scale and is not a motivator of priority unless the needs of love, self-esteem, social approval and self-assertion are fairly well satisfied.

For many people, work satisfies their lower-order needs in that it provides the means to purchase food and shelter. As individuals are promoted, their hierarchy of needs is met in other ways. However, as individuals set different priorities, managers should not assume that the factors that have motivated them in their work will also motivate others.

ERG theory

Alderfer has reworked Maslow's need hierarchy by refining his five needs into three – existence, relatedness and growth (ERG). The existence group of needs is related to the basic material existence requirements, i.e. the physiological and safety needs. The second group of needs refers to the desire to maintain important interpersonal relationships – the relatedness needs. The third group of needs involve the intrinsic desire for personal development. These include the need for self-actualization and the intrinsic component of Maslow's esteem need.

In contrast to Maslow, Alderfer's research showed that more than one need may be operative at any one time. In addition, when a higher-order need is frustrated, the individual may regress to concentrate on a lower-order need.

Herzberg's two-factor theory

Herzberg and his associates examined the relationships between job satisfaction and productivity among a group of accountants and engineers. They noted that the aspects of jobs that produced satisfaction were different from those that produced dissatisfaction. The satisfied worker was not a person in whom dissatisfaction was always minimal, as satisfaction and dissatisfaction were evoked by different stimulus conditions.

Dissatisfaction was caused by extrinsic factors such as pay, supervision, working conditions and company policies. However, the removal of these unsatisfactory extrinsic factors was not in itself satisfying or, indeed, motivating. It merely eliminated dissatisfaction. For instance, whilst low pay or bad supervision both could lead to dissatisfaction, good pay or good supervision may not necessarily lead to satisfaction. This was because satisfaction and motivation came from a different set of factors called 'motivators'. Motivators include recognition, achievement, responsibility, and personal growth.

Table 20.2   Integration of Maslow's hierarchy of needs with Herzberg's two-factor theory

Maslow's need hierarchy	Herzberg's two-factor theory	
Needs	Hygiene factors	Motivation factors
Self-actualization		Satisfiers: Achievement
Esteem		Recognition Work itself
Social		Advancement
	Dissatisfiers:	
Security	Interpersonal relations Supervision	
Physiological	Salary Working conditions	

The two sets of factors identified by Herzberg are called motivation factors and hygiene factors. Motivation factors relate specifically to work content and are the satisfiers. Hygiene factors relate to the work environment and are the causes of dissatisfaction (see Table 20.2).

Herzberg's two-factor theory can be utilized in information services as follows. To avoid dissatisfaction amongst individuals, the hygiene factors must be adequate. Salaries and other working conditions should be satisfactory, the work environment should be safe, supervisors should have good interpersonal and people management skills. They should have adequate professional and technical knowledge and be experienced in imparting their knowledge. Interpersonal relations between peers and between management and their staff should be good. By providing for these needs, the information services manager will not provide any motivational stimulus, but will ensure that the employees are not dissatisfied.

To create high levels of satisfaction and motivation amongst the staff, the information services manager will require a different set of factors. These include:

- the recognition of individual efforts;
- the setting of standards for achievement and the provision of mechanisms to enable others to strive to succeed;
- assigning responsibility to individuals for outcomes; and

- enabling personal growth by extending the boundaries or comfort zones of people, or providing different work experiences.

McGregor's Theory X

McGregor (1960) has listed some key assumptions which people hold in regard to others. There are two sets of assumptions, that are quite distinct. McGregor termed these Theory X and Theory Y.

Managers holding Theory X assumptions generally have negative or pessimistic views of the nature of people. They have a more autocratic management style and believe that:

- work is inherently distasteful to most people;
- most people are not ambitious, have little desire for responsibility, and prefer to be directed;
- most people have little capacity for creativity in solving organizational problems;
- motivation occurs only at what Maslow called the 'physiological' and 'safety' levels; and
- most people must be closely controlled and often coerced to achieve organizational objectives.

In contrast, Theory Y assumptions are positive. Managers holding these assumptions are more participative in their style. They rely upon self-control and self-direction for individuals, providing opportunities for personal growth and involvement. They believe that:

- work is as natural as play, if the conditions are favourable;
- individual self-control is often indispensable in achieving organizational goals;
- the capacity for creativity in solving an organization's problems is widely distributed throughout the organization;
- motivation occurs at the social, esteem, and self-actualization levels, as well as at the physiological and security levels; and
- people can be self-directed and creative at work if properly motivated.

The point of McGregor's work is not to create two management styles. Rather, it is the recognition that an individual's assumption about others affects the way in which they treat them. Individuals can develop Theory X and Theory Y assumptions based on their experiences, attitudes and predispositions toward people.

Motivation is a key to successful performance at both the individual and organizational levels. Motivational strategies can be developed and used at the organizational level and at the individual level. Both strategies depend upon managers understanding what motivates individuals and being flexible enough to tailor these strategies to meet individual needs.

References

Alderfer, C. P. (1969), 'An empirical test of a new theory of human needs', *Organizational Behaviour and Human Performance*, May, 142–75.

Hackman, J. R. and Oldham, G. R. (1976), 'Motivation through the design of work: test of a theory', *Organizational Behaviour and Human Performance*, August, 250–79.

Hackman, J. R. and Oldham, G. R. (1980), *Work Redesign*, Reading, MA: Addison-Wesley.

Herzberg, F. (1968), 'One more time: how do you motivate employees?', *Harvard Business Review*, January–February, 53–62.

Herzberg, F., Mausner, B. and Snyderman, B. (1959), *The Motivation to Work*, New York: Wiley.

McGregor, D. (1960), *The Human Side of Enterprise*, New York: McGraw-Hill.

Maslow, A. H. (1943), 'A theory of human motivation', *Psychological Review*, **50** (4), July, 370–96.

Vroom, V. (1964), *Work and Motivation*, New York: Wiley.

21 Conflict management

Introduction

Conflict occurs as the result of a disagreement, threat or opposition between individuals or groups, or within an individual or group. Whilst it may be destructive if it is not handled correctly, conflict can be a healthy sign of organizational growth and competition.

Both individuals and groups have two drives. These are to maintain psychological equilibrium and harmony, and to actualize their potential. Conflict arises when an individual or group perceives either a threat or opposition to one or both of these drives, when two antagonistic drives or needs have to be satisfied simultaneously, or where there is a tendency to simultaneously accept and reject a course of action.

Conflict has traditionally been viewed as destructive. A state of affairs that should be suppressed or eliminated. Managers now realize that there are some positive actions in conflict. In many instances conflict can be a sign of a healthy organization. Conflict of a competitive nature generally leads to improved organizational performance. In fact, if conflict within an organization ceased, stagnation could set in. Conflict can also serve as a unifying factor and a source of feedback. It acts as a safety valve and brings issues to the surface that may otherwise never arise.

Individuals who are faced with personal conflict may react in either of two ways – flight or fight. Whilst the source of the conflict may not be in the organization, its effects will be manifested through the individual's actions. When such actions begin to affect the output of other staff members, the information services manager must become involved to help resolve the conflict. There are various methods and styles for resolving conflict. Some are more effective than others. In most instances, it depends upon the conflict situation.

Sources of conflict

Conflict is inevitable. It serves as a catalyst for change which in turn leads to some form of adaptation that is necessary for the survival of any living species. In an organizational context the species can either be an organization or an individual. There can be many sources of conflict in information centres. These include the organizational structure, technology, role expectations, communication channels, interpersonal relations and behaviours, personal interests of individuals or groups, physical separations and the dependency of one party on another.

Organization differentiation

Individuals in information services and other parts of the parent organization perform different kinds of work. As a result, cost centres or work units have different time horizons, values, goals and management styles. The greater the differentiation between units or work groups, the greater the likelihood of conflict and the need for mechanisms that will integrate these groups. It is frequently the integration that is a source of conflict. Complex organizations often expect very different groups or work units to integrate their efforts towards accomplishing organizational objectives without having any understanding of their differences.

When groups of people are physically separated by location or shiftwork, the possibilities for misunderstanding and the opportunities for conflict are increased. Information services are particularly vulnerable to this type of conflict as employees often work in a number of physically separated locations (e.g. computing centres or branch libraries), or have to work rostered hours in order to support customer services.

External environment

There is a likelihood that internal conflict will build up as uncertainty and complexity increase in the external environment. To accommodate these complexities different skills and attitudes may be required. The uncertainty brought about by the necessity for change, the knowledge that new skills will have to be learnt or acquired through external recruitment, and concern for their future will leave individuals feeling vulnerable. New services may be needed to satisfy the demands of customers. A different internal structure either within the information service or the parent organization may be required and corporate objectives may need to be modified. This change and repositioning will inevitably lead to conflict between individuals or groups.

Uncertainty also leads to conflict. Where the future is certain, activities are routine and predictable. Rules and regulations are relied upon. In a rapidly changing environment, the basic rules and regulations may no longer be relevant. Individuals may feel threatened by change or uncertainty, conflicting opinions may arise, new problems may have to be solved and conflict is inevitably the result.

Organizational growth

As information services grow to meet new demands, regulations evolve to control behaviour. These are not always effective and so conflict occurs. Growth within the information service or its parent organization may create additional levels in the hierarchy. Conflict will arise as individuals and work units vie for the higher positions in the hierarchy. Takeover bids are likely to occur whereby individuals and work units inevitably win and lose.

Resources

Resources that are scarce and in demand, or determine the interdependence and independence of departments, are another source of conflict. Work units or groups that have to share resources such as access to video links may require them at conflicting times. To overcome this, units may strive for their independence, thereby creating further tensions and conflict as they demand their own technology systems. Where work units 'own' their own information or technology systems, they may not share their technology or information with others. Alternatively, they may seek to impose their systems or solutions on others. As a result, conflict over ownership often arises. Integrated systems overcome this to some extent, but conflicts will always arise over levels of authority to access scarce resources.

The possibility that conflict will arise is greater when one party is dependent upon another for performance of tasks or for the provision of resources, materials or information. Conflict will sometimes occur between management and individuals as management is dependent upon individuals to perform tasks to achieve corporate objectives. Likewise, individuals depend upon their managers to provide the resources, materials and information that they need to carry out their tasks. Conflict between work units can also occur because of dependencies upon other work units to provide resources, information or services that may or may not be forthcoming.

Professional terminology

Due to the complexity of modern organizations and their high degree of differentiation, communications between work units and within work units can easily become distorted and lead to conflict. Information services managers and specialists often use specific terminology associated with their area of expertise. This is not always recognized or interpreted by others in the same way. The use of technical terminology or acronyms to describe events or objects can also threaten people who do not understand their meaning.

Policies

Conflict can arise between individuals and groups over policies, practices and plans where these are not in the main interests of one of the parties. This is particularly so if the policy removes decision-making or responsibility from one party.

Role expectancies

Differences between individuals and managers in terms of role expectancies, goals or even personal characteristics are often sources of interpersonal conflict. Managers are used to directing, yet employees receive orders; managers usually work for a salary and negotiate for pay rises, employees often work for wages and work to keep their jobs. Managers often have higher-order, promotion-seeking goals and usually perform challenging tasks. Individuals' personal goals may be more aligned to activities outside of work. Their tasks may be more routine and sometimes boring. Often the dividing line between the responsibilities and tasks of managers and others is not clearly defined and overlaps. Jurisdiction becomes ambiguous and consequently there is a high potential for conflict.

Conflict of interests

Individuals may also experience personal conflicts of interests. For example, there may be a conflict of interests between their professional values and organizational demands. The information services manager has to compete vigorously for funds with other managers during budget deliberations, yet needs to co-operate at all other times with these peers.

Many information services personnel experience a conflict of interests in having to work long hours in order to obtain promotion in the information service, whilst at the same time balancing their home life, furthering their professional education, and pursuing their personal interests – all of which are important. The conflict may be identified through feelings of guilt or being pressurised to give more attention to one aspect of life than another.

Advantages of conflict

Conflict has a place within information services. It can serve as a unifying function within a group and as a source of feedback. Groups will find that their internal differences are overcome when they are faced with an external source of conflict. For example, under a threat of closure, work units will work more closely together to achieve a more productive output, that in turn may prevent the threatened closure.

Conflict provides feedback to management as it brings issues to the surface. Under stress, individuals are more likely to express their real feelings or problems. This makes it easier to identify and resolve the real issues of concern. Issues can be addressed that otherwise may never have surfaced. It can also act as a safety valve. Minor conflict can prevent pressure from building up to the point where it is destructive. Petty complaints are often examples of tension release.

Conflict is a test of power. At the organizational level conflict situations often test the power of management and their employees, or their unions if they are acting on their behalf. On an individual basis, conflict will test a person's willpower.

The main outcome of conflict is change. Changes will occur as an outcome of the resolution of conflict. Some of these will be creative or innovative. For instance, budgetary pressures can lead to new and imaginative methods of delivering customer services.

Competition is healthy as it will often result in the improved performance of each party as they strive to win the battle. Conflict can also lead to a better understanding of each party's problems. The discussions that take place may find issues that can be resolved to the advantage of both parties or basic common goals that were previously unknown or overlooked.

Personal conflict

When faced with conflict, the individual's natural instinct (which is common to all living things) is to react through either 'fight' or 'flight'. Either method of conduct is an attempt to adjust to the conflict situation.

If a reliable staff member suddenly begins to act unpredictably, their actions may be a symptom of conflict. The cause or source of conflict may not be within the information service, but its effect will most certainly be felt there. In such a situation, it is the manager's duty to try to help resolve the conflict either by providing advice or by referring the individual to an appropriate source of advice. If the source of the conflict lies within the information service's internal or external environment, the manager must help resolve the issue. If the source is beyond the manager's control, he or she can choose whether or not to be involved. However, their involvement becomes essential when other staff begin to be affected.

Fight or aggression can be identified by negativism, dominance, displaced anger or hostility. A member of staff may be contentious for no apparent reason or rebellious without cause. Some individuals may become domineering towards their peers or fellow workers, or instances of anger will be levelled at colleagues rather than management. Others may become sarcastic, or make cutting comments or criticize. All of these are symptoms of an underlying conflict that must be resolved.

Flight can be identified by absenteeism, apathy or hypochondria. A staff member who suddenly begins to arrive late for work or absences themselves from others by being aloof or refusing to become involved is using flight as an escape mechanism from a source of conflict. Other examples of flight are day-dreaming and absent-mindedness, an overindulgence in food, drink or drugs, or continual tiredness.

Occasionally other adjustments to conflict are made. The individual may establish defence mechanisms or perform attention-getting activities in an effort towards self-deception. Compensation tactics may be used in order to reduce the sense of uselessness. The individual may substitute satisfaction in one kind of achievement for the lack of it in another. For example, the person may put more personal energies into sporting activities than their work.

A less well adjusted form of compensation is used when an individual will bask in the reflected glory of another. Individuals may also push the blame on to someone or something else, such as the boss or personal computer, or attribute to others the faults that really exist in themselves.

To help individuals to adjust to conflict, there needs to be an understanding of what lies behind the conduct, in order to help the individual substitute acceptable and efficient attitudes and responses.

Managing and resolving conflict

The process of managing conflict is important if the conflict is to be turned into a positive force for organizational change. Management needs to recognize the existence and usefulness of conflict, to consider the management of conflict as one of their major responsibilities, and to encourage opposition. In so doing, they should define conflict management in such terms as to stimulate as well as resolve conflict. For conflict to be effectively managed, the information service's and its parent organization's objectives should be identified to all concerned.

In resolving work conflicts between management and staff three techniques can be used. These are win-lose, lose-lose or win-win.

Win-lose methods

In win-lose methods the manager or supervisor inevitably wins and the employee inevitably loses. Win-lose methods constitute an authoritarian approach to conflict resolution as legitimate or coercive power is often used to bring about the employee's compliance. Managers will pursue their own outcomes at the expense of others, and employees will be forced into submission, often by the use of threats. Majority rule and the failure of the manager to respond to requests for change are also considered to be win-lose methods. Whilst win-lose methods may prove satisfactory to the manager they result in employee resentment and can have negative effects on the performance of individuals and the organization.

Where the employees win in a win-lose situation the manager or supervisor will lose his or her position power. They may, as a consequence, build a resentment towards the individuals concerned. This can sometimes lead to grudges or retaliatory action, such as the assignment of awkward tasks to individuals. This may cause a further breakdown in the relationship and the associated loss of control will affect work output. In any event, respect for management will be diminished. They in turn will lose their self-esteem.

Whilst the examples here are described as dealing with conflict between management and staff, the techniques can also be used between other groups or individuals.

Lose-lose methods

Lose-lose methods leave no one entirely happy. One such method is the compromise. This is based on the assumption that half a solution is better than none. Another lose-lose strategy involves side payments. One party agrees to a solution in exchange for a favour from the other party. A third strategy is to submit the issue to a neutral third party. The results of this action may be disappointing as arbitrators frequently resolve issues at some middle ground between the positions held by the disputants. Although each gains something, the outcome is rarely satisfying to either side.

Win-win methods

Win-win methods provide a solution that is acceptable to all. Win-win conflict resolution strategies focus upon ends and goals, identifying the sources of conflict and then present these as problems to be solved. Superordinate goals (goals that are greater than those of the individual, work unit or cost centre) are established. These reflect the corporate objectives that all parties must work towards.

The identification of the superordinate goals reminds conflicting individuals or work units that, even though their particular goals are vitally important, they share a goal that cannot be achieved without co-operation. The win-win approach uses participative management techniques in order to gain consensus and commitment to objectives. The desired solution is one that achieves both individual or work unit goals and the organization's objectives, and which is acceptable to all parties.

Conflict management styles

Whilst it would be nice to think that all conflict was handled by managers in a positive and successful way, this is not always the case. Managers use different styles in managing conflict.

Avoidance style

Sometimes a manager attempts to dispose of the problem by denying that it exists or by avoiding the issue. He or she may try to remain neutral or withdraw from it. Examples of this can be found where managers are unavailable in their office, defer answering a memo, fail to return a telephone call or refuse to get involved in the conflict. In most instances the conflict will not go away. In fact, it will often escalate to a point where it becomes unmanageable.

The avoidance style is suitable in three instances:

- where the issue is of minor or passing importance that it is not worth the time or energy to confront it;
- where the person's power is so low in relation to the other party that there will be little or no positive outcome by being involved; or
- where others can more effectively resolve the conflict between themselves.

Smoothing style

The smoothing style refers to the tendency to minimize or suppress the open recognition of real or perceived differences in conflict situations, whilst emphasizing common interests. This style of management fails to recognize the positive aspects of openly handling the conflict. The manager acts as if the conflict will pass with time and appeals to the need for co-operation. He or she will try to reduce tensions by reassuring and providing support to the parties.

The smoothing style encourages individuals to cover up and avoid expressions of their feelings. It is effective on a short-term basis in three situations:

- when there is a potentially explosive emotional situation that needs to be defused;
- where harmonious relationships need to be preserved or where the avoidance of disruption is important; or
- where the conflicts are of a personal nature between individuals and cannot be dealt with within the organizational context.

Forcing style

The forcing style refers to the tendency of the manager to use coercive or reward power to dominate the other party. Differences are suppressed and the other party is forced into adopting the manager's position. This style results in winners and losers. The losers do not usually support the final decision in the way that the winners do and this can create more conflict.

The win-lose forcing style is appropriate when there is an extreme urgency and quick action is needed. It can also be used when an unpopular course of action is necessary for the long-term survival of the information service. It is sometimes used as a self-protection when a person is being taken advantage of by another party.

Compromise style

The compromise style is used when negotiating. There is often a tendency to sacrifice positions when seeking a middle ground for the resolution of conflict. Early use of compromise results in less diagnosis and exploration of the real nature of the conflict. The real issues often surface much later in the negotiating or conflict resolution process.

The compromise style is desirable when both parties recognize that there is a possibility of reaching an agreement that is more advantageous than if no agreement was reached. It is also useful if there is a likelihood that more than one agreement could be reached, or where there are conflicting goals.

Collaborative style

The collaborative style required the willingness of the manager to identify underlying causes of conflict, openly share information, and search out alternatives considered to be mutually beneficial. Conflicts are recognized openly and evaluated by all those concerned. Sharing, examining, and assessing the reasons for the conflict leads to a more thorough development of alternatives. Collaborative style is inappropriate when time limits are imposed to the extent that they inhibit direct confrontation of feelings and issues involved in the conflict, and, when there are no shared meanings (norms, values, feelings) between management and employees.

The collaborative style uses win-win methods to resolve conflict. It is used more by managers who are relationship-oriented than task-oriented. It is found more frequently in open organizations than in bureaucratic ones. The collaborative style is recommended:

- when individuals have common goals;
- when consensus should lead to the best overall solution to the conflict; and
- where there is a need to make high-quality decisions on the basis of expertise and information.

Each style has its purpose and, if used appropriately, will be successful. If a style is used to avoid or suppress an issue it will have a negative effect on individuals and the organization.

Detecting conflict

Grievance procedures

Conflicts can be detected through grievance procedures whereby dissatisfaction is communicated to management through official channels. Such procedures assume that the individual has the courage to submit their complaint for discussion and that the manager is approachable.

Observation

Direct observation may often identify interpersonal or intergroup conflicts. Conflicting motives are usually apparent when clashes between individuals or groups occur or work output deteriorates.

Suggestion boxes

Suggestion boxes may be used for information service staff as gripe boxes. Employees can make suggestions to overcome conflicts whilst preserving their anonymity. Alternatively, the open-door policy is used to create open communication and reduce conflict.

Exit interview

The exit interview can be one of the most reliable indications of subversive conflicts within information services. Employees may be willing to discuss such matters when they have no further affiliation with the organization.

Sometimes conflict may lead to the resignation of an employee and, in such cases, the employee may not be willing to discuss their dissatisfaction for fear that this may affect some future job reference. The interviewer should be impartial and stress the positive outcomes of the exit interview for resolving future conflicting situations.

Like power and politics, conflict is often viewed as a negative force within an organization. Conflict can also be a sign of a healthy organization if it leads to improved organizational performance through competition and change. Conflict also acts as a safety valve. The sources of conflict and the resulting actions do need to be managed to ensure that only positive outcomes arise from conflict.

22 Negotiation

Introduction

Negotiation can be defined as a process in which two or more parties try to reach a common agreement on matters where there are both common and conflicting goals. The parties deal directly with each other in an effort to persuade or compromise with the view to reaching a desirable conclusion. Negotiation takes place with varying degrees of formality.

Successful negotiating requires experience on behalf of both parties, confidence, and the possession of high-level communication skills. Time and information are critical factors in successful negotiations.

Negotiation is commonly used in the resolution of conflict and in the implementation of decisions. It is also used in the preparation and finalizing of budgets, industrial relations, contract management and policy development and implementation. Not all issues can be settled through negotiation. So it is pointless to attempt co-operation for co-operation's sake if the outcomes are likely to be less than those that can be achieved through other solutions.

Effective negotiation

Whilst compromise is the cornerstone to negotiating, effective negotiation uses both compromise and collaboration. Collaboration enables the realization of common interests, whilst compromising conflicting interests. Effective negotiating should result in shared meaning. That is, the convergence of values, views, attitudes, styles, perceptions or beliefs to enable a common view or action.

Negotiators have to strike a balance between being:

- steadfast in their desires; and
- sufficiently co-operative with the other party to allow negotiations to take place.

This is particularly true when personal interests are at stake. Emotions are prone to be far more volatile in these situations.

Negotiation requires trade-offs between short- and long-term gains. This is particularly true when negotiating the implementation of a decision, as it is inherent in this exercise that the parties will need to continue to work with each other after the event. Apparent honesty and openness are an important feature of the negotiating process. However, complete honesty can sometimes run the risk of exploitation by the other party. To overcome this, the motives of each party must be made clear.

In some situations, negotiators must be willing to give up more than they would like in order to obtain a result that is preferable in the long run. The result may be a less than the perfect solution, but one that has a better outcome than that provided by the next best alternative. Faces should be saved and the important working relationship should be preserved. A positive outcome of any negotiation process is that the parties learn a good deal more about each other than they may previously have known.

Good negotiators are experienced in the negotiating process. They have high aspirations, are articulate and have great presence and self-confidence. Their self-confidence arises out of their technical knowledge of the field in which they are negotiating and in their past negotiating experience. Effective negotiators are creative, yet determined and disciplined. They need a high frustration or tolerance level.

Age can make a difference. In their early years of negotiating, negotiators tend to be very competitive, showing signs of aggression or abrasiveness. In their later years there tends to be a higher tolerance of others. Ideally, the negotiator should be between these two stages – that is, experienced but still keen to be successful. Above all, the negotiator must enjoy negotiating and have an understanding of how to devise mutually beneficial alternatives.

Negotiation can be very much a personal process, even though the negotiator may be acting on behalf of other people. It is an exercise in predicting the other's position without the negotiator disclosing their own. However, there still needs to be some leeway to tempt the other party into wanting to know more about what is being offered.

Sensitivity to the behaviours of others will help the negotiator in his or her task. Negotiators are better able to anticipate and evaluate others' responses to the offers being made if they are:

- attentive to what is being said;
- able to distinguish between what the other is saying and what they really mean; and
- able to translate their offers and demands into what is the real situation.

The success of negotiation depends upon the people who are involved. Outer-directed people, whose values, skills and attitudes are gained from outside themselves, are easier to change attitudinally than inner-directed people. Inner-directed people resist group pressure, do things their way and have a sense of independence; all of which limits their sense of negotiation.

To be effective, the negotiator should be able to identify both their own role and that of the opposite number. The negotiator should also take steps to identify the apparent hierarchical structure of the opposing team. Each member will have their individual purpose and strategies. The studying of the non-verbal communications of the members of the opposing team will assist the identification process.

The role of a negotiator as an agent may range from being an emissary commissioned only to state the position, to a free agent with considerable latitude. This range of responsiveness is likely to affect the negotiation process. The effect of the 'person' variables in the negotiating process will be felt more strongly in instances where the negotiator has more latitude to manoeuvre.

The process of negotiation

The first stage

The initial meeting of the parties establishes the climate that prevails during the ensuing negotiations. The atmosphere created in the first few minutes of the meeting or greetings stage is critical. Tensions need to be relaxed so that common sense prevails, rather than outright confrontation. Non-verbal clues such as eye contact, posture, gestures and patterns of movement will add to the feeling of the meeting.

The physical properties of the negotiating room can affect the negotiating atmosphere. The shape and size of the table will either place participants in a compromising or contending position. Round tables are less threatening than square or oblong ones. Opposing parties will usually want to sit opposite each other. This allows them to pick up their opposite numbers' non-verbal communication signals and places each party in a competitive position. At times when a compromise is to be achieved, opposing parties may sit next to each other.

The first meeting is usually devoted to establishing the bargaining authority possessed by representatives on both sides. If the parties are unknown to each other, a 'pecking' order will be established and personal interactions developed. This stage may be omitted where all parties are known to each other. In situations where external people are involved, for example when negotiating a contract, the negotiating rules and procedures will need to be determined. This is not always necessary where internal negotiations take place. The negotiating rules and procedures should be well known throughout the organization; their norms being part of the corporate culture.

The second stage

The second stage is characterized by each side attempting to consider the opponent's position without revealing its own. Each side will try to avoid disclosing their key important factors in the proposal in order to avoid being forced to pay a higher price than is necessary to have the proposal accepted. Negotiators will also attempt to get greater concessions in return for granting those requests that their opponents want most.

The proposals may be discussed in the order of their appearance on the agenda or in some other sequence. The sequence in which they are discussed may also be a subject for negotiation. If the discussion of the most important issues is deferred until last, this can often serve as a leverage for gaining agreement on more minor issues that precede the important ones.

The settlement

A process of haggling, bargaining, and settling then begins. The proposals are resolved at a stage when agreement is reached within the limits that each party is willing to concede. The agreement is then ratified. In settling and ratifying the agreement, all the points and concessions of the agreement should be summarized and all actions accounted for. A document should be produced that provides a record of what was achieved. Finally, responsibility should be allocated to individuals or groups for the implementation of the agreement.

Problems in negotiations

Stress and tension

The environment of negotiators has been likened to a fishbowl, with everyone interested in the negotiating performance. The face-saving techniques that are often used and their associated anxiety, enhance the stresses and tensions of those who are involved in the negotiating process.

High levels of stress and tension can have a debilitating effect on negotiations. They may cause greater hostility among negotiators, leading to harder bargaining strategies. This can result in less successful outcomes. Increases in tension beyond a certain point may make members of either party less capable of evaluating information and making the fine discriminations necessary in order to achieve a mutually satisfying solution. It is important that negotiators are aware of their personal stress levels when undertaking any negotiating procedures. They should monitor their tensions, looking for physical symptoms such as aggression or tension headaches.

Conserving the position

The psychological need to impress others and maintain a position of strength is poignant in negotiation. Taken too far, it is likely to lead to rigid and contentious demands that may spoil the negotiating process. Skilful negotiators like their concessions to be seen as a willingness to deal from a position of strength rather than a weakness. They also like their concessions to be allowed because of their competency as negotiator.

Some negotiators find it tempting to commit themselves to tough negotiating positions, when discussions become bogged down, in an effort to impose such a considerable cost to the adversary that they will yield under pressure. However, it is a mistake to assume that all negotiators can be pressured into arriving at a settlement. The threat of an impasse being reached when time expires may be sufficient in itself for a result to be obtained closer to the time. To adopt the first attitude will result either in the perpetrator having to retreat to their former position, losing credibility in the process, or opening the way to subsequent exploitation by the other.

Emotions

The negotiation process is complicated by the fact that not all people are alike. Not everyone is a self-actualizer; not everyone wants to participate in the decision-making or negotiating process; some even may resist. Negotiators meet a multiplicity of emotions as they try to negotiate. These need to be understood if the negotiating process is to be successful.

Complex situations

A host of different negotiating strategies is necessary to suit different environments and different kinds of conflict. Negotiations become more difficult if people are not sufficiently knowledgeable or obligated to the issue at stake.

The complexity of the situation may cause different parties to develop different conceptions of the situation or prefer a different structure for handling the negotiations. This situation can also arise if a member of the party is someone who has not previously been involved in the decision-making process. An impasse may result from an inability to resolve the differences, and a mediator may be required to alter perceptions or definitions of purpose on behalf of either party. This could delay or jeopardize the implementation of the negotiations.

Factors for successful negotiations

Time frames

One of the most critical aspects of the negotiating process is time. Time can be either a constriction or an advantage. It is important not to let the opposing side know of any time constraints that the negotiator may have. Time pressures have two effects. First, as the deadline approaches, decisions will be made faster, leading to one party losing their demand power. Second, to declare any time constraint may result in the other party holding their real negotiating process until close to the deadline, in order to place the first party in a more vulnerable or critical position. The negotiator should be patient, realizing that the other party must have a deadline too. As the deadline of the other party comes close there may be a shift in power back to the first party.

Information

Information is also critical to the negotiating process. The negotiator should quietly and consistently probe the other party for information. They should listen rather than talk, asking questions rather than answering them. It may be useful to check the other party's credibility by asking questions to which the answer is already known.

Attentive listening and observation are critical. Often unintentional clues can be given out. Negotiators should have faith in their own problem-solving abilities.

Agendas

Momentum for results can sometimes be encouraged by placing easier items earlier on the negotiation agenda, so that both parties are able to build upon their successes. A mediator may serve as a valuable communications link between the parties, co-ordinating movement towards a compromise. Trust, too, is important, but it is the absence of distrust that makes negotiating more effective.

The opening bid should be put firmly, without reservation or hesitation. For the 'sellers' it should be the highest defensible bid. For the 'buyers' it should be the lowest defensible offer.

Breaking deadlocks

If a deadlock is threatened there should be a break in the negotiating procedures. This can either be achieved by using a time break such as lunch or morning refreshments, or by talking about some aspect other than that where a deadlock is threatened. A mediator or third party may also be used to help the negotiating process at this stage.

Effective negotiation can be used in resolving conflict and implementing decisions. It is a skill that can be learnt, building upon experience and utilizing high-level interpersonal and communication skills.

23 Change management

Introduction

Change can be defined as an alteration in relationships or the environment. Change has always been part of the human condition. However, external factors such as global competition, growing customer sophistication and revolutionary developments in technologies, products and management thinking are increasing the speed, complexity and intensity of change.

Continuous change is a necessary part of organizational life. It occurs as an adjustment to the altered states in the external and internal environments. For example, pressure for change can come from the introduction of new technologies, new external sources of competition, or simply the stages of development in the organizational life cycle. Continuous change is usually planned, allowing some control over outcomes and providing time for thought.

Discontinuous change occurs in response to an abrupt event in the environment. It can be described as a strategic shock. There is a rapid and fundamental shift in the organization's circumstances. Examples may be where a rapid downsize occurs as the result of a merger between two organizations, or where a totally different political philosophy is introduced overnight as a result of a change of government.

People and organizations will often be resistant to change. Resistance by individuals is usually caused by feelings of loss and uncertainty which in turn leads to insecurity. The most effective way of overcoming resistance to change is to encourage those involved to be part of the planning and decision-making process. Training, open communication and evidence of clear, tangible benefits as an outcome of change also facilitate the change process.

Business and process re-engineering are two approaches that are being used to rethink organizational activities in order to manage in a competitive and changing environment. These approaches take advantage of the potential for change that is offered through the introduction of new technologies.

Organizational change

Sources of organizational change

Organizational change occurs either as the result of changes in the external environment that impact on an organization or through internal forces. Some internal forces may be an indirect reflection of the external forces acting upon the organization.

External forces most likely to affect information services are those relating to:

- the introduction of new technologies such as Internet and other public access information systems that open up new mechanisms through which individuals can access information globally;
- changing political, economic and financial conditions such as an increased emphasis on outsourcing and full cost recovery for services;
- shifts in customer demands for services such as extended hours that impact upon the rostering of staff;
- changes in the behaviour of competitive organizations such as the introduction of electronic trading strategies; or
- changing cultural and social conditions that reinforce individual rights and probity.

Internal forces are most likely to come from:

- the involvement of the information service in the business and process re-engineering strategies within the parent organization, especially in the area of information flows;
- a revision of the information service's or its parent organization's objectives to incorporate a stronger customer focus;
- shifts in employees' socio-cultural values; or
- changes in work practices and attitudes such as more flexible work conditions.

Organization life cycles and change

An internal force for change is growth within an organization. For example, as an information service and its parent organization grow they progress through an organization life cycle. Changes in managerial structure, processes and style occur. The fundamental reason for this is found in systems theory. As systems grow they move in the direction of differentiation and elaboration with greater specialization of function. As differentiation proceeds, it is countered by processes that bring the system together for unified functioning.

When an information service is first established, the emphasis is on creativity. Services and information products are created and introduced in order to prove its worth. The founding person devotes his or her energies to establishing and marketing the services. As there are generally few staff, the organization and management style are informal and non-bureaucratic. There is often less differentiation and people perform a variety of tasks. Control is based on the manager's personal supervision. Long hours are experienced. There is often not enough time for proper procedures to be documented; most decisions are based upon professional knowledge.

As the service grows, more staff are added. People are promoted from within. It is an exciting place to work. However, the information service becomes in danger of losing direction unless the policies and goals have been formally documented. The founding person may not be interested in the operational details of management, more in his or her area of expertise. Strong management is needed to guide the information service through this stage.

If the leadership is strong, clear goals and direction are provided. Differentiation occurs, specialization takes place, work units are established to perform different tasks, and a hierarchy of authority is formed. This marks the beginning of the division of labour. Management systems are introduced for accounting budgets, inventory and acquiring items. Communication becomes more formal, and elements of bureaucracy are apparent.

As growth continues, restrictive practices begin to impede the service. First-line managers in charge of specific areas need to be able to exercise discretion. The more senior managers begin to delegate responsibility to others, concentrating more on long-term planning and co-ordination. The internal control systems have by now formalized communication to the extent that it becomes less frequent. New specialists and services are added. Consultants are often hired to review policies and procedures as the organization appears to be ineffective. As a result, task forces, project and matrix groups are formed to improve co-ordination, but the proliferation of systems and bureaucracy strangles innovation.

The solution to this crisis is in collaboration and co-operation. Managers develop skills for confronting problems and resolving interpersonal differences. Formal systems are simplified. Attempts are made to create a more open, reactive organizational environment.

The developments in the organization life cycle produce significant changes from one stage to the next. Each stage presents different challenges for management. For example, the first stage requires boundless energy and creativity in terms of establishing services, thinking of new ways of doing things, and letting people know about the information services and products offered.

The challenge of the second stage is to keep the creativity and energy going whilst establishing systems that assist rather than hinder service delivery. New positions and levels within the information service may be created. Whilst it may be desirable for members of the information service to fill these new positions, this may not always be possible. Those individuals who are unsuccessful in terms of promotion may need to be given other opportunities for personal development.

Growth needs to be managed in the context of the strategic direction of the parent organization. It is important for managers to recognize the stage at which their information service is in the organization life cycle in order to manage the change, prepare for the future and avoid the pitfalls.

Managing change

The strategies used in the management of change differ according to whether the change is continuous or discontinuous. Continuous change occurs where there is a gradual adjustment within the organization to environmental circumstances, examples being the introduction of new information services to meet a market need and the phasing out of other services that have lost their relevance to the business needs of the organization. In these situations classic change management techniques can be used. In discontinuous change situations, where there are major threats or changes to the organizational direction, rapid and radical change has to take place.

Strategies for managing continuous change

Continuous change can generally be planned for in advance. An example of this is where there are changes made to an organizational structure as a result of process re-engineering and/or the introduction of a new technology. In managing continuous change, the ability to incorporate planned change is preferable to having reactive change.

Planned change can be designed and implemented as far as possible in an orderly and timely fashion in anticipation of future events. Although it should be recognized that each action will always have some unplanned consequences. The reasons for this are that each successive step of change will affect other areas and reveal new information that must be taken into account to further progress the change. If a more piecemeal response begins to emerge to the problems as they develop, then the change becomes reactive.

In introducing planned change, the reason for the change and its implications should be explained to all stakeholders. In explaining the implications of the change, some of the anticipated concerns that individuals may have should be addressed. Change sparks powerful emotions in people, yet at the same time people are required to make changes in their behaviours. The changes in behaviour cannot be learnt if individuals are distracted by fear, anger or uncertainty. These feelings need to be openly acknowledged and dealt with as a natural course of events arising out of the change. The need to empower individuals to manage their emotional response is as important as providing them with the necessary skills and training for the new situation.

The magnitude of the change alters the way in which the change process should be managed. Radical or major changes that have the potential to affect the whole organization should be managed quite differently to minor changes affecting one or two people. Changes at a policy level also need to be managed differently from those at a procedural level.

The timing and frequency of the change need to be considered. Ideally, changes should be implemented at a time when the information service is least pressured and has been made ready for the change. However, this is not always possible, particularly in the case of reactive change. The frequency of change and the duration of the change affects the way in which the change is managed. Permanent change needs to be managed differently to short-lived change. Finally, the need for the change should also be considered. Change for change's sake has no inherent organizational value.

Strategies for managing discontinuous change

The difficulty in managing discontinuous change is that as the often radical changes are made quickly, the shock wave travels through the organization. The hard task is to identify where the shock wave will be felt most and what its impact will be. Crisis conditions frequently prevail. The resulting chaos and time factors may not allow measured consideration of the impact of the decisions.

The uncertainty brought about by the discontinuous change needs to be managed through strong and direct leadership. New roles, tasks and interim structures should be quickly put in place for the transition period. Strategic areas that are working well should be identified quickly and if possible quarantined in order to preserve and build upon their success. Areas within the information service that do not support the new direction should be dispensed with immediately.

Where radical change affects individuals, the information services manager should be aware that the way in which they treat any one individual sends signals to the rest of the people in the organization. These signals can be very powerful in determining the people's expectations as to how they may be treated, valued, rewarded or penalized. An information service that is in the middle of a crisis cannot afford to have the staff that will be retained demotivated or distracted to the extent that it adversely affects its performance and quality of service to customers.

Individuals view the changes through their own eyes, not those of the leaders of change. They interpret the messages about the change according to how they see others being treated, how they hear of changes through the grapevine, and through what they are officially told by their managers. These messages may not always be consistent or correctly interpreted. It is therefore important to ensure that any actions or signals send the correctly framed message. If the message is distorted because of other political agendas, or if mixed messages are received, people will quickly become despondent and confused. The message should be simple and clearly identify what needs to be achieved by the information service through the change process.

Strong internal communications and access to counselling may help individuals deal with their personal anxieties about their and the organization's future.

Managing the change cycle

As change occurs individuals and groups progress through four stages: denial, resistance, exploring and commitment. Each of the four stages have quite distinct behavioural reactions and need to be managed in different ways. As change occurs, it is unlikely that all individuals will progress through the four stages at the same time. Figure 23.1 illustrates the four stages of change.

Stage one (denial) is characterized by individuals ignoring any signals of change. They may experience shock if they could not see that change was required, or relief that the inevitable had actually happened. Individuals in this stage of change require information about what the change will mean to them and to the organization, with pressure to move forwards with the change.

The second stage of change (resistance) is characterized by negativity and

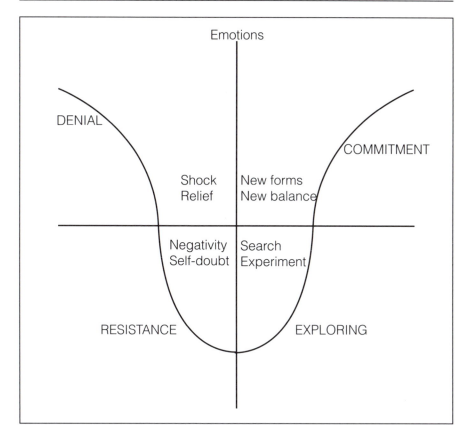

Figure 23.1   The four stages of change

self-doubt. This is often expressed in terms of sabotage, absenteeism, anger, anxiety, suspicion and cynicism. During this stage, the information services manager will need to deal with illogical arguments and hostility. The important management process at this stage is to listen rather than reason or argue. The manager should empathize with staff whilst trying to reconnect them to reality. Staff will feel a sense of loss and require support whilst still keeping the pressure to move forward.

The third stage (exploring) is the most critical stage as it is the point of transformation. The change process at this stage relies upon people being given tangible things to do that reinforce their new roles. Staff should be encouraged to acknowledge what has happened, reinforcing the positive things of the past whilst exploring the future. Individuals will still feel insecure but their hostility will be diminished. This marks the formation of the new team with new behaviours. The information services manager should provide information and support through discussion and problem-solving. People should be involved in all discussions and provided with opportunities to succeed in the new environment. To mark the transition there should be a launch of something new that signifies a change within the corporate culture. This may be a new logo, new stationery or new premises.

The final stage is commitment. The information services manager should have a watching brief at this point, being available for consultation. Staff should be allowed to get on with their work and own it.

Resistance to change

Individual resistance

In planning for change, the information services manager should take it into account that people will react to change in one of three ways:

- accepting and supporting the change;
- complying with the change in action but not in spirit; or
- they will resist the change.

There are a variety of reasons why people resist change. Often the uncertainty of impending change leads to anxiety, particularly in relation to people's ability to cope with a new situation. Familiarity with existing procedures and lack of psychological energy to acquire new skills or change direction add to this resistance. People often fear the thought of having to master something new and the possibility that they may not be able to do this immediately. They may argue that they are too old to learn new systems.

Resistance can also occur because of previous experiences in life. If the change is coloured by a previous negative encounter with a similar life experience, there will often be resistance. Change may also produce a threat to an individual's or group's self-interest or status. Their position of authority or power source may be threatened if they are placed in a situation of being dependent upon others whilst they are in a learning situation. The different perceptions of the employee's and management's assessment of the situation also add to the resistance.

Changes in organizational structure or workplace may cause the severance of old relationships with feelings of loss and disruption to existing social networks. The promotion of an internal candidate to a more senior position may sever the close relationships that existed beforehand between the candidate and their peers.

Organizational resistance

Change can also be resisted at the organizational level. Organizations have inbuilt mechanisms that produce stability. The selection process and culture of the organization create a persona that is difficult to change. Group norms may also act as a constraint to change.

Techniques for overcoming resistance to change

The most effective technique for overcoming resistance to change is by encouraging participation in the decision-making, problem-solving and planning processes. Employees who participate in planning and implementing change are better able to understand the reasons for it. Uncertainty is reduced and self-interest neutralized through the opportunity to express their own ideas.

Training and communication about the new work practices and anticipated results should also reduce resistance. If open channels of communication are established and maintained, uncertainty can be minimized. It is also helpful to introduce change gradually to minimize resistance and facilitate the unfreezing process.

To minimize resistance it is important that the change quickly results in a positive and relative advantage. The benefits of which should be clearly apparent to the individuals being asked to change. The sooner these benefits can be identified by those involved, the more likely they are to accept and continue their change related practices. The changes being advocated must be compatible with the existing values and experiences of the individuals other-wise they will be discarded as threatening or inappropriate. Change agents can also be used to facilitate and support individuals through the change.

If resistance to change continues it may be the symptom of one of two causes. Either the correct 'fit' between the change situation, change agent and persons involved has not been found, or, the proposed change is a poor strategy and is not in the organization's best interest.

Symptoms of unsuccessful change

A successful change will barely be visible. Unsuccessful change can be recognized by the absence of feedback, even though a feedback mechanism is available, or by strong feedback in the form of protests or complaints. A drop in productivity below that anticipated by the learning curve also indicates a problem. Likewise, withdrawal symptoms characterized by lack of co-operation, absenteeism, resignations or transfers indicate that something is wrong. When any one of these symptoms appear, it should be immediately investigated in order to isolate and correct the problem.

Re-engineering and change

The competitive environment within which information services and their parent organizations operate and the advantages being offered through new technologies require them to rethink and streamline their business and processes. These requirements have led to two change requirements: process re-engineering and business re-engineering. Business re-engineering requires the ability to fundamentally rethink the mind set or way in which organizations deliver their products and services in line with their business strategy. Process re-engineering is a narrower set of business re-engineering. It concentrates upon rethinking and streamlining the processes within an organization to achieve better outcomes either in terms of higher levels of efficiency or productivity and improved customer service. Instead of concentrating on functions, process re-engineering looks at the steps that contribute to the process of creating the outcomes as a value chain.

Business re-engineering

Hammer (1990, pp. 104–12) identified the notion of discontinuous thinking. He argued that organizations should use the power of modern information technology to radically redesign business processes in order to achieve dramatic improvements in their performance. Organizations could not achieve major breakthroughs in their performance just by trimming the fat or automating existing processes. Organizations needed to recognize and break away from outdated rules and fundamental assumptions that underlie operations in order to avoid simply speeding up inappropriate processes. His basic principles of re-engineering are as follows:

- *Organize around outcomes not tasks*: design a person's job around all the steps in the process instead of a single task.
- *Have those who use the output of the process perform the process*: use the technology so that the individuals who need the result of the process can do it themselves. When the people closest to the process perform it, there is little need for the overhead associated with managing it.
- *Subsume information-processing work into the real work that produces the information*: move the work of processing the information to the area that processes it. For example, let the section that receives the goods or services also process the payment of the account.
- *Treat geographically dispersed resources as though they were centralized*: use databases, telecommunications networks and standardized processing systems to get the benefits of scale and co-ordination while maintaining the benefits of flexibility and service.

- *Link parallel activities instead of integrating their results*: use databases, telecommunications networks and teleconferencing to forge links between parallel functions and co-ordinate them whilst the activities are in process rather than after they were created.
- *Put the decision point where the work is performed, and build control into the process*: let the people who do the work make the decisions. Build controls into the process through expert systems and the way in which the information technology is designed.
- *Capture information once and at the source*: overcome the delays, input errors and costly overheads of duplicated data in 'silo type' systems by capturing information at the source and using this throughout the information chain. Use bar-coding, document image processing, intranets, electronic commerce to provide better access and reduce processing time in the provision of better services to customers.

Business re-engineering requires commitment and drive from senior management. It is business strategy driven. A significant proportion of business re-engineering strategies are information related. As such, it creates a significant change process for any information service. The traditional functional and organizational boundaries are ignored. Cross-functional processes are emphasized. This necessitates the reshaping of job designs, information flows, organizational structures and management systems, not just the introduction of a new technology. There will also be an impact upon the motivation and reward systems, performance monitoring systems, and staff training and development. The focus should be on managing the cultural dimension of the organization as well as the people, technology and structure.

The impact is also found at the interface with the external environment. There is a stronger alignment of the core processes to the business strategy. Customer needs become a major driver. The relationships with stakeholders such as suppliers and customers change as they become part of the information chain. Negotiations will be required between them and the organization about the redesigning or elimination of processes and the choice and compatibility of equipment that is used at the interface between them.

Process re-engineering

Process re-engineering requires the bringing together and streamlining of multiple functions such as customer needs identification, budgeting, purchasing of materials and delivery of customer services to form a process that delivers a specific outcome. The emphasis is on the outcome of the process rather than the success of the individual functions.

The traditional approach of managing functions within an organization created situations where differing priorities and time horizons between functions led to delays in customer service. Those people performing the functions halfway through the value chain had little idea of the impact of any delay for the customer at the service delivery end. For example, a payments section could be very efficient about paying their accounts by the end of the month, but if urgently required software or library materials were held until the account was paid or delayed through the asset management process, the service delivery to the customer would be impaired. Process re-engineering changes this. Instead of streamlining the functions, process re-engineering manages the total value chain by seeing it as a whole and making improvements across functions. The bottom line is to maintain competitiveness in the market-place through the ability to increase the speed, quality and flexibility of services to customers at lower costs.

The transition from the functional state to the process re-engineering state requires analysis and planning so that value chains are created. Every process should be reviewed in order to determine the value that it adds to the business strategy and customer needs. Workflows should be analysed for bottlenecks and inefficiencies. The aim is to avoid doing things just because they have always been done.

Management's changing role

To manage the necessary change, the role of management must also change (see Table 23.1). Their channels of communication must be opened up, so that there is a free flow of information in order to build the vision, discuss any concerns with individuals, understand the impacts of the change and be committed to the change.

Managers now act as facilitators, enabling work teams to devise effective processes that fit the work unit's situation rather than imposing uniform processes from above. This approach is supported by empowering individuals with the relevant expertise to make decisions as compared with the more formalized, functional approach where only those in a formal line management position were allowed to make decisions. It is also reflected in the control and behaviour elements, where work teams and individuals are encouraged to devise their own measures of control and responsibilities to meet the specific needs of the work situation or process.

The role of the information services manager in the new process is to enable, motivate and empower people to make their own decisions, when dealing with their own staff and also in putting in place the appropriate information systems within the parent organization to support the change.

The only constant in the world today is that it is an era of continuous change. In this environment, change management strategies are important in

Table 23.1   Management's changing role

Element	Functional approach	Process approach
Channels of communication	Highly structured controlled information flow	Open. Free flow of information
Decision-making	Taken within formal line management position	Taken by empowering individuals with relevant expertise
Work emphasis	Formal procedures handed down	Individuals/teams devise own effective processes
Adaptability	Slow and reluctant even when business circumstances warrant change	Changes are made in line with continuous improvement
Operations	Uniform and restricted	Vary from business unit to business unit
Control	Tight through strict, formal systems	Individuals/teams devise own measures in line with fulfilling process role
Behaviour	Contained by need to follow job description	Individual/team roles and responsibilities evolve to meet needs of process
Participation	Little. Information is handed up, decisions down	Teamworking with co-operation between teams
Management role	Commands and controls	Empowers, enables and motivates

order to smooth the transition of change and, importantly, to initiate and manage the change itself for the strategic advantage of the information service and its parent organization.

Reference

Hammer, M. (1990), 'Re-engineering work: don't automate, obliterate', *Harvard Business Review*, July–August, 104–12.

Part 6

Managing and communicating information in the corporate environment

This part of the book looks at managing and communicating information in the corporate environment. It considers the communication of information at the individual level through the personal communication process and at the corporate or organizational level. It also covers the management of the organization's information as a corporate resource (see Figure P6.1).

Chapter 24 considers the human side of communication. It identifies the personal communication skills required of information service managers and their staff. It also describes the communication process and issues associated with interpersonal communication that may affect the communication process. These issues include self-image and attitude to others, listening, stereotyping and the 'halo effect'. Barriers to personal communication are also explored in this chapter.

Internal and external communications within the organization are separated into Chapters 25 and 26 respectively. Chapter 25 identifies how communications are used within the parent organizational environment. There is particular emphasis on the impacts of this for the information service. The use of formal and informal communication channels is explored. The chapter also describes how the corporate culture of an organization is communicated, and how managers communicate through reports and meetings. The chapter offers advice on how meetings should be conducted to be effective.

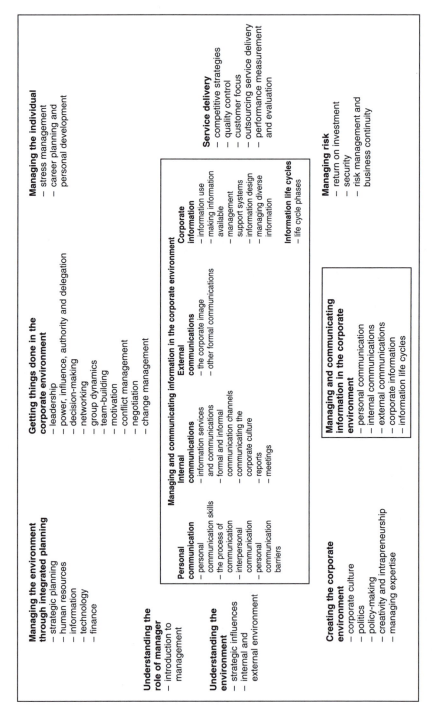

Managing the environment through integrated planning
– strategic planning
– human resources
– information
– technology
– finance

Understanding the role of manager
– introduction to management

Understanding the environment
– strategic influences
– internal and external environment

Getting things done in the corporate environment
– leadership
– power, influence, authority and delegation
– decision-making
– networking
– group dynamics
– team-building
– motivation
– conflict management
– negotiation
– change management

Managing the individual
– stress management
– career planning and personal development

Managing and communicating information in the corporate environment

Personal communication
– personal communication skills
– the process of communication
– interpersonal communication
– personal communication barriers

Internal communications
– information services and communications
– formal and informal communication channels
– communicating the corporate culture
– reports
– meetings

External communications
– the corporate image
– other formal communications

Corporate information
– information use
– making information available
– management support systems
– information design
– managing diverse information

Information life cycles
– life cycle phases

Service delivery
– competitive strategies
– quality control
– customer focus
– outsourcing service delivery
– performance measurement and evaluation

Managing risk
– return on investment
– security
– risk management and business continuity

Creating the corporate environment
– corporate culture
– politics
– policy-making
– creativity and intrapreneurship
– managing expertise

Managing and communicating information in the corporate environment
– personal communication
– internal communications
– external communications
– corporate information
– information life cycles

Figure P6.1   Managing and communicating information in the corporate environment

264

Chapter 26 looks at strategies for projecting the information service externally through communication. Information on managing the corporate image is included as well as other formal mechanisms such as annual reports and submissions to outside bodies.

Chapters 27 and 28 cover the management of the information resource as a competitive tool and an information utility. Chapter 27 identifies the uses of information within the organization and how appropriate information should be made available for decision-making. The information requirements of the different levels of management, customers and other stakeholders are identified, together with management-oriented support systems such as Executive Information Systems, Decision Support Systems and Management Reporting Systems that aid decision-making at the different levels of management. The chapter also considers how information and its supporting technologies should be designed to meet the corporate or organizational needs and to complement the organizational structure. The chapter makes the point that even though the information resource is diverse, it should still be managed in a systematic and consistent way.

Information resources have a life cycle similar to that of other resources. Chapter 28 steps through the five phases of the information life cycle and considers the information management strategies that are relevant to each phase.

24 Personal communication

Introduction

All human interaction is dependent upon communication for the exchange of information and the conveyance of ideas. For the information services manager, their ability to influence and get things done in the corporate environment is based on an ability to clearly communicate across organizational boundaries and with all levels of people within the parent organization. The nature of the activities of information services staff requires them to have highly developed communication skills as well as the ability to assess, select, manage, process and disseminate vehicles of communication to customers.

The passage of information or ideas between two people does not constitute communication. The message or idea must reach and be meaningfully understood by the other party to be part of the communication process. Communication occurs when the messages flowing between two parties arrive at a stage where the images and ideas that each is trying to pass to the other, have the same meaning to the receiver as to the sender.

Personal communication skills

The information services manager and others working in the information service spend most of their day listening, making judgements, evaluating, reasoning, providing advice, reassuring and appeasing their bosses, peers, customers and stakeholders. These activities all require highly developed verbal and non-verbal communications skills. The activities may take place in formal and informal meetings, over the telephone or by e-mail, through formal report writing or casual conversation.

Information services managers' and other employees' communication skills are extremely important. They have to communicate with each other to keep informed about operational issues within the information service and of the latest developments in service delivery. They also need to communicate continually with their customers.

The very nature of their job requires them to assess, select, manage, process and disseminate vehicles of communication in a variety of formats. They have to manage and use information in the form of databases, information systems, books, films, cassettes, office automation systems, electronic commerce, document imaging systems, CD-Roms and multimedia to provide information services to their customers. They must be expert in recognizing the most appropriate vehicle to communicate information and deliver interactive services to a large number of people. They are required to understand the widely differing communication skills of both the senders and receivers and to take this into account when designing services. They continually update their knowledge about new and emerging communication techniques to increase their productivity and provide better services to customers.

The information discipline is particularly strong in its use of technical terms and jargon. This can be offputting to those who do not have the same technical background. The information services manager has to communicate the technical issues to a range of people outside the information discipline without using the technical terminology.

The process of communication

Communication is a process that takes place and is interpreted at the individual level. This is true even if the individual is acting on behalf of, or interacting with, a machine, group or organization. In some situations, such as in the negotiating process, individuals may be communicating the views of others in their messages. However they will initially perceive incoming messages from their personal viewpoint.

The key elements of the communication process are a source, a message, a receiver, feedback and noise (see Figure 24.1). The source is the person or element who is responsible for encoding an intended meaning into a message. This may be the person who translates their thoughts (the message) into a language, such as French, English or technical terminology with the hope that it can be understood by the other person(s). The receiver decodes the message into a perceived meaning. If both parties speak the same language and share a joint perception of the message then they are communicating. Feedback from receiver to source may or may not be given. If it is, it serves either to confirm the message or to show that the message

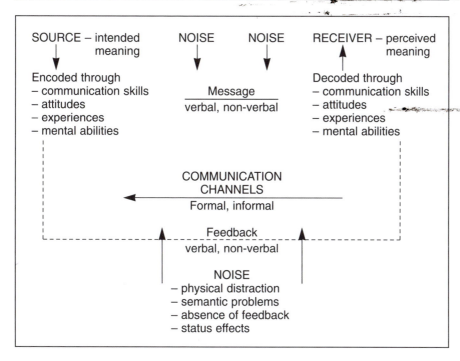

Figure 24.1   The communication process

has not been received correctly. In the latter case another message reinforcing the context of the first message is usually sent. 'Noise' is anything present in the perceived signal that was not part of the originally intended message. It may originate from the sender or the receiver, or it may be the preoccupation of either party with some other pressure that may prevent them from fully understanding the implications of the message. Noise distorts the original message.

Messages may be sent over more than one channel at a time. Whilst it is unusual for two people to continue to speak to each other at the same time, it is usual for non-verbal communication to be concurrently transmitted between people. This is often unconsciously acknowledged and interpreted by the other person, who may change or adapt their next verbal message as a result.

Interpersonal communication

Effective interpersonal communication can be achieved by focusing upon concrete evidence and issues rather than being vague or abstract. Opinions should be formed upon descriptive actions, not judgemental ones or inferences. The emphasis should be upon developing alternatives and the sharing of ideas and information, rather than the giving of advice.

Managers can enhance their interpersonal communication skills by being accessible and by defining each individual's or group's areas of responsibility. Goals should be kept clearly in mind. In situations where a person requires guidance, their actual behaviour should be focused upon rather than their personality. The manager should develop trust between all concerned and be frank with employees on plans and problems. Above all, effective listening skills should be developed.

To improve their interpersonal communication, individuals or groups must understand each other better. Interpersonal communication can too often be based upon subjective analysis of the other person(s) rather than the objectivity of the message conveyed. Strategies for understanding the other person include:

- seeking more information and exploring mutual ideas;
- empathizing and sharing an appreciation of their feelings; and
- reflecting upon their position and what they are saying.

Self-image and attitudes to others

It is helpful when communicating with others to appreciate and understand the complexity of interpersonal communication. The interpersonal aspect of communication has been described by Lippitt (1982) and involves the searching and understanding of the self and others' self-image, needs, values, expectations, standards and norms and perceptions (see Figure 24.2).

Self-image involves the perceptions of an individual about themselves or the group to which they belong. The concept of a group can also be extended to include a nationality. Self-image takes into account ego, pride, traditions and ambitions. Needs reflect requirements in order that psychological or physiological yearnings are satisfied. They include love, security, recognition and success. Values reflect subjective ideas held dearly. Expectations are anticipated outcomes, desired or otherwise, which are likely to be the consequence of actions or the lack of actions.

Standards are found in fixed norms that reflect cultural background and experience. Perceptions are preconceived ideas that may or may not distort an individual's views. To this may be added a background of stored information, understanding and knowledge based on the past, and an experience, understanding and knowledge of the present. None of these can be mutually exclusive, and all interact to influence the interpersonal communication process at the time.

Lippitt (1982) also describes interpersonal communication as being a

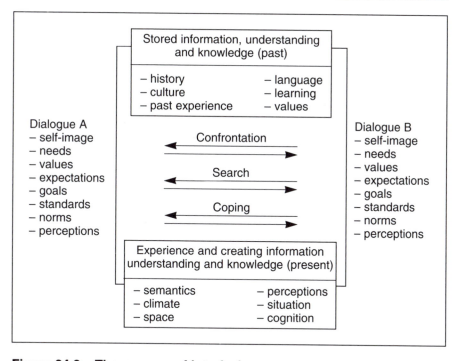

Figure 24.2   The process of interfacing
Source: Lippitt, G.L. (1982), *Organizational Renewal: a Holistic Approach to Organizational Development* (2nd ed.). (Englewood Cliffs, NJ: Prentice Hall).

circulatory process (see Figure 24.3). The individual has a picture of their self and an understanding of the kind of person they are. This is known as their self-image. Individuals also possess a set of attitudes towards the person(s) with whom they are communicating, which can either be positive or negative. As a result of the self-image and set of attitudes, intentions to behave in a certain way are formed. These intentions are coloured by past experiences in similar situations, and perceptions of the attitudes of the other(s) towards themselves.

Receivers filter the behaviour as it is being received according to whether they like or dislike the senders. The receiver also has some prior expectations as to how the sender should behave. Incoming behaviour is evaluated as to whether it meets these expectations. As a result of the valuation, the receiver responds to the sender. The original sender also filters the incoming behaviour according to their prejudices, attitudes, etc., and the process begins again.

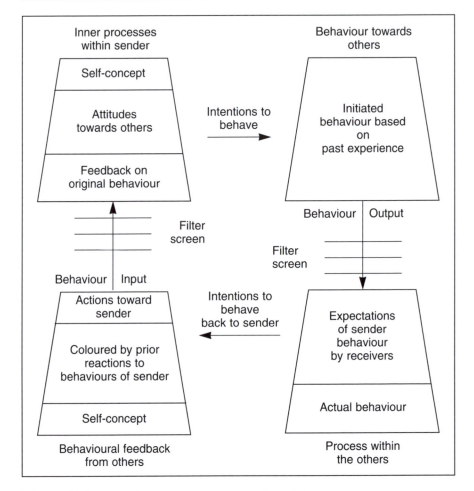

Figure 24.3   The circular process of interaction
Source: Lippitt, G.L. (1982), *Organizational Renewal: a Holistic Approach to Organizational Development* (2nd ed.). (Englewood Cliffs, NJ: Prentice Hall).

Listening

A good communicator is also a good listener. Poor listening is one of the most inhibiting features for the communication of ideas. Managers who are good listeners can often obtain invaluable information from their people, peers and stakeholders. Managers with effective listening skills also create an atmosphere of understanding and respect. This can lead to higher levels of productivity through increased motivation and the fact that people are more willing to co-operate.

Effective listening requires the individual to listen to what is being said in terms of what is being meant. Key words, inferences, prejudices, provide meaningful detail that explain underlying thoughts. Effective listeners also remember what has been said and the context in which it was said. They try to understand the viewpoint of the other party, even though it may be a contradiction to their own ideas and values. They ask pertinent questions thereby providing a feedback mechanism to the other party. This demonstrates that the listener is listening to what is being said.

Hearing is not listening. Listening involves interpreting non-verbal communication signals such as mood, aggression and nervousness, and incorporating these into the verbal message that is received. Active listening allows the listener to place themselves in the other party's position and look at things from their point of view.

Listening skills can be improved through practice, training and concentration. Good listeners do not interrupt or attempt to finish other's sentences. They are patient, allowing the other party plenty of time. They try to put the other party at ease and make an effort to remove or minimize distractions. Finally, good listeners never show anger or criticize the other party.

Stereotyping and halo effect

Stereotyping involves forming generalized opinions of how certain people appear, think, feel and act. It is an attempt to classify or categorize individuals so that they lose their individuality and are in turn assigned the characteristics of an entire group of people.

Stereotyping affects the interpersonal communication process because it keeps individuals from understanding one another. Stereotyping is 'noise' that prevents one party from hearing the message that the other party is sending. It colours attitudes and creates prejudices.

The 'halo effect' is a tendency to judge an individual favourably, or occasionally unfavourably. In many cases this judgement is made on the basis of one strong point on which the other party places a high value. 'Halo effects' can have positive or negative consequences for the other party. It affects the communication process in that anything that the person says is consistently interpreted in either a positive or negative fashion.

Personal communication barriers

The existence of various avenues or media for communicating does not always ensure that communication takes place. The communication process may fail for a number of reasons.

A significant barrier in communication is that no two individuals are alike. Individuals have different perceptions of people and situations that are governed by their past experiences, values, knowledge, attitudes, expectations and self-image. This can result in an inability to build a two-way communication process.

Differences also occur in listening abilities. These may be coloured by natural tendencies to judge and evaluate both what is being said and the person saying it. This leads to differences in the interpretation of the message.

Often there is a lack of distinction between information and communication and a lack of clarity as to who needs the information. Relevant information may not be able to be synthesized due to the overabundance of irrelevant information. Being over-informed is as inhibiting as being under-informed.

Problems may be oversimplified in the message or deliberately generalized, distorted or omitted. Alternatively, the receiver may be insensitive to the problems expressed in the message and so not listen properly to what is being said.

High-level interpersonal and communications skills are a necessary requisite of the information services manager and their staff. Personal communication skills are an integral part of information work. Information services personnel are required to communicate with all levels of staff within the organization as well as assess, select, manage and disseminate information to meet customer needs.

Reference

Lippitt, G. L. (1982), *Organizational Renewal: a Holistic Approach to Organizational Development*, 2nd edn, Englewood Cliffs, NJ: Prentice Hall.

25 Internal communications

Introduction

Communication is the process through which the management functions of planning, organizing, decision-making, controlling, motivating and leading are carried out. Managers communicate their needs, philosophies and decisions to their staff, policy-making bodies, peers, senior management, customers, colleagues within their area of discipline and other stakeholders.

Feedback is a necessary part of communication. Until feedback is received, the manager does not know how an employee or associate is feeling, nor can he/she assess the performance of the individual and if necessary what corrective action to take. Employees also require feedback in order to allow them to take their own corrective action.

Information services and communication

A considerable proportion of the role of the information services manager is to act as a change agent within the parent organization. The information services manager must persuade and influence individuals and change the way in which information is viewed within the organization. Information and its supporting technologies are corporate resources that can be used for competitive advantage, yet often people associate the information that they control as part of their personal power base. The information services manager has to be able to interpret the business information needs of the organization and its customers, understand the technology from a business perspective, reason with and convince people of the value of their intended actions.

To remain competitive, information services have to be on the leading edge in terms of applications and service provision. The information services manager must be a visionary, selling concepts to senior management and other stakeholders. The activities of lobbying, marketing, promoting, negotiating and liaison require high-level communication skills. The effectiveness of these activities relies upon the information services manager having an in-depth knowledge and understanding of the parent organization, and of the competitive and changing external environment. This information is obtained through the communication process.

In strategic planning, networks and other sources of information are used to obtain knowledge of the internal and external environments. Managers use their contacts with individuals and groups within and outside the information service and the parent organization. Information from reports and personal networks is used in the needs assessment and situation audit. The implications of managerial policies and overall objectives are discussed amongst senior management who drive the process. The strategies for implementation are discussed with the people who will carry them out.

Open communication is necessary to create a positive environment for change. The messages used should dispel fears and encourage initiative and innovation. Communication is also the basic ingredient in participative decision-making. The finding of methods to improve productivity and service delivery involves discussion and the sharing of ideas and information.

A further activity where communication is used is in ensuring an adequate level of resources so that the information service can achieve its objectives. Managers must constantly demonstrate, through various communication channels, that their:

- services are valued and appropriate; and
- resources are efficiently and effectively utilized.

In dealing with individuals, a manager or supervisor should clearly communicate what is expected of them and their areas of responsibility. This may involve either physically demonstrating the task or providing an actual example of what good performance looks like. Good work should always be rewarded; even if this is just a simple acknowledgement.

Immediate feedback should be given about the level of performance. Where possible encouraging feedback should be given to reinforce good behaviours. Feedback about incorrect performance should be quick, specific and pertinent. In correcting behaviour, only one aspect of the behaviour should be dealt with at a time. Attacks on an individual's value system should be avoided, so as not to damage the relationship between the person and the manager.

To avoid information overload, corporate information should be distinguished in its dissemination in terms of 'must know' and 'nice to know'. Information that is of a 'must know' nature is information that is immediate or critical to the functioning of the organization and it is imperative that all individuals are aware of its contents immediately. Information of a 'nice to know' nature is that which may be useful to an individual in their decision-making at some future point in time.

Mathews (1983) draws attention to the temporal context of communication. She advocates that individuals should be rostered to work directly with their customers during their best 'communicating' time. There are 'morning' people and 'late starters'. Desk duty rosters should be assigned on the basis of allowing information services staff to interact with their customers at a time when their communication skills are at their peak. People will then feel more comfortable and this will have a positive effect upon their approach to work and their customers.

Formal and informal communication channels

The extent to which formal and informal channels of communication are used within information services depends upon the complexity and stability of the environment, and the size, nature and corporate culture of the parent organization.

Generally speaking, the level of formality in the communication process increases as the organization grows or becomes more complex. Rapidly changing, complex external environments require less formal communication in the organization. In contrast, bureaucratic-type structures create situations where procedures and regulations are followed and communication is much more formal.

If the information service is small, there is little or no need for formal communication within the service. However, communication with external stakeholders and the parent organization will probably be both formal and informal.

Formal channels of communication

Formal communications are often used by management to inform people of significant corporate issues and to provide answers to routine questions. Policy or procedure manuals, corporate plans, appraisal forms, job descriptions and e–mail or bulletin board communications memoranda are all examples of written forms of formal communication. These may be in electronic or hard copy format. Formal communication can also be oral. Addresses or speeches, meetings, appraisal interviews and formal discussions or conversations are all used to convey important messages. Formal communication should be open and timely in order to engage trust and keep people informed. As far as possible, people should be advised of important events that may affect them before they occur, not as they occur or afterwards.

Managers should encourage individuals to provide formal feedback and ideas for improvement. Feedback can act as a measure on how they are managing and how services are meeting the needs of customers. Individuals should be encouraged to provide formal feedback whenever they wish, not just when management wants to hear it. Managers should be aware that some feedback may be distorted. For example, people may screen out any unfavourable or negative aspects in an attempt to impress them. Alternatively, they may try to enhance their image by highlighting others' problems or lack of contribution. Occasionally the original message is clouded by an individual's personal anxieties, aspirations, beliefs or values.

Formal channels of communication are also used to convey messages to peers, customers and other stakeholders. Examples include newsletters and home pages. Electronic messages may also be exchanged between work units and individuals about problems, decisions that have been made or activities that may affect them. Electronic forms of correspondence or reports are often copied to work units and individuals for information purposes.

Informal channels of communication

Informal communication occurs as part of the social relationship of people. It is not confined to hierarchies, work relationships or work practices. Informal communication supplements formal communication; in the absence of good official communication, informal communication may supplant it. Informal communication channels distribute information that is often not communicated officially.

The 'grapevine' is the mostly widely recognized form of informal communication. It is fast, highly selective and discriminating. It provides management with insights into employee attitudes, helps spread useful information and provides a safety valve for employee emotions. The 'grapevine' has both positive and negative implications. Whilst the rumour and hostility that make up the grapevine may psychologically help people by releasing emotions, they can be disturbing to others. Grapevines may also spread false rumours. This can be a problem as the grapevine has no permanent membership and so cannot be controlled.

Communicating the corporate culture

The corporate culture of an organization is a consequence of the communication processes within it. The culture is learnt and maintained through the interaction of the people in the organization. People interact by exchanging words, tones and pitches and non-verbal behaviours such as gestures, appearances, postures and special relationships. This interaction forms patterns that, after repeated use, become accepted as norms. Meaningful behaviour patterns are passed on to others through modelling, instruction, correction and their wish to comply with norms.

Cultures are also sustained and transmitted through the communication processes of languages, story-telling about the heroes and villains of the past, and through rituals and ceremonies. Managers consciously and unconsciously signal values and goals to information services staff through statements, metaphors and physical symbols. Logos are organizational symbols and communicate values created specifically for customers and employees. Employees identify with the symbols and feel an integral part of the organization.

The consolidation of all cultural forms is to be found in rites and ceremonies. In performing the activities of rites or ceremonies, people make use of other cultural forms – language, gestures, ritualized behaviours, artefacts and settings. This heightens the expression of shared meanings appropriate to the occasion. Events such as receptions for visitors, annual dinners, board meetings, Christmas functions, retirement functions, presentations, professional conferences are rites in which the corporate future is displayed. They are efficient and effective methods of communicating and instilling beliefs into an organization.

Corporate stories, legends, slogans, anecdotes, myths and fairytales are all important as they convey the information service's shared values. Anecdotes and stories provide the opportunity for people to share their experiences. The significant stories are those told by many people. These are the ones that are active in the cultural network and provide evidence of the corporate culture. Newsletters and memoranda are examples of indoctrination. To be effective the messages portrayed must be sincere and backed up by action.

Stories of 'heroes and villains' provide an insight into corporate values and the personal qualities of employees who are likely to be successful or unsuccessful. The attributes of the 'heroes' who are held in high esteem emulate those qualities likely to be found in successful employees of the information service and its parent organization. 'Villains and outlaws' are those whose values or attributes were opposed to those of the organization. They provide the corporate guidance of 'what not to do'. Villains are remembered long after they have left the organization for their 'sins'. They are the outlaws.

Communication rules are also part of the corporate culture. These are tacit understandings about appropriate ways to interact with others in given roles and situations. They are generally unwritten and unspoken. As prescriptions for behaviour, they function to co-ordinate, interpret and justify interactive behaviour and act as self-monitoring devices. They provide guidelines as to what is acceptable interactive behaviour within the information service and its parent organization.

Communicating through reports

Information services managers are called upon to write and submit reports on a regular or irregular basis. The purpose being to communicate information to senior management and stakeholders upon which informed decisions can be made. In their role as information disseminators, managers write or commission annual reports, monthly or quarterly reports, reports relating to specific issues, submissions and budget papers.

Regular formal reports provide continuous feedback to senior management. They usually contain statistical information and reports on activities. Issues of concern can be raised through these reports for further action. Regular reports usually follow a specific format that is established by the parent organization.

Regular reports can be supplemented by reports on specific issues. These can include papers for discussion and/or action, requests for the introduction of additional services or changes in service level, requests for changes in policy or reports relating to future planning. Reports such as these vary in length. They begin with a summary of the reasons for the report and contain details of background, progress to date, legal or resource implications and recommendations. Specific reports are either commissioned or written by in-house specialists. They use corporate data and data from external sources. They are written for senior management so that appropriate action can be authorized and taken.

Budgets are a form of report in that they identify the requirement for, and proposed use of funds. They communicate the need for funding, priority services and major areas of expenditure to senior management, employees and stakeholders.

Communicating through meetings

The purpose of a meeting is to bring together a group of people with a common interest to accomplish a goal. Meetings can be scheduled or unscheduled. They can be held on a regular or irregular basis.

Participants in meetings use communication skills to share knowledge and experiences, to plan and make decisions, to solve problems, to negotiate and evaluate, to consult and to disseminate information. Handled effectively and efficiently a meeting will result in creative thinking, multiple thought input, enhanced group cohesiveness, commitment to the outcome, co-operation and better decision-making. Handled ineffectively or inefficiently a meeting can waste time, stifled creativity and foster aggressiveness, or result in attacks on others. This can lead to a breakdown in communications between the participants that in turn creates more problems.

Purposes of meetings

Meetings are a useful tool in decision-making where the decision requires judgement rather than calculations or expertise, or where a pooling of ideas improves the chances of a good decision. They are also important where it is necessary to get the participants' acceptance of the decision. Figure 25.1 explains some of the purposes and types of meetings that can be held in information services.

Meetings should not be called to solve routine problems or where it is difficult to demonstrate the correctness of any one particular solution to others. Neither are they useful as a vehicle for briefing individuals about issues upon which they have little control or that are unrelated to work.

Meetings are useful to establish contact between work units. This ensures that they are all moving in the same direction to achieve the organization's corporate objectives. Managers and specialists from other parts of the organization should be invited to attend the information service's meetings when decisions likely to affect their area(s) are made. If time permits, they may also be invited to attend at other times in the interests of good communications and to encourage their input, experience and potential different point of view. This can result in mutual understanding and increased co-operation between the information service and the other work unit(s).

Where time permits, meetings that are attended by different levels of management can improve relationships, boost productivity and allow direct communication between all levels of staff. Less experienced members greatly benefit from the knowledge and expertise of the more senior members, whilst senior members in their turn should obtain valuable feedback as to the beliefs and values that flow through the organization.

Meetings are sometimes held for political reasons. This is inadvisable as the more experienced attendees will quickly recognize the motives. Examples of such instances are image-building exercises that are used to

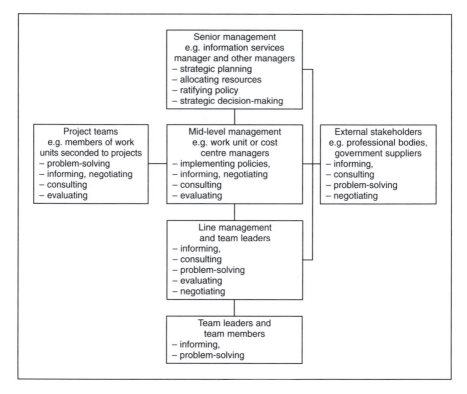

Figure 25.1   Purposes and types of meetings held in information services

conspicuously demonstrate that things are happening in the area or that are to impress the boss.

Framework for effective meetings

The agenda should communicate a well-defined purpose for the meeting and a sense of direction for the participants. It should prepare participants for the tasks that they need to accomplish during the meeting and afterwards. The agenda should provide details of date, time and place of the meeting. Time refers to both the starting and ending time as open-ended meetings invite time-wasting procedures. A time may also be set for each item on the agenda. It is also useful to label agenda items according to their desired outcome, for example, 'for discussion', 'for decision', 'for information'.

The agenda should be circulated to participants in advance to allow time for reading, research and consultation with others. Background material such as reports, statistics, proposals should be distributed with the agenda.

To ensure that the meeting is effective and productive, participants should be those:

- who are stakeholders in the decision-making process;
- who can contribute through relevant knowledge or appropriate level of expertise;
- who can communicate and contribute to the meeting in a positive, creative and open fashion.

If the wrong people attend they can stifle creativity and waste their own and others' time. If too many people attend, or if those who are not directly involved in the agenda issues attend, there is a risk of too much time being spent on explaining the background. Agenda issues may also become side-tracked.

In some types of meeting the make-up of the committee determines who should attend. For example, the members of the corporate executive automatically attend any executive meeting by nature of their positions. In other instances, particularly if it is an *ad hoc* meeting, the chairperson has a right to stipulate who is to attend.

The ideal number of participants in a meeting is between four and eight. This number allows all participants to contribute their views. Any less than this number may mean that not all of the relevant issues are explored; any more can result in too much diversity and a lack of control and input.

The role of the chairperson is to keep the pace of the meeting brisk. They should ensure that participants do not waffle or get side-tracked on to issues not relevant to the agenda. The chairperson should facilitate open communication and dissipate potential personality problems to make it easy for all participants to put their point of view. Individuals should not be allowed to dominate meetings. The chairperson should have a knowledge of group dynamics in order to steer the participants in a creative fashion to the desired outcome. A skilled chairperson is able to persuade participants to think again and get proposals accepted where less experienced colleagues may fail.

The chairperson should ensure that all decisions made at the meeting are recorded, together with details as to who is responsible for follow-up actions, what these actions are and when they should take place.

The meeting environment

It is important that meetings are held in non-threatening environments. If people from different organizations or work units are attending, it is preferable for the meeting to be on neutral territory such as a conference room. The room and seating arrangements affect the outcome of the meeting. A round or oval table is better for problem-solving and group discussion. Participants should be comfortably seated in a business-like manner with room to move and the ability to clearly see all members. People likely to be in conflict or confrontation with each other should not be placed opposite each other. There should be no noise, distractions or interruptions. In the case of long meetings, breaks should be scheduled with refreshments of non-alcoholic beverages. The size of the room should give the impression of being comfortably full but not crowded. Large premises are threatening and stifle discussion.

The information service can play an important role in the internal communications of the parent organization. It is also incumbent on the information services manager to ensure that the staff of the information service are kept informed of organizational issues and of what is required of them.

Reference

Mathews, A. J. (1983), *Communicate: a Librarian's Guide to Inter-Personal Communications*, Chicago: American Library Association.

26 External communications

Introduction

The ability to manage the communication with the external environment is as important as managing the communication internally. This includes managing the corporate image of the information service. The management of the corporate image is important, for if the perceptions of the information service differ from reality then:

- the quality and value of the information service may be underestimated;
- the information service may be missing part of its market share;
- the wrong impression of the service could be projected.

Other examples of formal external communications include the writing of annual reports and submissions for external consumption, and obtaining competitive intelligence from the external environment.

The corporate image

An important aspect of the boundary-spanning role of the information services manager is to manage the corporate image. The corporate image is the set of beliefs, ideas and impressions that individuals have about an organization. Managing the corporate image comprises the following activities: identifying the target audience, determining the communication objectives, designing the message, selecting the communication channels, allocating the budget, managing the process and measuring the results.

Target audience

The target audience consists of the people or organizations towards whom the information service needs to project a favourable image. This is with the objective of building an awareness of the services provided and increasing market share, ensuring the continuation of funds or simply communicating the image of a valued and quality service. The target audience for the information service can include all or any of the following: current and prospective customers, senior management in the parent organization, other information services, suppliers, professional bodies and other stakeholders.

Determining the communication objectives

Having identified the target audience, it is important to establish how familiar the target audience is with all aspects of the information service as well as the value they place on it. This provides information for the image gap analysis, that is, the difference between the desired image that the information service wishes to project and the current image that it is projecting. It also identifies the gap between the target audience's awareness of the information services offered and those provided, and their perception of the quality of the information service as compared with that provided.

The next stage is to determine the required audience response in relation to the results of the image gap analysis. This may be to change the customer's attitude to the information service, to alert customers to services that could fill latent needs, to provide a better understanding of the information service, or to engender the support of senior management and other stakeholders to ensure that the information service continues to receive adequate financial support and conviction.

Designing the message and selecting the communication channels

The aim is to design a positive message about the information service. There are many different messages and communication channels that can be used including:

- personal communication, e.g. word of mouth recommendations, personal representation;
- print, e.g. a brochure or strategy report;
- oral, e.g. a description of the services that the information service offers being played whilst a person is 'on hold' on the telephone;
- multimedia or video presentation aimed at a particular audience;
- advertisement in the local press, television or public area; or

- electronic information on a public access system such as the Internet or a kiosk service.

The choice and mix of the messages and communication channels will depend upon the purpose of the message and the target audience.

In addition to the above, the physical surroundings of the information service will also create an atmosphere or image. The choice of colours, type of office furniture, wall decorations, floor coverings and spaciousness of the surroundings will communicate an image about the information service.

The house style of the information service's reports and stationery also communicate a corporate image. The house style should also be continued and included in any multimedia presentations and other information published in electronic form.

Colour and style in the physical surroundings and in the house style are also important. Colour exerts a powerful influence on the mind and emotions. Each colour has a symbology of its own:

- red – leadership, energy and vitality;
- orange – excitement, creativity, self-confidence;
- yellow – clarity;
- green – balance and harmony, wealth;
- blue – power.

The way in which information service staff interact with customers and stakeholders will also project an image of the information service. The image conveyed should be friendly, welcoming and helpful, although in some environments a more formal approach may be necessary. Interaction includes the way in which individuals answer the telephone, and the articulation and wording of the greeting on the telephone answering machine. If music (rather than information about the information service) is used for the 'on hold' interval whilst people are waiting on the telephone, the choice of music will influence the person's perception of the information service.

Allocating the budget

Not all of the strategies for managing and promoting the information service's image cost money. A proportion of the image promotion rests with the information services manager and their staff projecting a positive image and 'selling' the service in their interaction with customers, senior management and other stakeholders.

Budget allocation for the more formal mechanisms of promoting the information service's image should be based upon the specific objectives, the tasks to be performed to achieve the objectives and the costs of performing the tasks.

Managing the process

The wide range of communication tools and messages make it imperative that these be co-ordinated to ensure consistency. Co-ordination is also required to ensure that the correct message is sent through the correct medium and communication channel to reach the correct target audience.

Measuring results

To measure the results of the promotion, the information services manager will require feedback from the target audience. This will involve talking to or surveying the target audience about how they feel about the service, what level of awareness they have of the information service, and any other information that provides feedback on the communication objective.

Other formal communications

Annual reports

At the end of the calendar or financial year, managers are often required to produce an annual report for the information service or provide copy for the parent organization's annual report. Sometimes they need to do both. The annual report serves several purposes. It can be used:

- to provide an account of the information service's activities for the year;
- as a source of information about the information service. It may contain information about key managerial positions, holders of such positions and their qualifications, an organizational chart, mission statement and corporate objectives;
- as a source of information for benchmarking or comparative purposes, as it often contains statistical data;
- as a public relations exercise in that the achievements of the year are reported;
- to account for the use of resources;
- to highlight problems that prevent the information service from carrying out all of its activities;
- to reconcile the use of funds, staff, etc. (inputs) against activities (outputs); and
- to measure the organization's level of performance.

Annual reports are often distributed to other related organizations. The format and presentation of the report are powerful mechanisms to project the information service's image. It will send a message about the organization's culture and its willingness to make an impressionable image on stakeholders. For example, some organization's annual reports are glossy publications and considerable prestige is attached to their contents and format. Others are very formal. Some are very plain as they are only seen as an operational requirement to report on activities once a year.

Submissions to outside bodies

Managers and in-house specialists may also draft submissions to government bodies and other organizations relating to external issues. These submissions can be either reactive to external impacts on their services or functions, or proactive in terms of positioning the information service or its parent organization in the external environment. Examples are a submission on the implications of proposed changes to copyright legislation or a submission that suggests new ways of providing electronic services to the community.

The information services manager, or his or her staff, will usually draft the submission on behalf of the parent organization. In this case, the submission may need to be ratified by senior management before being forwarded to the appropriate body.

Obtaining competitive intelligence

Competitive intelligence is information that supports management's role in managing customers, competition and change. It:

- provides an early warning of developments in the external environment, in particular the industry, technology, economic or legislative change, that could adversely affect the business success of the organization;
- identifies new product or services, process or collaborative opportunities to create new markets and business opportunities; and
- creates an early understanding of the competitive environment so that surprises can be eliminated or their impact lessened by allowing a longer time and better opportunity to respond.

Competitive intelligence-gathering is not spying or undertaking industrial espionage. Good intelligence-gathering is based on information that can be obtained from sources through legal and ethical means. Published sources of competitive information include trade publications (electronic and hard copy), market analysts' reports, aerial photographs, job advertisements, government reports and filings. Other information can be obtained through the continuous monitoring and surveillance of competitor actions for key events or changes, the following of leads, checking of sources and the surfacing of ideas. The art is in knowing what information is relevant, where to find it legally and how to convert it into intelligence for the basis of management decisions and actions.

Competitive intelligence involves obtaining information about:

- which competitors are vulnerable;
- which competitors are likely to make moves that could endanger the organization's position in the market; and
- the requirements of the competitor's customers.

An ability to communicate the desired message and obtain information from the external environment is of equal importance to an ability to communicate and obtain information within the organization. The information service assists both aspects of communication.

27 Managing corporate information

Introduction

To utilize information as a competitive tool, the information service should ensure that information is managed as a corporate rather than an individual or work unit resource. The corporate information concept lessens duplication, empowers individuals, opens up the flow of information and ensures that decisions are based on the same information. Real-time information is delivered to all levels within the organization. It is not a privilege to any group or individual.

Appropriate information should be made available for decision-making at all levels within the organization and to customers and stakeholders. Information and its supporting technologies should be designed so that relevant information can be easily identified and retrieved by those who need it, whilst preserving privacy and commercial confidentiality. Appropriate security measures should be in place.

The information and its supporting technologies should be designed and managed to complement the organizational structure. The architecture needs to be flexible to withstand organizational restructures and changes to business direction. The diverse information resources and systems within the organization should all be accessible in a seamless and consistent way.

Information use

The effective management and use of information as an organizational resource creates a strategic weapon to support the business strategies, objectives and activities. It enhances competitive advantage by:

- delivering increased productivity;
- reducing service and product development and marketing life cycles;
- increasing the understanding of customers' needs; and
- facilitating business and process re-engineering.

It can also be used across the organization as an information utility to:

- support strategic planning and policy-making;
- meet legislative and regulatory requirements;
- protect the interests of the organization and the rights of employees and customers;
- support research and development;
- support consistent and rapid decision-making;
- enable effective and efficient utilization of resources;
- provide evidence of business transactions and activities in the case of litigation;
- identify and manage risk; and
- evaluate and document quality, performance and achievements.

Successful organizations are able to design and manage their information and the supporting technologies as a strategic weapon as well as an information utility. This requires information to be readily available on an as-needed basis to staff, management, customers, suppliers and other stakeholders. It is not just a matter of having the right information delivery mechanisms in place. It requires a selective approach to what is provided and individuals having the information skills to make informed judgements on their use of the information.

Making information available

The availability of information as voice, video, image and data is fundamental to the decision-making process. Decisions are made within the organization at strategic, operational, programmes and activity levels, and by customers and other stakeholders who also need access to corporate information. To evaluate alternative courses of action as part of the decision-making process, it is essential that appropriate information is available when required.

Information for strategic business decisions

The information required to make decisions about an activity within a work unit differs from that required to make strategic business decisions in terms of the degree of detail and comprehensiveness (see Figure 27.1). For example, senior management deals with issues related to positioning the organization within the external environment. Most of their information comes from external sources such as information about new markets, competitors, business trends, new technologies, or new or impending changes to legislation that may affect the business strategy.

Some management information is sourced internally; the majority of this relates to internal performance and strategic planning. A large proportion of information is obtained verbally, either in meetings, presentations or during conversations with their peers. Other information is summarized in reports, electronic mail messages and executive information systems. Due to constraints on their time, senior management is only interested in a highly summarized view of the organization's internal information. They often employ research or executive assistants to provide these summaries for them.

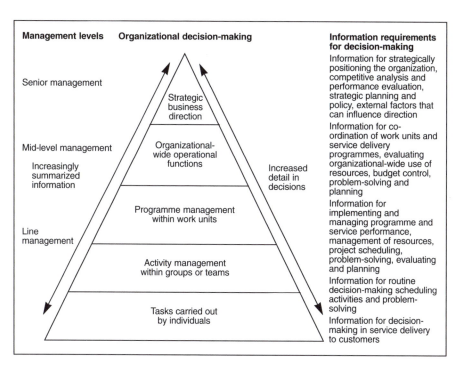

Figure 27.1   Information needs and decision-making activities of the various levels of management

Mid-level management information requirements

Mid-level management deals with information from both external and internal sources. They require information for decision-making to support the organizational-wide functions of resource utilization, budget control and co-ordination at a more strategic level, as well as the co-ordination of service delivery programmes and work unit outputs to achieve the organization's objectives.

Mid-level managers are usually interested in the gross performance of the work units and in implementing large projects. Data is gathered from in-house sources relating to the allocation of human, financial and technological resources, budgeting and performance measures. It is combined with other information from external sources. This is used for evaluative and comparative purposes to measure performance, to help make decisions and solve problems, and to prepare reports that are presented to senior management. This information is also used to influence strategic planning and policy-setting processes at the senior level.

At this level of management, external information is significantly different in source and character from internal information or that received by senior management. It often comprises telephone conversations, hearsay and overheard snatches of conversations. If such information is intended to be used effectively in any decision-making processes at mid-management level, its reliability and relevance must be determined beforehand.

Line management information requirements

Line managers and team leaders require information for routine decisions relating to the scheduling of activities, accounting for the use of resources and for problem-solving.

They obtain nearly all of their decision-making information in-house, using a very restricted subset of the organization's internal information. They receive instructions from mid-level management and gather data relating to individual and group or team activities at a transactional level. They have to make operational decisions related to day-to-day matters, or specific activities such as rostering of staff, based upon policies and operational requirements.

Service delivery information requirements

Staff at the front counter or in the field require information for decision-making in service delivery. This includes information about the customers, their customers' history and their specific service requirements. They also need access to information about the parent organization, the services and products that it offers, customer service policies and procedures. This is so that they can inform customers of the products or services offered by the organization, answer their questions quickly and provide a better service.

Customer information requirements

The customer needs information to help them make a decision about their choice of service or product. They may already have information about the competitors' products and services, and require information to allow for comparisons in making their choice. Customers and other stakeholders may also have legal access to any of their personal information that the parent organization holds under privacy or data protection and freedom of information legislation (see Figure 27.2).

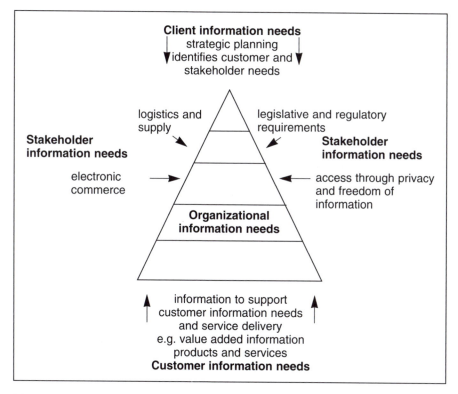

Figure 27.2   Relationships between customer, stakeholder and organizational information flows and needs

Other stakeholder information requirements

Stakeholders such as suppliers have information requirements for ordering and logistical purposes. Some may utilize electronic commerce for the ordering, supply and payment of goods and services. Finance and insurance companies also require information returns. There are also legislative and regulatory requirements for information to be lodged with government agencies. These include industrial relations agencies, corporate and securities commissions, revenue collection and taxation agencies. Increasingly, this information is provided or lodged electronically.

Management support systems

Management-oriented information systems provide support to various levels of management. Executive Information Systems (EIS) allow executives to see where a problem or opportunity exists. Decision Support Systems (DSS) are used by mid-level management to support the solution of problems that require judgement by the problem-solver. Line managers utilize Management Reporting Systems (MRS) for routine operational information. In addition, other application systems support decision-making for business processes and the delivery of products and services to customers (see Figure 27.3).

Executive Information Systems

Executive Information Systems (EIS) provide access to a wide variety of internal and external information. Typically this information is presented in graphic form with the ability to 'drill down' on more detailed data (see Figure 27.4). They assist senior management identify trends, opportunities and problems. EIS rely on databases being updated daily. They provide highly summarized corporate data, often with forward projections, in a timely and easily handled manner.

Decision Support Systems

Decision Support Systems (DSS) are flexible interactive information systems that support managers in reaching decisions concerning ill-structured problems. They provide analytical models and support the consideration of alternatives ('what if' scenarios). Using DSS, mid-level managers are able to apply quantitative and statistical models to the data as well as causal relationships.

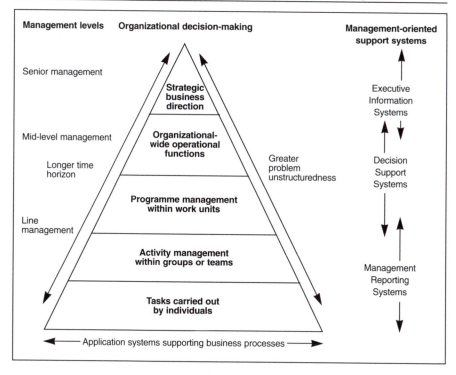

Figure 27.3   **Management-oriented information systems**

Management Reporting Systems

Management Reporting Systems (MRS) provide lower and mid-level management with reports and inquiry facilities. They generally handle situations where the information requirements are reasonably well known and are expected to remain relatively stable. They are oriented towards reporting the past and present rather than projecting the future. MRS focus on reporting internal information and have little analytical capabilities (see Figure 27.5).

Information design

Information and its supporting technologies should be designed so that relevant information can be identified, retrieved, manipulated and made available to appropriate individuals across the organization, for this is where the strategic business advantage lies. The information and technology

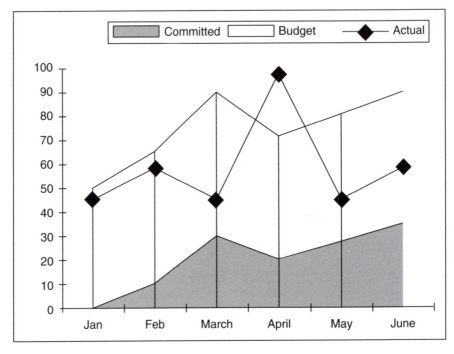

Figure 27.4   An extract from an Executive Information System

should be streamlined so that there is less likelihood of error.

Information should be well defined, and have a standard or corporate classification scheme, language control and index which fit the business needs of the parent organization. These ought to be devised by the information service in consultation with users, and maintained to reflect changing business needs. Information services staff and other employees within the parent organization need to be educated in the use of the corporate classification scheme, language control and index. Everyone should be able to base their decision-making on the same information and employees should only need to check one source. The intention being to increase customer satisfaction as information can be obtained more readily and faster, the requirement for analysis time is shortened and so the decision can be made more quickly.

Design criteria

Information and its supporting technologies ought to be:

● accessible – information must be able to be accessed easily and quickly at

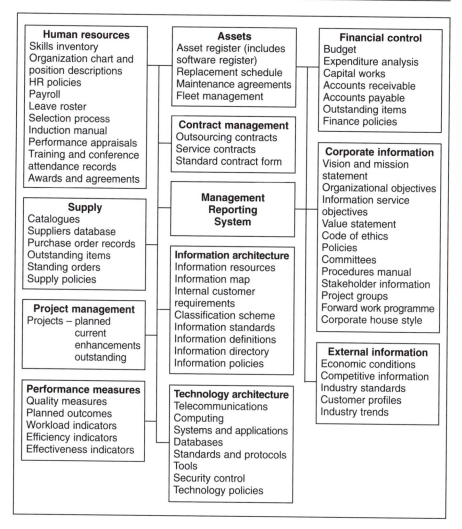

Figure 27.5   A Management Reporting System for an information service

the right time and in the right place by the appropriate people. Access should be seamless, regardless of source or format, and must take into consideration any necessary security and privacy considerations;

● comprehensive – information should be useful, related to need and appropriate to the level of the decision-maker. There is a difference between providing information that is comprehensive enough to satisfy information needs and information overload. Too much information can be as problematic as too little information;

- accurate – information must be accurate, complete, reliable and current;
- appropriate – information content, information flows and delivery mechanisms ought to be appropriate to the business processes, decision-making and information needs of management, employees, customers and other stakeholders. Irrelevant information is costly in terms of capture, storage and use. Information should also be presented in a manner that is meaningful and best fits the skills and competencies of the user.
- timely – the information should be continually kept up to date, although in some cases, historical data is required;
- clear – information should be free from ambiguity. The source and purpose for use ought to be immediately obvious to the individual so that they can make informed choices as to the usefulness of the information;
- flexible – the systems and information content should be designed to be flexible to allow for growth and change within the parent organization, and allow a variety of users to navigate through the system(s) to locate the required information;
- verifiable – the information content should be capable of being verified in terms of source, accuracy and authenticity;
- free from bias – the information content should not be entered, modified or displayed in such a way as to influence the user's course of action;
- consistent – data definitions and terminology ought to be consistent across the organization regardless of format, storage device or location; and
- compliant – where international or national information or technology standards are used to support the parent organization's objectives and business strategy, all information and its supporting technologies within the organization should accord to the chosen standard.

Complementing the organizational structure

Information and its supporting technologies should be designed to complement the organizational structure. In most traditional organizations, information flows upwards and commands are passed downwards. The information is prone to distortion and manipulation. Decentralized, highly integrated informal organizations require technology architectures that enhance information flows and extend across work group boundaries visibly and simultaneously.

The new organizational structures that utilize teams and group work require networks, electronic mail and messaging facilities in order that they all receive the same information at the same time. They also make greater use of collaborative processing and groupware applications that support more flexible work patterns and teamwork. Not only is hard information required, teams and groups rely upon more qualitative information in both external information and internal information such as members' experiences, views, successes and problems.

Information and its supporting technologies can also be designed to overcome distance and time barriers. People from diverse geographic locations and those whose personal situations require them to work from home or during non-traditional hours can work together in the same team to create a boundaryless organization with the use of the right technology and human resource management policies.

The information architecture and its supporting technology architecture, classification scheme, language control and index should be designed to be used across work units and be flexible enough to withstand organizational restructures and changes to business direction. For accountability purposes, it should also be capable of tracking ownership of business decisions and records over time. Information architecture is the vehicle for determining organizational information needs. It shows how activities and information that the activities require can be grouped and sequenced, allowing the information service to plan the information and its supporting technology architecture around the business objectives of the parent organization.

Managing diverse information

A systematic approach should be applied to managing the diverse forms of information within organizations to ensure that it:

- meets the business and customers' information needs;
- protects the interests of the organization, its customers and stakeholders;
- results in a complete, reliable and accurate documentation of the organization's business activities and transactions (including accounting and finance);
- meets all legal, evidential and accountability requirements.

The systematic approach should include:

- the creation of adequate records for voice (sound), video, image, text, multimedia and data;
- consistent definitions;
- the design, establishment and operation of accessible systems to support business activities and organizational objectives; and
- the management and security of the organization's information transactions.

Whilst the information resource and systems within an organization are diverse (see Figure 27.6), they should still be managed and made accessible in a consistent way.

The artificial boundaries that occur by reason of media or format, location or work unit ownership should be removed. Standard forms of identification and retrieval procedures ought to be used as far as possible for all information.

Access to the diverse information resource should be:

- user friendly;
- seamless;
- tailored to need;
- cost-justified;
- low maintenance;

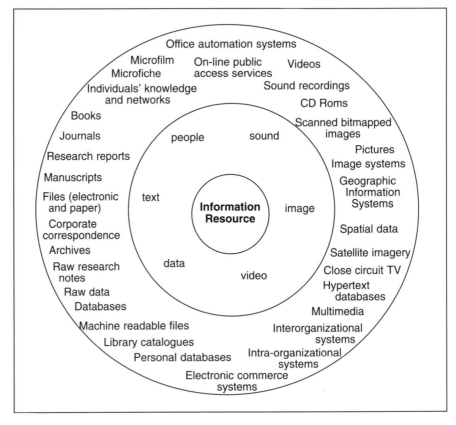

Figure 27.6   Diverse information systems and resources

- adjustable; and
- protected.

Inefficient information management practices

Inefficient information management practices can be costly in terms of time, money and lost business opportunities. Inefficient practices include:

- collecting and storing information when it is no longer used;
- disseminating information too widely (information overload);
- not making information accessible to potential users; or
- duplicating information across the organization.

Efficient management practices empower individuals, enable accurate decisions and assist the organization to remain productive and competitive.

28 Managing the information life cycle

Introduction

Information resources have a life cycle similar to that of other resources. The life cycle comprises five phases: planning, acquisition, maintenance, exploitation and retirement (see Figure 28.1). The information service has a responsibility for ensuring that all information, regardless of source or format, is subject to a managed life cycle.

The life cycle phases

Planning

The first or planning phase involves identifying the information and supporting technology needs to assist the business strategy and to meet the information needs of customers and stakeholders. It incorporates the information and information technology planning processes that are described in Chapters 6 and 7.

Acquisition

The acquisition phase involves strategies to capture, collect or purchase information that is relevant to the business needs of the parent organization and its customers' information needs. There are many mechanisms through which information is acquired. For example, information may:

- be created internally and captured;

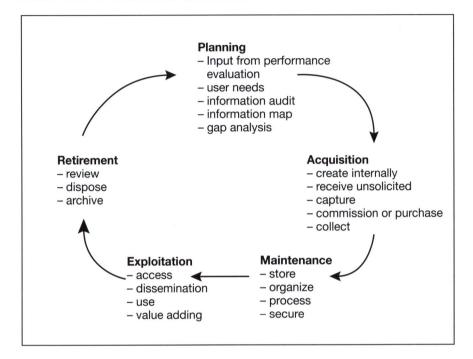

Figure 28.1   The information life cycle

- originate from an external source such as in electronic messaging services;
- be received unsolicited such as external correspondence; or
- be collected as part of case management such as medical records.

In some government departments and libraries, electronic data and information and printed materials are obtained through a legal requirement to deposit certain material. Information is also purchased in the form of databases, subscriptions to journals and electronic information services, and the commissioning of reports.

Information may be acquired in a variety of formats such as electronic mail, published and unpublished reports, spatial information in geographic information systems, video and satellite imagery.

To ensure its accuracy and reliability, information needs to be captured as close as possible to the original source of the information. The capture and use of some information types and formats of information may need specialized technology. For example, moving imagery and large volumes of spatial information require higher speed, broader capacity bandwidth to manage the transfer and use of the information.

For accountability purposes, the information may need to be registered on receipt or creation. Examples of formal registration processes are:

- entering details of the item in an asset or acquisition register;
- registering a file or document upon its creation or receipt; or
- logging the transaction in a system.

Copyright may also need to be cleared for the use and reproduction of the information by the parent organization. The information service may have to identify the copyright holder and obtain their permission for a specific use of the information. In some cases, payment may be required by the copyright holder in return for the right to use the information or copyright work.

Maintenance

In the maintenance phase, information must be stored, organized, processed, tracked and secured in such a way that it is easily identified and accessible to those authorized to use it, whilst being protected from unauthorized use or misuse. Storage requirements in electronic and physical forms may be assessed according to the:

- physical characteristics of the information;
- business objectives and customer needs of the parent organization;
- source and level of risk; and
- required level of security.

Security classifications may need to be assigned to different types of information or its content in order to ensure that only authorized persons have access.

Information must be organized and managed so that there is consistency and connectivity. It can be accurately described in information directories and indexes so that its source, relationships and other attributes are known. Standards can be employed that encourage the sharing and integration of the information. The use of standards must be cost-effective. Information should not be maintained at a higher level standard than is necessary. The choice of standard should be based on a business case. Data dictionaries and data models can also be used to provide a clear picture of the information that is available.

In the case of electronic information, the maintenance phase includes additional responsibility for managing different electronic versions of the same information. This can include managing the version control of information contained in reports, and ensuring that all information is kept in a form that can be read by the software and hardware in current use. As new technology or versions of software are introduced, the information on disks must be upgraded so that the information can be used at a later date. This particularly applies to significant documents or reports that have been produced on word-processing or desktop publishing systems and that require continuous use.

Vital or valuable information that is to be retained within the organization not only needs to be secured, it also needs to be preserved.

Exploitation

The exploitation phase provides the return on investment for the information service and its information resource. Unless the information service exploits its information to its fullest extent, the rest of the efforts in planning, acquisition and maintenance will be underutilized.

The exploitation phase involves being proactive about doing more with the organization's information resource. It entails looking at strategies and activities for designing and adding value to the original information to meet new market needs or in identifying new uses for the existing information. This may include the combining or overlaying of information in a system or in presenting the information in a different way.

The exploitation phase also requires consideration of the means of use of the information as well as accessibility, dissemination, distribution and delivery mechanisms. Customer requirements to access information ought to be met whilst protecting copyright, privacy and confidentiality. The background, skills, knowledge and perspective of the customer will influence their ability to use the information. The customer may also have a particular preference for information in a certain format or language, or may wish to use a particular distribution method such as facsimile or electronic mail.

The physical environment in which the information is to be used can influence the method and format in which the information is distributed. For example, information may be required to be updated continuously or in batch mode at a remote site, or individuals may work in all weathers and climates and require information in a format that is durable in inclement weather.

Retirement

The retirement phase involves decisions about information that has been identified as redundant. Information becomes redundant when it is superfluous to requirements, outdated or inactive. Not all information reaches a redundant stage. A significant proportion of information in live information systems is continually updated, although the information systems can become redundant if they no longer fit the purpose, objectives or business needs of the organization.

The retirement phase requires consideration of if, how and when the information may be disposed. Information should not be kept beyond its useful life as this leads to unnecessary and inefficient use of storage space, equipment, staff and resources. Not all information can be destroyed. Legislative and regulatory considerations require certain corporate information to be kept for a minimum period of time. Some information may also be of archival value. Vital or valuable information may be identified and be made subject to corporate retention and disposal schedules.

Information should be retained, removed or destroyed in accordance with authorized processes. If the information is to be removed off-site or off-line, such as to an archive facility, the security and ease of retrievability should be considered. Information should be deleted from hard and floppy disks before either the computer or disk is disposed of. If printed information is to be destroyed, it should be burnt, pulped or shredded. It ought not to be disposed of through normal refuse disposal facilities.

Information has quite distinct phases in its life cycle that require different management techniques. A knowledge of the information life cycle enables information to be managed in a quality manner.

Part 7

Managing the individual

This part of the book concentrates on managing the well-being of the people who work in the information service (see Figure P7.1). This is important from a duty of care perspective as well as being strongly connected to motivation and productivity factors.

Managers have a responsibility for the well-being of their staff. However, in a busy and competitive environment the fact that the individuals who work in the information service are its most important asset is sometimes overlooked. Where the management of the well-being of individuals appears to be overlooked it can adversely affect the information service in terms of lack of employee commitment to the organization and expose the service to breaches of occupational health and safety requirements.

Chapter 29 considers stress management. It explores why some individuals are vulnerable to stress at certain stages in life. It identifies factors in the workplace that can be stressors and different personality types that cause some people to handle certain types of pressure better than others. Finally, the chapter considers personal and workplace strategies for the management of stress.

Chapter 30 is about career planning and personal development. Employees' personal satisfaction with themselves, their lifestyle and their work, and their sense of purpose in their career and life goals, can be supported through the activities of career planning and personal development. The chapter looks at the relevant responsibilities for the information service, the information services manager and the individual in career planning. It considers a holistic approach to lifestyle planning using a

311

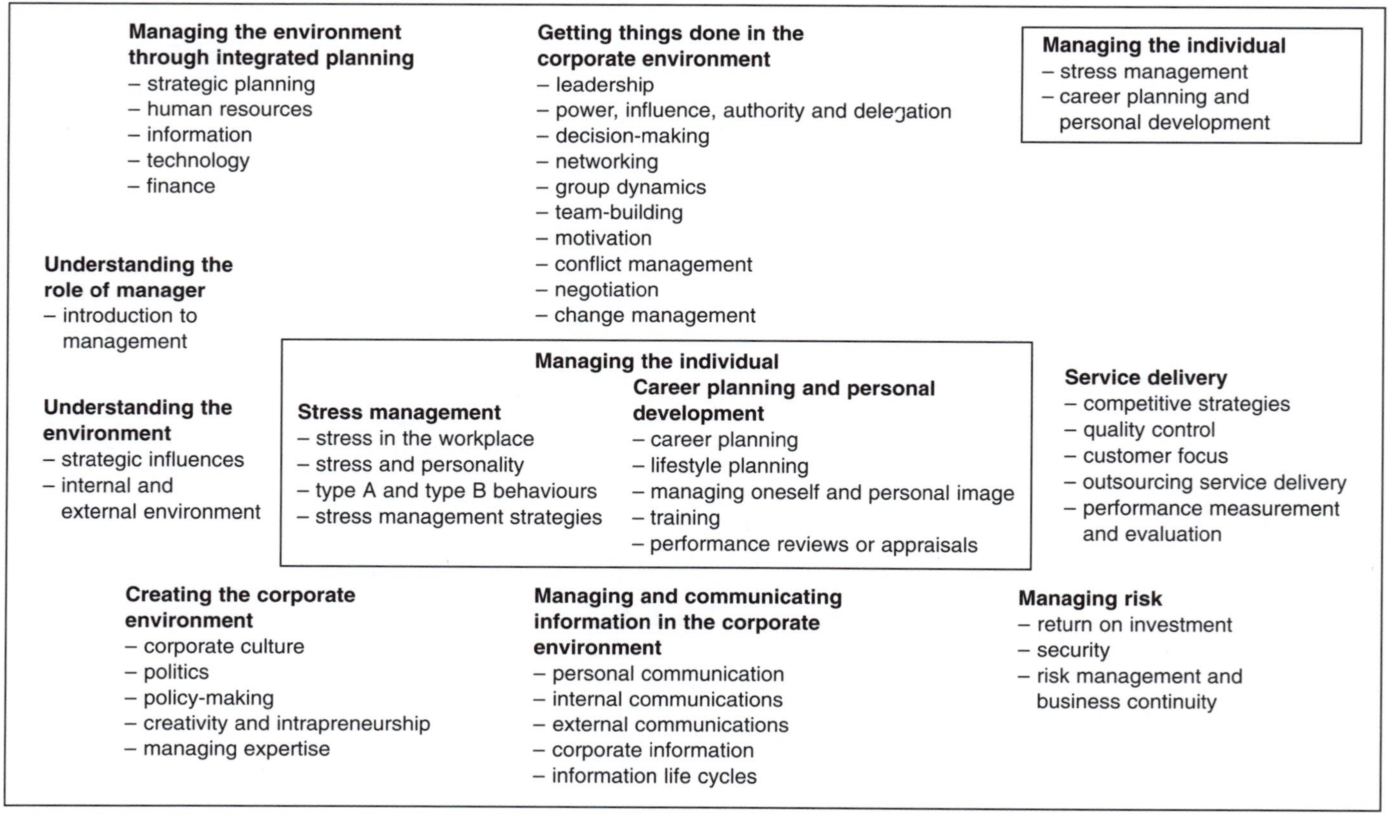

Managing the environment through integrated planning
– strategic planning
– human resources
– information
– technology
– finance

Understanding the role of manager
– introduction to management

Understanding the environment
– strategic influences
– internal and external environment

Creating the corporate environment
– corporate culture
– politics
– policy-making
– creativity and intrapreneurship
– managing expertise

Getting things done in the corporate environment
– leadership
– power, influence, authority and delegation
– decision-making
– networking
– group dynamics
– team-building
– motivation
– conflict management
– negotiation
– change management

Managing the individual

Stress management
– stress in the workplace
– stress and personality
– type A and type B behaviours
– stress management strategies

Career planning and personal development
– career planning
– lifestyle planning
– managing oneself and personal image
– training
– performance reviews or appraisals

Managing and communicating information in the corporate environment
– personal communication
– internal communications
– external communications
– corporate information
– information life cycles

Managing the individual
– stress management
– career planning and personal development

Service delivery
– competitive strategies
– quality control
– customer focus
– outsourcing service delivery
– performance measurement and evaluation

Managing risk
– return on investment
– security
– risk management and business continuity

Figure P7.1   Managing the individual

312

mind map exercise. Managing oneself and personal image is also covered.

Chapter 30 also includes the topic of training. It covers the identification of training needs, designing the training programme, maintaining the behaviour learnt in the training programme and evaluating the training programme. Finally, it considers performance reviews and appraisals to provide feedback to individuals on their performance and as a mechanism for identifying training and personal development needs.

29 Stress management

Introduction

Stress is an environmental force, either real or imagined, that acts on an individual's tolerance to have a motivational or stimulatory effect. Stress is the response that the human system makes in adjusting to the demands of activating life events. It is not the event itself. The life event is known as the stressor. All individuals are victims of stress: being constantly exposed to life events that are threatening. However, stress tolerances differ between individuals, some being more able to control or manage their responses to stress than others.

Stress is not necessarily unhealthy. Everyone needs a certain amount of stress in order to function well. It is constant or excess stress that produces unpleasant or harmful side-effects. If the stressor's force exceeds the individual's stress tolerance level it will have a debilitating effect upon the individual.

Stress is a physiological state. The conditioned responses to aid the body, characterized by arousal to meet the situational demands and relaxing when the task is accomplished, are natural characteristics of survival in transitory stress-producing situations. If these responses are allowed to accumulate beyond the adaptive capacity of the body they can result in physiological or psychological illnesses. This is because the build-up of physical energy inside the body is inappropriate to the modern life situation. Man is no longer a primitive animal requiring sudden bursts of energy for survival.

Vulnerability to stress

Stress implies a vulnerability to a stressor. Individual vulnerability to specific stressors varies widely. Vulnerability alters with age and is related to phases involving change and failures in the life cycle. Vulnerability also changes according to day-to-day events, moods and individual experiences, roles of individuals in particular settings, perceptions of expectations held of the individual by others and the ability to control or alter the situation. Stressors produce symptoms only when context and vulnerability are ripe. The individual must be particularly vulnerable or be in a generally threatening environment to experience the effect of the stressor. Personality has a particular relationship to stress. Certain characteristics predispose individuals to experience more or less stress than their peers.

Occupational or status level bears no relationship to the incidence of stress-related disease. Stress is only related to vulnerability. However, each stage of life has its particular vulnerability. It is important that these stages are recognized by the information services manager so that they may assist themselves and their people to manage their stress levels. The stages are:

- young adult, the stage of transformation from child to adult. This is characterized by growing, maturing and learning;
- the twenties, a stage of establishing a home and career;
- the thirties, this stage provides minor crises of uncertainty concerning career choice;
- thirty-five to fifty-five, the so-called mid-life crisis stage. This is a potentially stressful stage when most people reach their status in life. It is a time associated with reflection, significant changes in occupation, interpersonal values and commitments, and role conflicts between family and career. The more ambitious a person is, the more they are likely to suffer; and
- the latter work years, this stage may be associated with apprehension of retirement or feelings of competition from younger members of staff.

Stress may be controlled or reduced by management techniques that can be employed at individual or organizational level.

Stress in the workplace

Managers and their staff experience potential stressors in their everyday work situation. Role conflict, role ambiguity, role overload and role underload all have the potential to be stressors depending upon the vulnerability of the individual.

In their boundary-spanning role managers will be involved in investigating complaints, troubleshooting and interacting with the environment, all of which may cause stressful situations. Planning, decision-making, interacting with others, motivating, controlling and having responsibilities are other managerial tasks that have stress potential.

The organization's structure and climate, government legislation, external group activities, economic or time pressures, technological change, obsolescence, organizational and work group values are factors in the information service's environment that can produce stress.

Potential stressors for any individual in the workplace can be found in job insecurity, lack of work autonomy, bad work relationships, group conflict, constant work interruptions, lack of a defined career path, organization demands, promotions, demotions or transfers, or management's attitude to employees. Some individuals are guilty of perfectionism and place excessive demands upon themselves. These types of people are their own stressors.

Employees sometimes feel that changes imposed from above are solely for the benefit of the information service. Strategies to improve working conditions, reduce stress or increase opportunity, pay or security are interpreted as being intended to meet the goals of management, to increase productivity or reduce costs. This can create a lose-lose situation for management who have often tried very hard to improve the conditions.

The physical work setting, and health and safety practices, can be a stress source. Photocopiers, printers and other equipment that continually break down, lack of light and ventilation and poorly designed work areas can inhibit productivity and cause conflict, and these in turn become potential stressors for people.

Dual-career families and single parents, where individuals have heavy responsibilities have implications for work-related stress. For example, they may feel guilty about putting either their work or home responsibilities first, they may worry about the possible impact of promotion or relocation on their family or partner, and they may experience role conflict between their responsibilities for their career and family.

Despite all of this, work (either voluntary or paid) is a vital part of coping with life stress. Without work, the potential for boredom and meaninglessness is increased immeasurably. Work is the primary means through which people feel useful in society and life, and so develop a sense of identity. Work may be a form of coping and a refuge for personal distress.

Stress and personality

Stress that is attributed to pressure is highly related to individual personalities. Certain personality characteristics predispose individuals to experience more or less stress than their peers. Information services managers will find that some of their peers and staff will handle pressure better than others. Their tolerance for stress will also differ according to the stressor. For example:

- *Introverted people* are often not very sociable and cannot easily cope with interpersonal tensions from others. A promotion may trigger a strong stress reaction if it results in a job that involves working with other people. The additional responsibility is not the problem, just the act of being placed in unknown company.
- *Extroverts* are people who need other people for various reasons. They work well in jobs requiring the establishment of interpersonal relationships but this need makes them vulnerable as they are dependent upon something apart from themselves. If they are confined to a lonely job they can become stressed.
- *The rigidly structured individual* is security oriented and afraid to take risks. They are stressed by anything that upsets their routine. They are uneasy in implementing new ideas or solutions that have not been tested.
- *The hard-driving, work-oriented individual* is stress-prone. They compulsively push activities to capacity and are extremely performance conscious and goal oriented. They seek honour and recognition but rarely achieve self-confidence as they are always looking at acquiring ever-increasing skills. This stress-prone individual's outlook causes continuous work overload.
- *The stress-reducer* may be as serious as the stress-prone about getting the job done, but will seldom become impatient. They are less competitive and less likely to be driven by the clock. They work without agitation and find time for fun and leisure. Aware of capabilities and confident about themselves, they lead a fuller, less stressful, richer life than their stress-prone counterpart.
- *Risk-avoiders* are excessively careful. They are afraid of making decisions as this threatens their security. They experience constant inner tensions through feelings of inadequacy and dependency. Restrictive in innovative thinking, they avoid exploring new ideas. They will also avoid transfers or promotions, clinging to positions that have given them security and success in the past.
- *Flexible people* usually have healthy, mature egos and can adapt to changing situations, whilst tolerating a high degree of stress. Challenges may be seen as stressors, but this will not impede their ability to cope.

Individuals who have a high self-esteem can deal with stress and frustration more easily. Faced with a pressure situation, performance is likely to improve. There is a strong sense of confidence in their ability to conform and an optimism in their approach to performance. Individuals with low self-esteem will be overwhelmed and show a sharp decrease in performance if stress is applied. This is particularly true if stress is associated with a new job.

Type A and Type B behaviours

Type A individuals

Type A individuals have behaviours that are typical of many managers. These behaviours are highly linked to stress-induced illnesses. Type A personalities are extremely competitive, constantly struggling with the environment at work, in sport and at social functions. They focus upon gaining power, recognition, money and possessions in a short period of time, and portray excessive strivings for achievement accompanied by underlying feelings of hostility towards other people. This is caused by their perception of people in their environment as being roadblocks. The hostility may be subtle or undetected until people stand in their way.

Whilst Type A personalities are outwardly confident and self-assured, they have an underlying insecurity. They often overreact and are generally hypercritical both of themselves (to themselves) and of others.

Type A individuals are fast-talking, having a sense of urgency concerning time. They thrive on deadlines, create them if they are not set and become impatient if goals and objectives are not achieved. Their work habits and their interpersonal relationships are critical in contributing to the fact that Type A personalities are three times more likely to develop cardiac disease or hypertension than Type B personalities.

As Type A behaviours typify successful managers, these behaviours should not be reduced. Rather, managers should learn to manage, or seek assistance to manage, their stress and so reduce the risk of illness.

Type B individuals

In contrast, Type B personalities have an easy-going relaxed approach to life. They hold a rational approach to achievement and recognition. They experience positive interpersonal relations and maintain a balance between work and other events. They rarely have desires to become materialistic.

Stress management strategies

Professional and personal relationships are among the most useful weapons against the distress of work and people's demands. A manager who is willing to delegate will get instrumental support for their projects and will be able to accomplish much more.

Communication is also important. Effective listening skills and the seeking of further information, advice and/or feedback will make decision-making less reactive and crisis oriented. Individuals should always be truthful and honest in their working relationships as mixed messages or inaccuracies can be stressful to deal with. In building up supportive working relationships, work stress will be reduced. The social support offered by the relationships has a buffering effect upon the job demands, providing psychological and emotional support for the individual's well-being.

Personal planning processes can provide coping mechanisms for achievement-oriented individuals. The analysis of an individual's strengths and weaknesses and the periodic reassessment of their vocational, societal and personal goals and aspirations may allow more realistic goal horizons to be set.

Good time management skills are also a means of reducing the negative impact of stress. Knowing their daily cycle will result in individuals being more productive and increase their sense of well-being. For example, the most demanding parts of the job should be handled during the high part of the daily cycle when the person is most alert, whilst the less important events should be scheduled in the lower part of the cycle.

Meditation, appropriate exercise and rest, progressive relaxation techniques and moderation in diet and drinking alcohol will also help alleviate stress.

Preventative stress management strategies can also be employed in the work environment. Stress is often the result of an interaction of an individual with a demand. By altering, modifying or eliminating unnecessary or unreasonable organizational demands, managers can reduce stress in the workplace. Second, necessary coping skills can be provided. These should be aimed at improving the individual's response to, and their management of, organizational demands.

Quick and Quick (1984, pp. 24–34) have produced a model of preventative stress management for organizations. This model advocates that organizational stressors have to be diagnosed before they can be managed. On the basis of the diagnosis, and the individual's own personal response to the stressors, appropriate individual and organizational actions are taken. Actions can also be used as preventative measures by both individuals and the organization.

At the organizational level stressors are found in task, role, physical and interpersonal demands. Task and physical demands can be prevented by task redesign, participative management techniques, flexible work schedules, provision for adequate career development and the design of the physical work settings. Role and interpersonal demands can be prevented from being stressors by team-building, providing social support, goal-setting programmes and role analysis techniques.

Individual stressor demands can be controlled by the individual managing their perceptions of stress, and by managing their work environment and lifestyle. Individuals should also have access to physical and emotional outlets such as sporting activities, exercise routines and interpersonal relationships. Counselling and psychotherapy may also be needed.

The positive results are found in what Quick and Quick term 'eustress', or individual and organizational health. Negative results are found in distress that have psychological, behavioural and medical consequences for the individual and direct and indirect costs for the information service.

The ability to manage the well-being of individuals who work in the information service is important from a duty of care perspective as well as from a motivational viewpoint. It is an important management role to ensure that the physical setting, health and safety practices, work relationships and job structures do not create unnecessary stress for individuals. The ability to assist individuals to manage their responses to stress and to minimize the stressors in the workplace will also result in a happier and more productive workforce.

Reference

Quick, J. C. and Quick, J. D. (1984), 'Preventative stress management at the organisational level', *Personnel*, September–October, 24–34.

30 Career planning and personal development

Introduction

Career planning and personal development are two strategies by which the information service can sustain and increase individual productivity and prepare their people for the future. Individuals can be better equipped to cope with the changing world by planning their career and lifestyle, knowing themselves better and managing their personal self and image, training and work experience to fill knowledge and skills gaps, and by obtaining feedback on their performance.

Personal development strategies should extend individuals' capacities and utilize their maximum capabilities so that there is:

- improved personal performance and relationships;
- increased job satisfaction; and
- improved quality of life.

These strategies should not be limited to the workplace. The person's total lifestyle can be managed, including the home environment, social relationships, interests and career. Whilst these are not within the immediate boundaries of responsibility for the information service, a person's sense of well-being is directly related to their levels of motivation and productivity. As a responsible corporate citizen, the information service can provide lifestyle training and access to counselling services to assist individuals manage and balance their lifestyle.

Career planning

The largest increase in jobs to the year 2000 is forecast to be in the service and information-handling sector leading to an increase of new and varied positions in this field. As a result, career planning will take on renewed importance as opportunities develop for alternative career paths in information services.

Career planning is a joint effort involving the parent organization, the information services manager and the employee. The information service and its parent organization can provide the structure, career path opportunities and climate to encourage career planning and personal development. Individuals will look for evidence of organizational direction and career path opportunities when determining where their own future lies.

The information services manager has a responsibility to ensure appropriate assignments, coaching and counselling to assist individuals in the realistic planning and attainment of their career objectives. They can develop the talents of their people by providing encouragement and support to extend the boundaries of personal growth and development. As part of the appraisal system they should assist individuals choose goals that can stretch them and help identify the means to attain them. From a professional point of view the manager can act as a role model, providing personal and professional qualities that individuals may strive to achieve.

The individual also has to accept responsibility for their growth and development. This includes identifying their long-term career plans and seeking assistance from the organization's resources and development programmes. Action plans can be developed to assist in career planning by:

- identifying critical achievements in their work and personal lifestyle;
- producing an inventory of their current skills and knowledge together with their anticipated future needs (a 'where am I now?' analysis);
- identifying the ideal job and lifestyle position ('where do I want to get to?'); and
- defining the opportunities, constraints and critical success factors in achieving the ideal position ('how can I get there?').

The action plan determines the strategies, qualifications and skills necessary to achieve the ideal position ('what will I do?').

The motivation for successful career and personal development can be damaged if an individual perceives a lack of progress in their chosen career path, or if there is a lack of challenge in the current position and no foreseeable prospect of change. The lack of a foreseeable career path for a person within any organization is increasingly becoming an issue. Business re-engineering and downsizing invariably cut into the mid-level management positions that previously created the career opportunities.

Career development is also affected when there is a conflict of interest between personal loyalty, professional loyalty or organizational loyalty, since failure to reconcile loyalty dilemmas can cause stress and a feeling of futility or confusion. Problems with immediate supervisors can also lead to a sense of frustration in career progression. Mentors can provide encouragement and support in these cases. Mentors can also help to develop people's talents and often open doors to the future.

Lifestyle planning

Lifestyle planning includes making the most efficient and effective use of personal time at the operational (daily) and strategic (long-term) levels. Operational planning incorporates balancing the competing interests of work, home, family and relationships, travel time, personal fitness and other interests such as hobbies and cultural activities. Strategic planning includes longer-term personal goals and retirement planning. To achieve a better balance in their lifestyle and make more efficient use of their time, individuals may plan options such as working part-time, or telecommuting from their home.

Lifestyle planning can be assisted through the use of mind maps (see Figure 30.1). A mind map exercise allows the participant to identify and map out the important areas of their life as branches out of a central trunk. Each major branch indicates a significant personal development or lifestyle issue for the participant. This can be further divided into more specific issues.

A mix of concrete and abstract issues can be used. For example, concrete issues may be work, home, religion, relationships, travel plans, training and development. Abstract issues may be the future, missing items in the lifestyle, things to avoid. Each of the branches is then colour-coded as follows:

- colour one – areas to develop further
- colour two – dissatisfiers
- colour three – satisfiers.

Self-management of lifestyle begins by the individual knowing or finding out more about themselves. This is done by critically analysing personal strengths and weaknesses, assets and liabilities. The mind map exercise can help achieve this.

This exercise can also assist in creating a more balanced lifestyle as it will identify:

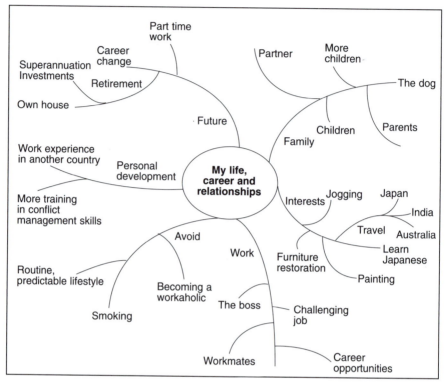

Figure 30.1 Mind map

- those areas that are going well (satisfiers) and those of concern (dissatisfiers);
- areas to develop;
- areas of intense activity and those that are lacking in activity.

Finally, personal attitude and enthusiasm for life will influence the choice of lifestyle. For example, risk takers will be more likely to have unpredictable lifestyles than those who are cautious or conservative.

Managing oneself and personal image

Managers devote many hours to managing organizations and others in order to achieve corporate objectives, but rarely is time given to managing themselves and their own personal image.

Managing oneself involves:

- valuing personal time, effort and energy;
- acting confidently and believing in personal talents and skills to achieve goals;
- being prepared to say 'no' at times;
- being prepared to make decisions about personal future and take responsibility for the outcomes; and
- learning from the past rather than regretting it.

Individuals may also review:

- their successes to reinforce their self esteem;
- personal motives to question their true direction;
- their time management in order to allow time to have personal needs met such as daily exercise and the enjoyment of simple things; and
- sources of conflict at work, in the home, and elsewhere to create more a positive attitude and reduce tension.

Management of personal image is important if individuals are to be confident and have positive attitudes towards themselves. Image is a communication tool. It conveys an impression and message to others. If the information services staff project an image of being confident, approachable and successful, that image will be reinforced to the customers of the information services who will in turn reinforce it to others.

Individuals should be encouraged to identify and manage the image that they feel most comfortable with. This includes identifying the message that the person wishes to communicate about themselves and reinforcing this. The image can be likened to a human package. It is communicated through mannerisms, appearance, dress, movement, speech patterns and personality. Facial expressions, posture and eye contact provide important information for others to judge levels of confidence. The sound, quality, intensity, rate and inflection of speech also projects a powerful image. The ways in which people stand, sit, move and dress influence others' first impressions.

Training

Training as a mechanism for personal development will only be taken seriously within the information service if senior and mid-level management demonstrate their commitment in terms of funding, time and the provision of opportunities for all staff. Training is also important to ensure that all employees are knowledgeable about the organization, its services and its future direction.

Senior management should ensure that the organization's training and career development policies and practices are promoted. Unfortunately during times of economic pressure, the training budget is often the first to be cut, although this represents a false economy. It is a management responsibility to ensure that all staff are adequately trained and that they have the skills and knowledge to carry out their tasks. Staff that are knowledgeable about the information service and its parent organization, their services, products and delivery procedures make fewer mistakes and can answer customer questions more readily. They can also inform customers of other services offered, providing better service and increasing the market share.

Identifying training needs

The training programme requires the same detailed and judicious planning as any other function of management. Training does not consist of just one activity, the training session. Provision must also be made for support systems, policies and/or follow-up programmes to ensure the individual's effective use of their newly acquired knowledge, skills and attitudes on the job.

It is essential that training programmes are based upon identified needs. Other possible problem sources should be investigated before it can be assumed that training, or rather the lack of it, may be the particular cause of a problem. For example, low productivity may be the result of inadequate training. It may also be a symptom of inadequate or unsuitable technology, low morale, a supervisor's lack of skill in training people how to make optimum use of the technology, or the supervisor's lack of skill in recognizing inadequacies in the use of the technology.

Individual training and personal development needs can be identified during the performance appraisal interview. The performance appraisal interview may also identify areas where specific training is required across the information service. Changes in policy or the introduction of new technologies will also present the need for training or retraining of those affected.

Designing the training programme

A good training programme is based upon the knowledge and skill requirements of the individual participants. The course content must be relevant, understandable, able to be absorbed and associated with the work environment. Learning materials should be varied in order to avoid boredom. A combination of didactic and experiential methods is necessary. Didactic training methods include lectures, reading, demonstration and panel discussion. Experiential methods of training can be provided through field trips, structural discussion, brainstorming, case studies, role playing, sensitivity training and encounter training.

The work environment provides the greatest continuing opportunity for personal development and job-related learning on an individual basis. Opportunities include planned job rotation, job exchange systems or secondments and acting in higher-level positions. Courses, seminars, conferences and other training activities supplement rather than substitute on-the-job opportunities for personal growth.

The training programme ought to be designed so as to be problem centred rather than content centred. Adults learn in significantly different ways to children. They see themselves as self-directing in their learning needs, expecting to be able to answer some of the questions from their own experiences and not just to be told. They need to test new concepts and behaviours against what they have previously learnt. Participants should be stimulated to introduce past experiences into the process in order to re-examine these experiences in the light of the new information.

The potential use of the new skill, knowledge or behaviour influences the type of training programme to be provided. If the planned outcome is that of increased knowledge, there is generally less need for discovery learning. If the learning is to be applied in an innovative way, then more experience-based learning is needed. If the desired outcome is to have frequent learning-on-the-job applications or it is to be used in an operating mode, there needs to be more experiential learning. Retention is another aspect to consider. The longer the participants need to retain what is learnt in the training programme, the more experiential the training programme needs to be.

If the training programme is to result in attitude or behavioural changes as an outcome of the learning process, attempts to change the participants' behaviour ought to be incorporated into the programme. The training programme should be designed to contain a great deal of simulation, group and individual participation, role play and case discussion in order to create the desired behaviour and provide immediate feedback on the success or failure of that behaviour to participants.

Maintaining behaviour acquired through training

Maintenance of behaviour is anything that keeps an acquired skill or knowledge up to a performance standard. Examples include getting feedback on the quality of one's work, and having the opportunity to use the skills.

A good training programme will result in newly acquired knowledge, skills or behaviours. It should also enthuse participants to want to master these new 'tools' and to practise them in the workplace. For the newly acquired knowledge, skills or behaviour to be locked in, they must be applied on the job. There must be active support and involvement in the workplace for this to happen. The immediate supervisor should be involved in pre-training and post-training meetings with the participant(s) to determine the purpose of the training programme, to set individual goals and objectives of the training session(s), to look at ways in which the newly acquired behaviour can be reinforced in the workplace, and to evaluate the outcomes of the training programme.

Evaluating the training programme

At the end of a formal training programme a review may be held between the organizer, the presenter (if it is a course) and participants to gather information and evaluate the training session. It is preferable for this to be done whilst the programme is still fresh in everyone's mind. Items for review may include the pace of the training session, problems with materials, groups, the presenter and general housekeeping problems.

The evaluation process may be a mutual activity between the participants, the organizer and the presenter. As a mechanism for the reappraisal of needs and interests, it can be an information-gathering and decision-making process. The evaluation should be confined to the outcome of the training process and not any other outside factor that could influence a change in behaviour.

Performance reviews or appraisals

All employees should undertake an annual performance review. This includes senior management. Performance reviews can be conducted in formal appraisal interviews by the immediate supervisor, although some organizations undertake what is known as 'skip' interviews. These skip a level so the individual is appraised by their boss's supervisor.

Performance reviews have several important uses. They are a means of improving staff motivation and expertise; they provide feedback to employees on their level of performance, allowing them to capitalize on their strengths and overcome their weaknesses; and they can be used to develop an inventory of human resources that forms the basis for career planning and skills inventory from an organizational point of view.

Performance reviews provide a method of career counselling and encouragement for staff members to plan for their future. They allow the supervisor and individual to set mutual goals for the future and outcomes to be achieved during the following year. The opportunity to sit down and plan individual strategies to achieve the information service's objectives can result in more rational and consistent goal-setting down the line.

Whilst feedback on performance is formalized in the annual appraisal interview, monitoring of performance and coaching should be on a continuous basis. Praise or criticism relating to individual events is best given at the time of the event, not held back until the annual appraisal interview. The word appraisal or performance review infers some judgement on an individual's performance. However, the interview should also focus on the training and personal development needs of the individual concerned. This is because improvements in performance cannot take place without adequate skills and knowledge development.

If the performance review system is valued by the organization, then it will form part of its culture. Management and staff hold the belief that the appraisal interview system is worth while and necessary, appraisals are given priority by management and care is taken to ensure that they are properly conducted. There is an emphasis upon personal development within the organization, with good personal performance being valued by a reward system based upon results. Promotion is based on capability, not necessarily seniority. Regularly scheduled appraisal interviews allow managers to confer with their people and translate individual and organizational goals into a joint commitment, leading to a mutual agreement about what needs to be achieved and a culture where co-operation is a norm and feedback a value.

Measuring individual performance

There are a number of different methods for measuring individual performance. One of the simplest methods is the graphic rating scale.

A graphic rating scale identifies certain factors to be related, such as neatness, personality, leadership, initiative, loyalty, dependability, appearance, and quantity and quality of work output. Employees are assessed as to their performance in each factor with either four or five degrees of rating.

The graphic rating scale is one of the most popular in use, but it is time-consuming to complete when a large number of people have to be assessed (see Figure 30.2).

Career planning and personal development should also be managed from a duty of care and motivational viewpoint. The organization's investment in its people in providing education, training and personal development is also an investment in the organization's future in terms of increased commitment and productivity, and the general well-being of its employees.

Staff Assessment Form

INFORMATION SERVICE	WORK UNIT		POSITION NUMBER			
SURNAME	FIRST NAMES					

Employees should be rated according to an objective assessment of the person's actual performance. Consider only one factor at a time. Carefully read each description and mark the one most closely associated with actual performance.

These headings are not necessarily in order of importance nor do they carry equal weight.	A	B	C	D	E	COMMENTS
ATTENDANCE AND PUNCTUALITY. Is the officer regular or irregular in attendance?	Frequently away and/or late	Very seldom away or late	Rarely away but sometimes late	Regular and punctual	Rarely late but sometimes away	
APPEARANCE AND DRESS. What is the officer's personal appearance?	Excellent	Neat and tidy	Passable	Untidy	Unsuitable and extreme tastes	
INTEREST. What degree of interest does the officer display?	Lacks interest generally	Shows lack of interest to a marked degree	Exceptionally keen and enthusiastic	Displays above-average interest	Displays a reasonable amount of interest	
ALERTNESS AND COMPREHENSION. How readily does the officer grasp what is required?	Readily comprehends	Slow to comprehend and adapt	Exceptionally quick even in a new area	Very slow and dull	Very quickly understands	
APPLICATION. What is the officer's application to the task in hand?	Keen and industrious	Steady worker	Usually industrious with occasional lapses	Poor worker and can distract others	Exceptionally energetic and enthusiastic	
KNOWLEDGE OF THE JOB. To what extent does the officer possess the knowledge and ability necessary for the job?	Has barely sufficient to cope with general requirements	Needs to refer too frequently even on routine matters	Very well informed with unusually sound knowledge	Well informed with good knowledge of work area	Able to cope fairly well with most aspects	
WORK OUTPUT. What is the officer's effective output?	Consistently slow, tending to hold up the office	Very fast worker, consistently producing considerable volume of work	Quick worker with greater output than normal	Normal output and keeps up with work flow	Rather a slow worker	
ACCURACY AND RELIABILITY. How accurate and reliable is the officer's work?	Exceedingly accurate and reliable	Rarely makes errors	Normally accurate and reliable	More errors and omissions than normal	Many errors and omissions	
LEADERSHIP. To what extent can the officer organize and inspire others	Leads and organizes efficiently	Shows indications of leadership	Job does not normally require leadership	A bad influence on others	Outstanding organizer and leader	
Signature *Assessor*	Position			Date		
Signature *Interviewee*	Position			Date		

Figure 30.2   An example of a performance assessment form using the graphic rating system

Part 8

Managing risk

This part of the book concentrates on managing risk within the information service (see Figure P8.1).

Chapter 31 considers the management issues associated with projects to ensure that they deliver the return on investment for the organization. It also provides details on how the return on investment for information products and services can be enhanced, and strategies for charging for information products and services.

Chapter 32 addresses the issue of security. The objective of security measures is to preserve the confidentiality, integrity and availability of information. Responsibility for this is found at all levels of the organization. The chapter identifies different security threats and how these can be overcome through the appropriate management of people, information, physical environment and the technology.

The choice of security level is a management issue. Chapter 32 considers the issues that influence the choice of security level. It also addresses access controls and lists other good management practices that maintain the integrity, availability and confidentiality of information.

Chapter 33 identifies major risks that can affect information services. It also considers business continuity issues and treats disaster recovery as a component of business continuity. The chapter advocates that a business perspective should be taken for each, including the need to plan according to the event and its impact on the business of the organization.

Managing the environment through integrated planning
– strategic planning
– human resources
– information
– technology
– finance

Understanding the role of manager
– introduction to management

Understanding the environment
– strategic influences
– internal and external environment

Getting things done in the corporate environment
– leadership
– power, influence, authority and delegation
– decision-making
– networking
– group dynamics
– team-building
– motivation
– conflict management
– negotiation
– change management

Managing the individual
– stress management
– career planning and personal development

Managing risk

Security
– confidentiality, integrity and availability
– roles and responsibilities
– security threats
– managing security
– choosing the right security level
– acess control
– good housekeeping practices

Return on investment
– planning the return on investment
– increasing the return on investment
– charging for information

Risk management and business continuity
– risk management
– business continuity
– disaster recovery

Creating the corporate environment
– corporate culture
– politics
– policy-making
– creativity and intrapreneurship
– managing expertise

Managing and communicating information in the corporate environment
– personal communication
– internal communications
– external communications
– corporate information
– information life cycles

Service delivery
– competitive strategies
– quality control
– customer focus
– outsourcing service delivery
– performance measurement and evaluation

Managing risk
– return on investment
– security
– risk management and business continuity

Figure P8.1 Managing risk

31 Return on investment

Introduction

Return on investment shows how well the information service is using its resources by relating the outcomes and outputs to the investment in the assets. It is also used to decide the worth of new project proposals.

From a management viewpoint, the return on investment involves:

- the relative delivered cost – maintaining high productivity, low outlays in the value chain; and
- the relative performance – ability to offer differentiated or highly desirable products and services.

Good planning ensures that organizational investments in large projects fit the business purpose and provide a high rate of return.

The ability to charge for information products and services will also influence the return on investment. Different pricing strategies for information products and services can be used. These will be influenced by the nature of the customer and the type of information product or service.

Planning the return on investment

Good project management is only the tip of the iceberg in ensuring a return on investment (see Figure 31.1). Seven other important factors need to be taken into account for project proposals. These are economic viability, alignment with the business needs of the organization and the information needs of its customers, environmental sensitivities, financial strategy,

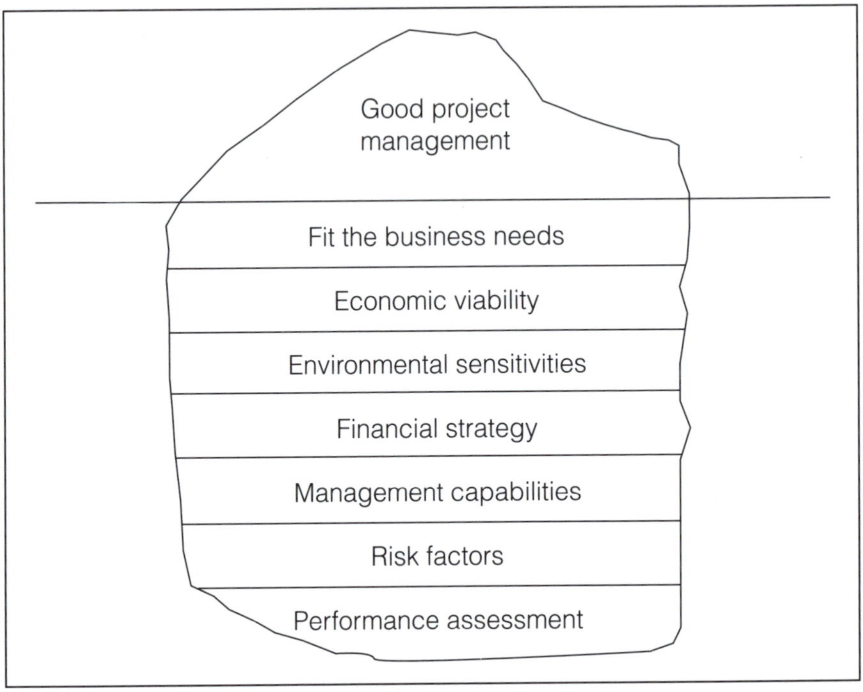

Figure 31.1   Iceberg factors affecting the return on investment for projects

management capabilities and responsibilities, risk factors and performance assessment.

To ensure an optimum return on investment, the information service must plan projects and utilize its resources in the most cost-effective way. The project management strategies should take into account issues such as conversion and changeover, managing the organizational change, the need for process re-engineering, staff training and data conversion or takeup. Projects can be managed through project steering committees involving all the stakeholders associated with the project.

Projects and resources should be planned and managed to fit the business needs of the organization and the information needs of its customers and stakeholders. Projects may be assessed according to how they will be utilized in the business activities, the value chain, and the resulting services and products. Projects and activities can be prioritized according to anticipated outcomes and benefits. In times of economic constraint, projects that are critical to the business needs or assist in developing or maintaining competitive advantage should be given the highest priority.

The long-term economic viability of the project must be considered. The project should be assessed according to its attractiveness as an investment opportunity in terms of potential for market growth, profit improvement, or ability to spawn new products or services. A cost-benefit analysis ought to be undertaken. Tangible and intangible benefits can be considered, as well as all direct and indirect costs. Any associated revenue or savings should be costed into the project. Cost schedules, budget statements and cash flow figures should identify the true costs, ensuring that there is no double counting.

External environmental sensitivities must be assessed, particularly those that can affect customer demand and the longer-term outcomes of the project in a changing environment. These include the competitive positioning and likely strategies of key competitors in undertaking a similar project, the scale or likelihood of major technology change that could quickly render the project obsolete, or consumer patterns that may affect customer demand.

The financial strategy will identify how the project is to be funded and the impact of this on the organization. Alternatives such as leasing services rather than having an up-front capital investment may be investigated. The financing decision must consider short-term and long-term needs for working capital and what other business opportunities might be forgone by investing in the project.

Before embarking on any project the management requirements and existing in-house capabilities should be assessed. Options for outsourcing or joint venturing the project may be considered. The decision to involve others will be affected by the level of commercial sensitivity and level of risk in the project, the availability of external capabilities, as well as the level of existing expertise within the organization.

Risk factors must be identified. This includes what could go wrong, the magnitude and impact of the risk. The amount of risk varies according to the size of the project, the amount of money at stake, the amount of attribute uncertainty, and the amount of confidence in the project. High-risk strategies are generally less attractive than low-risk strategies. The riskiness of the project also depends upon how easy it is to predict the future impact of the project. The formula for risk is:

$$\text{Risk} = \text{Magnitude} \times \text{Probability}$$

This is the scope and extent of the risk multiplied by the likelihood or probability that it will occur.

Performance assessment should not only identify desired outcomes and outputs; project milestones should be set throughout the life of the project.

Increasing the return on investment

The value of information to an organization can be as:

- a consumption good – the organization sells the information as a value-added product;
- a customer service good – the organization provides information as part of its services; or
- an investment good – the organization uses it for decision-making to achieve competitive advantage.

The return on investment for information products and services is enhanced by:

- adding other information to the original information;
- reprocessing and repackaging the information to meet market or customer demands;
- making information more accessible to customers; and
- refining the information to meet individual needs.

These are regarded as enhancements to the value chain.

Charging for information

Information products and services are not free. There are costs associated with capturing or purchasing data and equipment, storage, processing, production, distribution and exchange. Depending upon the information service's policies the cost to the customer can be:

- fully subsidized – information products and services are made available at no cost. The total cost being absorbed by the information service or parent organization as part of a community service obligation;
- partially subsidized – information products and services are made available at nominal cost. The information service or its parent organization exercises partial cost recovery and funds the remainder of the costs of providing the products or services internally; or
- full cost recovery – information products and services are made available either at market rates (cost and profit) or at the rate required for total cost recovery from the customer.

Charging strategies

Different charging strategies can be used to set market rates for charging for information products and services. The price charged can be influenced by:

- product or service intensity – information products such as maps that contain very detailed information or services that are provided in depth will often command a higher price that others that have less depth or detail;
- product life of the information – information that is rare or offers a new perspective will be of greater value. The price can be set much higher than for information that is older. Out-of-date information has no value unless it is of historical value;
- supply time – the faster information is made available, the higher the price can be set;
- customer's ability to pay and type of customer – organizations that rely on information products and services for their competitive advantage will recognize that information is a critical resource and will build provisions in their budgets accordingly. Customers requiring information for more personal reasons will be less willing to pay;
- medium or format – the medium or format influences the cost of dissemination of the information product or service;
- extent of the value added processing – information that is tailored to meet specific or individual needs and is highly processed will command a higher price than a more generic information product or service;
- intended use of the information – information that is used for commercial purposes may be priced at a higher rate than information that is used as a social good.

The nature of some information, particularly that which is provided as a customer service good, is that its value and optimum return on investment lies in it being fully subsidized. An example of this may be an energy, telecommunications or water utility that offers information under a 'Dial before you Dig' programme free of charge. The cost associated with offering this type of service is more than offset by the financial costs and disruption that could be incurred by the utility and the community if the pipeline or cables were severed.

Other information products and services have a value to specific customers in that they are designed and offered to fit a specific market need. These fall into the category of a consumption good, an example being where a library may offer specific research services tied to its local history collection to architects who specialize in restoring old houses. These services can be made available on a full cost recovery basis.

Ensuring the return on investment in the information service is a complex issue that is directly related to planning and managing projects to fit the business needs of the parent organization and the customers' information and service needs. It also requires consideration of how the return on investment can be increased at the different stages of the value chain, and charging strategies for information products and services.

32 Security

Introduction

Information security is a management rather than a technical issue. Security should be managed according to the level of risk and potential threats to the organization. The level of risk is influenced by the type of organization, its business and its objectives. An organization that operates in a highly competitive environment, depends upon large-scale information processing for its business, or manages a large proportion of personal or commercially sensitive information will have a higher security risk than an organization in a more stable and less sensitive environment. For example, the level of risk in the banking industry is much higher than the level of risk in a public library.

Security can be managed through a series of general and application controls that either:

- prevent threats; or
- detect and control the effects of damage if a security violation, disaster or failure takes place.

The efficiency of these controls should be tested through regular audits, monitoring and critical incidence reproduction.

Confidentiality, integrity and availability

The objective of security management is to ensure confidentiality, integrity and availability of information.

Ensuring the confidentiality of information includes protecting privacy, commercial and competitive information from unauthorized access and use. Maintaining the integrity of information relies upon the ability to protect it from unauthorized manipulation or processing. The continued availability of information to those authorized to have access and use the information requires mechanisms that ensure that the information is resilient, backed up and that steps are in place to quickly restore and maintain access levels in times of degraded activity. The testing of data recovery should be performed on a periodic basis to confirm that the backup process is effective and that correct and usable information is available.

Roles and responsibilities

Responsibility for security can be found at all levels. The Chief Executive is ultimately accountable for the confidentiality, integrity and availability of the organization's information resource and systems. Senior management has a responsibility for ensuring that there are appropriate standards, policies and procedures on security that reflect the level of risk within the organization, that staff are aware of and understand the policies and procedures, and that adequate security procedures and practices are in place to manage the risk. Individuals are responsible for ensuring that they follow the correct procedures and practices. The information services staff are responsible for periodically testing to ensure that the correct procedures and practices are in place and followed.

Security threats

Threats to security can be found in human error or deliberate human intervention, natural and political disasters, hardware and software failures. Examples of human error include incorrect keying of input data, errors in program development or maintenance, or operator error.

Security can be deliberately violated through:

- unauthorized access – access to critical information or systems with or without causing damage;
- damaging information – by damaging, contaminating, destroying, erasing, manipulating or rendering it meaningless;
- fraud – manipulating data to obtain a financial or other advantage.

Natural and political disasters include earthquake, flood, fire, industrial sabotage, terrorism and war. These have the potential to threaten, either partially or totally, access to information and the functioning of the supporting technology. They can also severely degrade the functionality of the organization.

Hardware and software failures include power failure, failure of equipment, network failure or systems malfunction. These can lead to loss of information and functionality for the organization.

Managing security

Security is achieved through the appropriate management of people, information, physical environment (including buildings) and the technology (including networks and systems).

People management

People are often a source of security violations. The security risks are found in human error, theft, fraud or the misuse of information and facilities. Apart from deliberate actions, an unfortunate aspect of security violations is that a considerable number are unintended. Security violations often occur through ignorance and negligence in following proper procedures.

Security should be addressed in the recruitment stage and monitored through the individual's employment. Employees must be made aware of information security threats, the importance of maintaining proper security and backup controls, and, be equipped to support the organization's security practices and procedures during their work.

If the parent organization continually deals with sensitive information or operates in a highly competitive environment, all new personnel must be screened before being appointed.

All employees and third parties utilizing the organization's information and supporting technical infrastructure ought to sign a confidentiality (non-disclosure) agreement with the organization. Employees and third parties should be advised in writing of their rights and restrictions of levels of access, and the security requirements of the organization.

Information classification

Information has varying levels of sensitivity and criticality. Some information may require an additional level of security protection or special handling, examples being some types of personal information or commercially sensitive information. Information classification systems can be used to define an appropriate set of security protection levels and to communicate the need for special handling requirements to users.

Information that is classified as high security will require specialized storage and restricted access and circulation provisions.

Information security policies and procedures should relate to information in electronic and hard copy form. Documents, paper records or microfiche are equally at risk for security breaches as information stored in electronic form.

Library collections

Libraries face particular risks in terms of physical security and wilful or accidental damage to their collections. This risk increases where there is open access to the collection. Damage can occur at both the collection level and the item level through:

- theft of an item of stock (such as a journal or video);
- wilful damage to an item or part of an item of stock (such as the cutting out of an journal article or picture in a book);
- accidental damage (such as an animal chewing a book);
- fire, storm or other damage.

Many libraries have installed security devices that either scan customers as they exit the premises, or provide videotape footage of movements within the building in order to minimize this type of damage.

Libraries such as National Libraries that house valuable and unique collections must weigh accessibility and ease of access against the security of the collections.

Physical environment

Critical or sensitive business activities should be housed in secure areas where they can be protected from unauthorized access, damage and interference by a defined security perimeter with appropriate entry and exit controls, and security barriers.

The physical environment that houses the supporting technology such as file servers, mainframes and network controllers should have hazard detection and suppression controls that minimize risk from damage through fire, water or other disasters. Support facilities such as power supply and cabling infrastructure must also be well protected. A battery-based or independent uninterruptive power supply ought to be installed to provide continuous operations in the case of a total or partial power failure. Equipment (including workstations) should also be protected against power spikes.

Physical access to storage locations may be restricted to minimize the risk of disgruntled employees or competitors destroying original and backup copies of information and software programs.

A 'clear desk' policy can be in place to reduce the risk of unauthorized access to information, sabotage or damage.

Technology

Information-related technology (hardware, systems, networks etc.) should be physically protected from security threats and environmental hazards such as water damage. The technology should also be protected against loss, damage and interruption to business activities or wire tapping.

Advanced planning should take into account future requirements so as to ensure the availability of adequate capacity and resources.

Security procedures can protect against virus control. Disks should be scanned before being introduced or exported from organizational equipment. Virus detection software ought to be installed on all personal computers and used as a matter of course. The software must be continually updated to take into account new viruses. Only authorized software should be used, and the downloading of information or software programs from remote sources such as bulletin boards should be controlled.

Choosing the right security level

The choice of security level is a management issue. The requirement for an appropriate level of control ought to be balanced against the need to make information easily available for decision-making. The level of security should take into account:

- the level of risk;
- ease of use;
- relative cost;
- feasibility; and
- availability of resources.

The level of risk can be calculated according to the amount of damage or loss that could result due to a security exposure, multiplied by the probability (or frequency) that this may occur.

Modern technology environments encourage access to systems from widely dispersed workstations or personal computers. Security features need to control unauthorized access without introducing barriers to legitimate use.

Security features can be expensive in terms of the capital costs for the security devices, additional costs for encryption facilities in messaging and telecommunications and labour costs in maintaining security. The level of security should match the level of risk. It is not cost effective to introduce a higher level of security than is necessary. In fact this could lead to a loss in productivity for the organization.

The level of security should be chosen to be feasible and practical. It ought not to inhibit work or information flows to the extent that it is detrimental to the organization's activities. It must also match the organization's level of expertise and resources.

Access control

Access to information and its supporting technologies should be controlled to prevent unauthorized use or access.

Authorizing use of organizational-wide networks and systems

There should be formal procedures that control and document the allocation of access, from the initial register of new users to the deregistration of users who no longer need access to services. The allocation of privileged access that allows users to override systems controls should be on a very restricted basis.

Network and computer access control

To prevent unauthorized network or computer access, technology facilities that service multiple customers must be capable of:

- identifying and verifying the identity, terminal and location of each user;
- recording successful and unsuccessful accesses;
- providing a password management system to allocate, check, maintain and prompt the user to change quality passwords;
- restricting the access times and connection times of users where appropriate or when not in use;
- providing enhanced user authentication facilities such as dial-back, smart card tokens or key-based encryption;
- logging audit trails; and
- automatically disabling or disconnecting users when a small number of consecutive incorrect passwords are entered.

Access to network addresses, controls and configuration files must be managed in a secure and controlled manner.

Application access control

Logical access can be used to control access to applications and information residing on computers. These should be protected from any utility software that may be capable of overriding the application, and should not compromise the security of other systems.

Access to systems administration menus and critical system files must be restricted so that only authorized personnel are able to access these to maintain authority and user level controls.

There should be a periodic review of users' access permissions to ensure that access permissions continue to be valid. Audit trails should be designed to track access and changes to applications and the information in order to confirm that any changes are valid and authorized.

Physical access

Access to rooms housing equipment should be strictly controlled. The employees and visitors must be appropriately identified. Badges or other means of identification should be worn at all times, registers (either electronic or manual) need to be kept for when people enter and leave, and closed circuit monitors should be actively monitored by security personnel.

Information access and privacy considerations

The protection of an individual's personal information is a democratic right. Privacy and data protection can be safeguarded through legislation. Where this is absent, the organization can develop its own code of conduct that:

- guards against the indiscriminate collection and use of personal information;
- ensures confidentiality in its information practices;
- provides individuals with the right to view their personal records, to challenge and have corrected (or noted) any incorrect personal information about themselves; and
- holds senior management accountable for the security and use of personal information that is in the possession of the organization.

Good housekeeping practices

In addition to the specific security requirements mentioned above, good housekeeping practices and routines maintain the integrity, availability and confidentiality of information. These include (but are not restricted to):

- maintaining and periodically revising security plans so that they remain relevant to the level of risk, are complete, and reflect the current business environment;
- a regularly maintained backup copy of critical information and software stored off-site;
- a register of security incidents to enable the organization to regularly review all security incidents and identify commonalities to improve the approach to security;
- controlled access to networks and systems by third parties;
- instilling norms of ethical behaviour amongst employees;
- accountability procedures for all assets;
- protection from the introduction of software containing viruses and other programs that can make unauthorized or unknown modifications to either the software or information; and
- the continuous monitoring of equipment performance.

The overriding factor in the management of security is that it should be managed in accordance with the level of risk and potential threats to the organization. The requirement for a high level of security should also be balanced against the need to make information available for decision-making. Ultimately, the choice is a management rather than a technical issue.

33 Risk management and business continuity

Introduction

Planning for adversity is the key to overcoming adversity. Risk management strategies identify the potential for adversity and plan to manage the event or situation according to the probability of it occurring. Information services have traditionally considered security and disaster recovery to be the main elements of risk management. There are also other risk issues that should be managed by the information services manager and senior management.

In the event of a major outage (failure or disaster), business continuity plans protect critical business processes from their adverse effects. The emphasis for the information services is on protecting and ensuring the continuity of access to information and its supporting technologies. However, other business aspects such as alternative sites for the total business operations must be considered.

Risk management

Risk management involves the identification of risk, analysing the probability of it occurring and the magnitude of potential risk, and introducing appropriate strategies to manage the problem. Significant risks that can affect information services include:

- fraud – this can be financially detrimental to the information service and its parent organization or result in a loss of customers if their relationships with the organization are affected. If the fraudulent person is a member of the information service's staff, this can have an adverse affect on the morale and levels of trust amongst staff members;

- security violations and computer crime – these can result in the loss of competitive information or severely affect the operations of the organization's systems through the use of logic bombs, computer viruses, etc.;
- inefficiency and waste – these lead to high costs, low profitability and low productivity;
- legal exposures – adverse legal action may be financially and organizationally debilitating;
- loss of public reputation, image or regard for corporate citizenship – the loss of an organization's reputation or image can severely affect its standing in the market;
- lack of contingency planning and business continuity strategies – this may result in the information service or its parent organization being unable to continue its business activities during times of degraded conditions;
- loss of key staff and expertise – this can leave the information service or its parent organization vulnerable in terms of a loss of business knowledge and expertise. It may also result in an organization's intellectual property being transferred to a competitor;
- public liability – this can have financial and image implications for the information service or its parent organization;
- insurable risks such as property damage – these may inhibit the operations of the information service and its parent organization if access and movement within the organization's building are restricted;
- unlawful acts, vandalism and terrorism – as well as the potential for property damage, acts of vandalism or terrorism can have a major impact on the safety and psychological well-being of staff;
- occupational health and safety issues – an unsafe workplace not only exposes staff to health and safety risks, there is an adverse effect on the morale and productivity of staff. The organization can be subjected to the threat of litigation. The use of information technology equipment such as screens and mobile telephones have been identified as possible sources of radiation that may be a health hazard to users over a long period of time.

Contingency plans should be in place to manage these risks according to the level of risk for the information service and the parent organization.

Business continuity

Business continuity differs from disaster recovery in that it is more comprehensive and provides alternatives for all resources and activities so that critical business functions can continue. Disaster recovery only considers the loss of computer-related and network facilities, and provides alternatives for data processing at other locations. It does not cover issues such as the requirement for office space or alternative work facilities, emergency telephone systems, operational facilities to support staff who may be disoriented by the changes or the business impact associated with the inability of customers to access services.

Business continuity addresses business scenarios. For example:

- planning for known events such as the continuity of operations at the end of an outsourcing contract, whilst the service provision is either being transferred to another vendor or being brought back in house; or
- what to do when the information related facilities are still working, but employees of the information service or parent organization are denied access to the building because of an incident.

Business continuity requires a process to be developed and maintained for the speedy restoration of critical business processes and services in the event of a serious business interruption. The processes will differ according to the event and level of risk. For example, the strategy to maintain business operations in the aftermath of a terrorist bombing of the office building in which the organization operates will differ from the strategy to maintain business operations during a period of industrial unrest that causes the power supply to be continually interrupted.

Disaster recovery

Disaster recovery should take a business perspective. It should:

- highlight preventative actions that may be taken;
- seek to minimize the impact of the disaster on the information service, the parent organization and its customers; and
- improve the organization's ability to recover efficiently and effectively.

Impact analysis

Before designing the disaster recovery plan an impact analysis should be undertaken. This describes the types of events that may cause an outage and analyses their impact on the business. The impact analysis links the development of the disaster recovery plan to the business needs of the organization. It also identifies the priorities within the business operations, so that critical processes can be restored first. The business impacts include:

- loss of business opportunities;
- likelihood of penalty clauses in contracts that may be affected by the outage, such as penalty fees for delaying the completion of a project;
- loss of important material; and
- impact on staff, customers, stakeholders and senior management.

The disaster recovery plan

The disaster recovery plan is part of the business continuity management process. It specifies how an organization will maintain its information services necessary for its business operations in the face of an outage or disaster. The disaster recovery plan has four components:

- emergency plan – this specifies the type of emergency and the actions to be taken that fit the emergency situation;
- backup plan – this specifies the facilities required (including data restoration, disks, computing equipment, telecommunications and networks, work stations) as a recovery site and to maintain operations;
- recovery plan – this specifies how the processing will be restored, including the responsibilities of individuals and a priority list for the retrieval of important material; and
- test plan – this specifies the frequency and manner in which the components of the disaster recovery plan will be tested.

Disaster recovery site

Arrangements need to be made for alternatives for a recovery site. The alternatives for a recovery site can be:

- backup facilities that are owned by the parent organization – if the organization operates out of a number of geographic locations, a site (or a number of sites) can act as the backup facility for others;
- right of access to facilities offered by organizations that specialize in providing disaster recovery sites – the organization may undertake a contract with a specialist organization for the use of a mobile, hot or cold site as a contingency measure. A hot site is a facility that operates equipment compatible with the organization. A cold site is a building that is designed so that it is able to accept equipment at short notice;
- facilities at another establishment – a reciprocal agreement may be undertaken with an organization that operates compatible equipment for each to act as recovery sites.

Managing the recovery

The recovery plan should be regularly updated, known and understood. Senior management must know how it will be managed and in what order so that business processes can be restored as quickly as possible. The recovery plan should be maintained in paper as well as electronic form, and copies stored off-site such as in bank vaults, the recovery site and the homes of senior management and key staff members. As the recovery plan will include sensitive and competitive information, it should be secured off-site.

A consolidated contact list should be maintained. This should contain the names, addresses, contact numbers and responsibilities of the people required to implement the recovery process. The contact list should be stored alongside the recovery plan.

In addition to the people directly involved in the recovery process, the contact list should also include details of suppliers, vendor contacts, business partners such as electronic trading partners and key customers. One of the first management tasks will be to advise those on the contact list of the event and the actions taken to restore business processes to normality.

Risk management and business continuity strategies are proactive management strategies for the identification and management of risk, and for ensuring the continuity of access to information in a working environment that may be operating under degraded conditions.

Part 9

Service delivery

This part is the key to service delivery in information services. It deals with defining and managing the end products and services that result from all of the other activities in the book. It also considers alternative strategies that can be used to deliver products and services as well as the performance criteria to establish whether these products and services are meeting customer needs (see Figure P9.1). As a reflection of its level of importance, this part could easily be at the beginning of the book. However, it has been located towards the end as it builds upon all the other practices and processes that must be in place within the information service and its parent organization to support service delivery.

Chapter 34 considers strategic marketing strategies to increase the competitiveness of the information service. It outlines the process of a strategic marketing exercise and explains the marketing mix, or 'the four Ps' of product, price, place and promotion in the context of information services. The chapter also outlines how markets can be divided into market segment groups of need markets, geographic markets, product markets and demographic markets.

Market targeting can be undertaken through three strategies: undifferentiated marketing, differentiated marketing and concentrated marketing. Each strategy is explained drawing upon examples in information services. Chapter 34 supplements the information on the information service's image contained in Chapter 26 by considering image analysis in the context of determining service provision. Image studies measure the perceptions that people have about the information service.

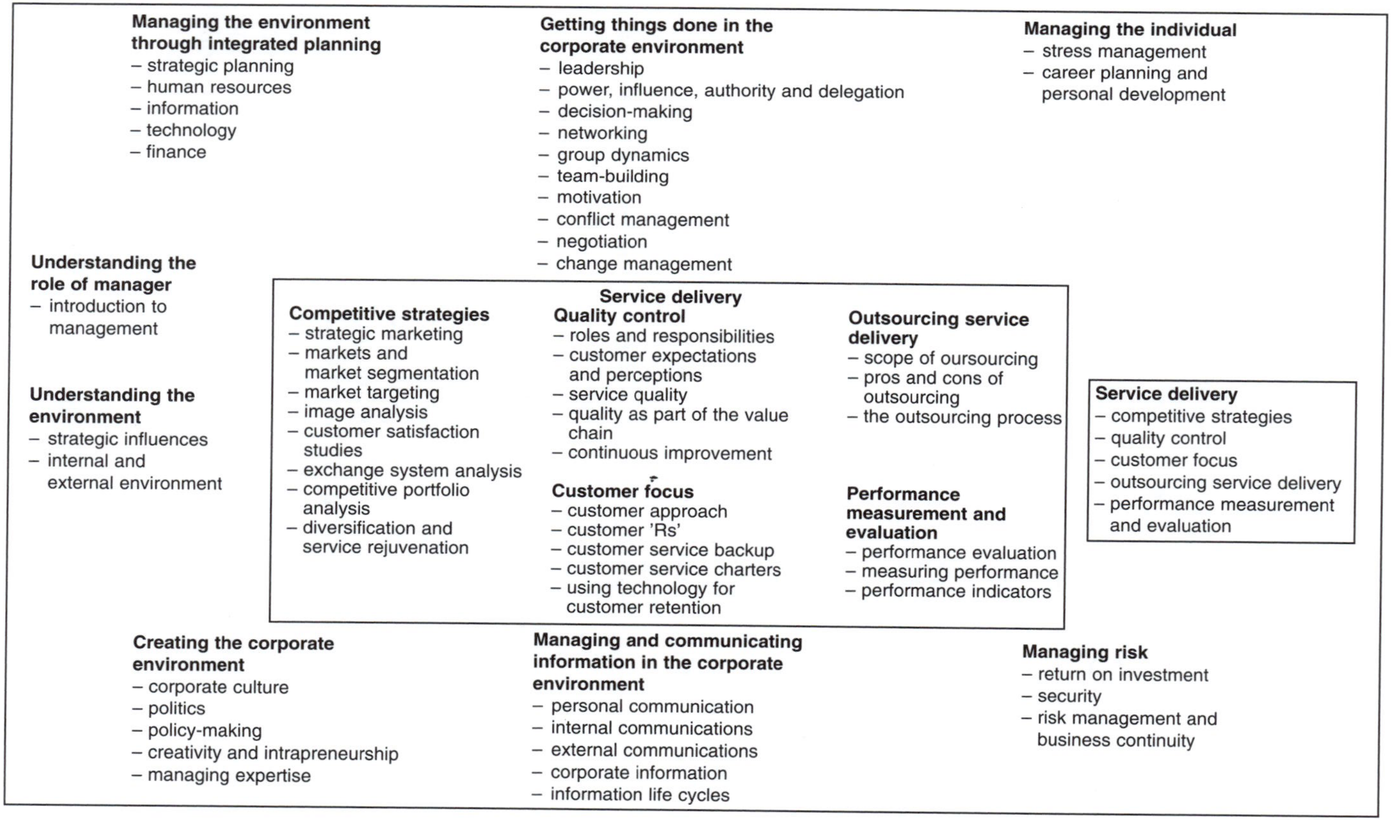

Managing the environment through integrated planning
- strategic planning
- human resources
- information
- technology
- finance

Understanding the role of manager
- introduction to management

Understanding the environment
- strategic influences
- internal and external environment

Getting things done in the corporate environment
- leadership
- power, influence, authority and delegation
- decision-making
- networking
- group dynamics
- team-building
- motivation
- conflict management
- negotiation
- change management

Managing the individual
- stress management
- career planning and personal development

Competitive strategies
- strategic marketing
- markets and market segmentation
- market targeting
- image analysis
- customer satisfaction studies
- exchange system analysis
- competitive portfolio analysis
- diversification and service rejuvenation

Service delivery

Quality control
- roles and responsibilities
- customer expectations and perceptions
- service quality
- quality as part of the value chain
- continuous improvement

Customer focus
- customer approach
- customer 'Rs'
- customer service backup
- customer service charters
- using technology for customer retention

Outsourcing service delivery
- scope of oursourcing
- pros and cons of outsourcing
- the outsourcing process

Performance measurement and evaluation
- performance evaluation
- measuring performance
- performance indicators

Service delivery
- competitive strategies
- quality control
- customer focus
- outsourcing service delivery
- performance measurement and evaluation

Creating the corporate environment
- corporate culture
- politics
- policy-making
- creativity and intrapreneurship
- managing expertise

Managing and communicating information in the corporate environment
- personal communication
- internal communications
- external communications
- corporate information
- information life cycles

Managing risk
- return on investment
- security
- risk management and business continuity

Figure P9.1 Service delivery

356

Tied to this, customer satisfaction studies provide an indication as to whether existing information service customers are satisfied with current services.

Underlying the marketing concept is a system of exchange. The theory behind exchange system analysis is explained in the context of information services. A further analysis that can be used in marketing is the competitive portfolio analysis. Chapter 34 explains how the product life cycle and the Boston Consulting Group's portfolio matrix can be used in a competitive portfolio analysis. A specific example of how the competitive portfolio analysis can be used in managing library stock is explained. Finally, Chapter 34 describes the rejuvenation strategies that can be used to recover some services' lack of use over time or to stop the decline in the product life cycle.

Chapter 35 introduces the reader to quality control. It makes the point that people have differing perceptions of quality according to how they judge it and their cultural background. The chapter lists the main determinants of quality and identifies five gaps that can cause unsuccessful service delivery. The role of quality in the value chain is covered, as is the need for continuous rather than one-off improvement.

Chapter 36 reflects a customer approach to management. It describes these in terms of 'Rs' that stand for retention, requirements, refined segmentation, etc. The chapter points out that the delivery of the service or product is only the beginning of the relationship between the organization and the customer. Service backup is extremely important to deliver a total quality service. Suggestions for a customer service charter are included. Finally, the chapter describes how technology can be used by organizations to retain their customers.

Chapter 37 covers outsourcing. The outsourcing of services, particularly information-related technologies, has increased exponentially over the last few years. The chapter identifies the scope of information related services that may be outsourced, and the pros and cons of outsourcing. The outsourcing process is described in detail and covers determining the right objectives and strategy, determining what to outsource, assessing the benefits, determining the risks, selection of the vendor, negotiating the contract, structuring the relationship and managing the risks.

Chapter 38 provides strategies for measuring and evaluating performance. It describes the performance evaluation process and how performance can be measured in different work units. This requires consideration of outputs and outcomes, quality and value, cause and effect. Information has specific qualities that make the measurement of its value more difficult. Different mechanisms for measuring its value are explored. The chapter also includes examples of performance indicators that can be used in information services and identifies some criteria for performance indicators.

34 Competitive strategies: strategic marketing

Introduction

Marketing is part of the total planning process. Strategic marketing makes use of many of the concepts and functions of strategic planning. Strategic marketing strategies ensure viable market positions and programmes for the survival and success of the information service. Any proposals for new services or extending existing services to new markets must be in line with the information service's objectives. Sufficient expertise, human, technical and financial resources should be available to support such services.

Market segments comprise individuals or groups who are actual or potential customers of the information service. Markets can be divided according to need, product, demography and geography, each market having its own particular characteristics.

Market targeting involves the evaluation, selection and concentration on the desired market segments. There are three strategies for market targeting: undifferentiated marketing, differentiated marketing and concentrated marketing.

There are various analyses that assist marketing strategies. These are exchange system analysis, image analysis, customer satisfaction studies, competitive portfolio analysis and product life cycles. The exchange system analyses is useful as it enables the information services manager to identify what the customers are prepared to exchange for the services that the information service offers. Its importance lies in the fact that both tangible and intangible items can be identified, including the more esoteric values that the information service community may hold. This may be useful information when planning new services or in justifying existing services.

Image analysis is exceptionally important in determining the information service's image to the funding and governing bodies, and its customers. As a result of the image analysis certain market strategies may need to be undertaken. Customer satisfaction studies determine whether customer expectations for services are higher or lower than those being provided. Product life cycles and product portfolio matrices help the information service to determine which areas have the potential for growth.

Finally, diversification and service rejuvenation can help to instil new growth into ailing services.

Strategic marketing

Strategic marketing takes place within the strategic management process of organizations. Strategies are developed that ensure viable market positions and programmes for the survival and success of the information service. Strategic marketing has been defined by Kotler et al. (1980, p. 56) as: 'A managerial process of analysing market opportunities and choosing market positions, programs and controls that create and support viable businesses that serve the organization's purposes and objectives.'

The strategic marketing process builds upon the information already obtained through the strategic audit undertaken during the strategic planning process. This includes information about the present and future environment, stakeholders, the external and internal environment, mission, programmes, and performance evaluation and review. Additional information relating to markets, customers and the resources is gathered by researching:

- the primary market for the information service;
- the main market segments in this market;
- the market segments to focus on;
- the needs of each market segment;
- market awareness and attitude to the information service;
- how potential customers learn about the information service and make decisions to use its services;
- customer satisfaction levels;
- the major strengths and weaknesses in staff, resources, programmes, facilities, etc.;
- opportunities to increase resources;
- key customer groups of the information service;
- key customer needs to be satisfied;
- main competitors; and
- the competitive benefits that can be offered to the target market through market positioning.

A SWOT analysis can also be used during this process to identify new opportunities that are in line with the objectives of the service. Other analysis tools that can be used to gather information include needs analysis, image analysis and customer satisfaction studies.

Proposed opportunities for information services are then analysed by considering market segmentations, the size and growth rate of the customer base, consumer behaviours, possible exit barriers and some forms of measuring and forecasting the attractiveness and effectiveness of the services in the future.

A new service or market opportunity is attractive if:

- it is of good size – that is, if many people use the service;
- it has the potential for growth;
- it is cost-beneficial on both a short-term and long-term basis;
- there are adequate financial and technical resources and a competent and trained staff;
- there are low exit barriers; and
- the service is in line with the information service's mission and objectives.

It may be the case that an opportunity satisfies most of these criteria, but that it has to remain dormant until financial or technical resources can be found or staff trained to provide the service.

The target market, that is the particular group(s) to which the service is aimed, needs to be identified. This is followed by a process of competitive positioning. This involves researching competitors' services and the needs of the target market in order to find a market or market niche. This determines whether the information service is in a strong or weak competitive position, whether the programme is attractive and whether there is high or low alternative coverage.

Once a target market has been defined and the service's competitive position determined, a market strategy is devised. This includes the development of the marketing goals and objectives. Goals may include such aspects as increasing the quality of the information service, its participation level or its satisfaction level. Funds need to be allocated to the marketing budget. New services that are designed to meet new markets should have the important values explained to staff before commencing the service.

Finally the market strategy is implemented and controls put into place to ensure that the information service's resources, service and objectives are correctly matched to the right markets.

Marketing mix

A marketing mix is a key part of the marketing strategy. A four-factor classification called 'the four Ps' has been defined by McCarthy (1971, p. 44). These are product, price, place and promotion.

Product refers to the information services and involves the special features offered, the way they are offered and level of service provision. Price relates to whether a direct fee is attached to the service such as a debit to the cost centre or payment for an on-line search or a photocopy. There may be price modifiers such as discounts or community service obligation allowances. Place concerns the logistical provision of the service and locations of service points. These generally correspond to the work units. Promotion involves the advertising and publicity campaigns, the message communicated, the media used and the timing of such. Promotional campaigns should be realistic and affordable.

Markets and market segmentation

A market is a set of individuals, groups or institutions that are actual or potential customers for a product or service. Markets can be divided into groups with specific requirements; this is called market segmentation. In information services there are need markets, geographic markets, product markets and demographic markets.

Need markets

Need markets consist of individuals or groups who have a common need. Information services cannot satisfy all their customers' demands just by providing one type of service. Their customers have diverse needs for electronic mail and facsimile services, information in varying formats (such as electronic and printed information), for personal computer support and records management services, for housebound services or story-telling sessions. Yet there are certain groups within the information service's community who have similar needs. For example, within a public library the need market for a homebound service would be the frail, the physically impaired, those people who are convalescing at home after surgery or hospitalization, young and old patients with terminal illnesses who are living at home, elderly people who can no longer drive and for whom public transport to the information service is inaccessible, and others who for some reason cannot regularly visit the library.

Officers working in a government department would need a records management service, personal computer and software support, an information dissemination service, and access to electronic mail and other on-line information services such as the Internet.

Geographic markets

Geographic markets consist of those customers who live or work in a region or a particular geographic locality. Geographic markets determine the type, size and setting of the information service together with the operating hours and services offered. For example, residents living in outer metropolitan areas and who spend long hours commuting may require the public library to be open later hours than those operating in the inner city. However, the dense population of inner cities may place more intensive demands on the service than those of outer metropolitan areas or semi-rural localities. Rural areas having isolated pockets of population may be best served by a mobile library service.

Information services serving organizations that have branch offices situated in regions or states need to consider the specific requirements of each location and develop their services accordingly.

Each market has its own particular characteristics. Using the public library example, the need market for a housebound service differs from that of a geographical market requiring a mobile library service. Whilst each is served by a 'library on wheels' the library services offered to the housebound differ from those offered to people using the mobile library. This is in terms of the time, length and frequency of visits, and choice and format of material.

Product markets

Product markets are determined by a demand for a particular product or service. A product market may be those people who have a demand for access to electronic information services from their desktop. This market could be further segmented according to specific scientific or technical information requirements.

Demographic markets

Demographic market segmentation is one of the most popular methods of distinguishing market segments in information services. These market segments have clear market needs, and information relating to these markets is usually readily available. Demographic markets may be identified by age, nationality, or physical needs such as the physically impaired who may need specialized equipment such as large computer screens or ramp access.

Markets that can be subdivided into identifiable segments or subsets may require individual marketing strategies. The information services manager should be aware of their:

- market segments' current and potential future size;
- main customers and potential customers, and their locations;
- customers' and potential customers' current levels of awareness of the range and levels of existing services;
- customers' needs and motives for using the services; and
- customers' concepts of competitive alternatives to the information service.

The strength in the market segmentation approach lies in the fact that it is based upon the customer rather than the product or service. The customer is assured of a service that satisfies as far as possible their individual needs rather than a mass-market offering. This is in line with the societal marketing concept.

Individual needs cannot be taken to the stage of a one-off situation, since this would not be cost-effective. Instead, the information services manager must search for broad classes of customers who have similar requirements. This is called a customer's product (service) requirement.

Such an example can be seen in a weekly story-telling session for preschool children in a public library. The session may satisfy many needs, some of which may not have been foremost in the library staffs' minds when they proposed the service, but which exist all the same. Examples of such needs may be: a need for an only child to socialize with others of its age group; a need to provide the beginnings of a lifelong association with information and the library; a need to begin the learning process through books and stories; a need for a baby sitting service; a need for the parent to get out of the house and talk to other parents; a need to promote the library to children of all ages; or a need for recreational activities. The story-telling session satisfies up to seven diverse needs of parents, library staff and preschool children.

Market targeting

Market targeting involves the evaluation, selection and concentration on specific market segments. There are three strategies for doing this: undifferentiated marketing, differentiated marketing and concentrated marketing.

Undifferentiated marketing

In undifferentiated or mass marketing the information service focuses upon the needs that are common to all people. Services are provided that appeal to the broadest number of customers. In concentrating on these basic services, the information service attempts to achieve excellence. Undifferentiated marketing is often pursued in times of financial constraint, when additional or specialist services are curtailed and basic services consolidated. Costs associated with providing specialist services can be saved, but whether this is an effective strategy is debatable.

Differentiated marketing

In differentiated marketing an information service decides to operate in at least two segments of a market and designs separate services and programmes for each. In a large corporate organization this could mean differentiating services to research and development staff and to senior management. A variety of programmes to suit the diverse needs of different information service customers are provided. The aim of this approach is to provide services catering for specific needs that strengthen the information service's overall identity within the organization and increase its use. However there are costs associated with this. Specialist services may involve additional staff with specialized skills and expertise, administrative and promotional costs.

In differentiated marketing some information services may be heavily promoted, these are called saturate segments. Others may be designated as hold segments. In this case services are offered but not heavily promoted.

Concentrated marketing

Concentrated or niche marketing occurs when the information service concentrates upon a small number of submarkets. Instead of spreading itself thinly, being all things to all people, the information service provides in-depth services in a few areas, serving a small percentage of the market-place. It purposefully determines a small number of target markets and sets out to concentrate on these. As a result, it achieves a strong market position through its detailed knowledge of its market segments' needs and its subsequent reputation.

For example, the information service may consciously decide to concentrate on one suite of office automation products in order to provide a quality service. This choice would be written into the information service's objectives. Organizational members would remain free to exercise their own choice in the suite of office automation products, but only the chosen package would be supported by the help desk. Everyone would be aware of this and would make an informed assessment of the consequences of choosing any other office automation package. Information services staff would either be recruited or trained to provide high-level, knowledgeable support of the chosen package. The primary duties of the information service staff on the help desk would be to support the chosen package and promote its functionality.

A concentrated marketing strategy may also be used when establishing a new information service. After determining several target markets and having regard for financial resources and the level of staff expertise, it may be considered prudent to concentrate upon providing a few market segments with a quality service, rather than to spread the market base too thinly.

The establishment of a new information service requires procedures to be put into place, staff to be trained, policies and routines to be established. These initial activities are time- and energy-consuming. If too wide a market base is selected in the initial establishment phase, it may be difficult to provide a high quality service. As an initial favourable impression is critical to the future of the information service, quality rather than quantity becomes a factor in service provision. Later, when all operations are running smoothly, a decision can be made on whether to broaden the service or product base. This called a segment 'roll out' strategy.

No single strategy is superior to the others. In adopting a particular target strategy the information services manager must base their decision upon the type of information service; the financial, technical, human and information resources available; the availability of competitive services; customer and potential customer needs, and the types of services having the potential to be offered. The information services manager must then decide which strategy is the most attractive given the constraints and opportunities of the information service's external environment, and its own strengths and weaknesses.

Image analysis

This section deals with image analysis in the context of determining service provision under the marketing concept. The management of the corporate image is covered in Chapter 26.

Image studies measure the perceptions that people hold about an information service. They determine what people respond to, which may not necessarily be the same as what the information service really does. All information services need a positive image in order to attract funds, potential staff members and customers. However, the image differs according to particular groups, their main interests and the way in which they perceive the services offered. Young adults have a totally different perception of a public library than an elderly person or a preschool child. Senior management may view an information service according to its return on investment, which is often different to the customers who are the recipients of the services.

The information service's customers and stakeholders can have multiple attitudes, some of which will be positive, whilst others may be negative. Different sectors of the information service's community or target audience should be surveyed in order to determine its image and profile in terms of service provision. This includes surveying stakeholders, customers and non-customers regarding their attitudes and awareness, interest and desires in an effort to ascertain a spectrum of responses within each dimension. This can be done by asking two simple questions for which multiple choice answers are provided on a rating scale (see Figure 34.1).

The survey questionnaire should indicate the sector of the target audience to which the respondee belongs. This information should be obtained by the person conducting the survey questionnaire. A code can then be applied to identify the group's responses for follow-up activities.

The responses are then plotted on a matrix graph (see Figure 34.2).

Quadrants B, C and D in Figure 34.2 indicate the need for some development in the information service's image about the services offered. To do this, the information services manager needs to have a mental picture of what the image should be. This should be based on the vision and strategic direction of the information service. This is then compared with the existing image of the information service. The image gap is the difference between the desired and actual images.

It may not be necessary to target all sectors of the target audience in trying to change the information service's image. The matrix graph identifies both those groups most in need of targeting and those groups for whom the information service's current image should be maintained in its present position. Changes in image may be to make the information service appear to be more efficient or relevant to corporate objectives, or more responsive to certain customer sectors. Alternatively, a sector of the customer base may have unrealistic expectations of the types of services that should be offered. In which case this sector requires re-educating about the services that can be realistically delivered within the operational and budgetary framework. The reality–expectations gap is the difference between the level of an adequate service and the level of a service to meet real expectations.

Image Analysis Survey

1 Community sector _____ (staff use only)
   (Please assign the appropriate identification code in box provided)

2 How familiar are you with the information service?
   (Please tick the most appropriate response)

   — Never heard of it

   — Heard of it

   — Know a little about it

   — Know a fair amount about it

   — Know a great deal about it

3 How favourable is your attitude to the services it provides?
   (Please tick the most appropriate response)

   — Very unfavourable

   — Somewhat unfavourable

   — Indifferent

   — Somewhat favourable

   — Very favourable

Thank you for your participation in the survey.

Figure 34.1   Proposed survey questionnaire to ascertain an information service's image

Customer satisfaction studies

Customer satisfaction studies provide an indication as to whether existing information service customers are satisfied with current services. Customer satisfaction studies are a marketing tool as they can be used as an argument to maintain existing funding levels if the results are good, or for increased funding if the results show that customer expectations for services are higher than those provided.

The results of the customer satisfaction study can be plotted onto the

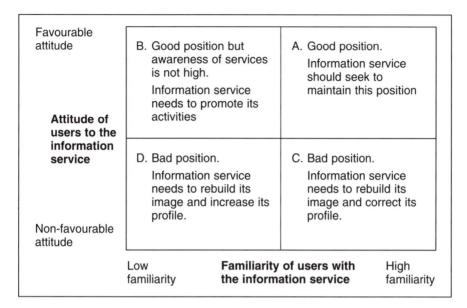

Figure 34.2   Matrix graph of information service's image

matrix graph according to their performance rating and importance (see Figure 34.3). This will determine which services need improved performance and which services should be discontinued.

Services falling in quadrant A are important services that are being well provided. Services in quadrant B have possibly too high a performance level for their importance. The information service staff can afford to pay less attention to these services. Services that fall into quadrant C have only a low priority and performance is deemed as low. These services can be the first to be abandoned if resources are few, in order to concentrate on those services in quadrant D. Quadrant D includes those services that are acknowledged to be important, but where the information service is performing badly. Information service staff need to concentrate their attention and resources in this area.

Exchange system analysis

Underlying the marketing concept is a system of exchange. The potential for exchange exists when two or more parties possess something of value that may be exchanged. This may be goods, services, money, a favour or goodwill. The simplest exchange is between two parties, and such an exchange may be seen in a public library where a customer exchanges

Extremely important	D. Service is important but level of performance is low. Information service needs to concentrate on services in this area.	A. Level of performance is high, service is important. Information service should maintain current position.
Importance of service Slightly important	C. Low priority, service fair. Service may be abandoned	B. Service is less important, level of performance is high – possible overkill. Information service can afford to pay less attention to these services
	Fair performance	**Level of performance in offering the service** Excellent performance

Figure 34.3   Matrix graph to determine level of performance and importance of services

money for a photocopy of a page from a reference book. Government departments may provide information services through kiosk services in exchange for monies received from rates and taxes. There is no direct exchange between the customer and the department as the rates or taxes that fund the service are paid to the department authorized to collect the revenue. Information service staff also exchange their knowledge and expertise, time and energy in return for salaries and other fringe benefits from the employing organization.

Multiple-party exchanges occur when three or more parties are involved in exchanging something of value. In the case of the story-telling session example in the public library, the parents require that their children meet others of the same age, engage in a learning process and be happy. They are exchanging their time for social and educational processes for their children. They also require that the library staff are friendly and that the library is clean and safe. In this instance they are exchanging monies paid in rates for services and safety. The children who attend want to have fun, perhaps learn something and therefore obtain their parent's approval. They are exchanging their time for their parent's love and acceptance. The public library, in holding the story-telling sessions, wishes to promote the library as a fun place and as a lifelong institution for information and self-education. The story-telling session must meet all of these needs in the exchange process.

Competitive portfolio analysis

The product life cycle and the product portfolio matrix are used to make strategic marketing decisions in commerce and industry as part of the competitive portfolio analysis. Whilst they are based upon products rather than services, their general concepts are useful for information services managers as they help to distinguish which services have potential for growth. Growth or decline in services affect budget allocations, technology, staff levels and the future direction of the information service.

The product life cycle is based upon the concept that products or services, like living things, have a finite life span. The basic proposition is that market growth and competitive characteristics change from one stage of the product life cycle to the next (see Figure 34.4). These changes have important implications for marketing and planning strategies.

The introductory stage of an information service is usually marked by slow growth in use, heavy advertising and promotion. Staff must develop the service to suit customer needs, and much enthusiasm is needed. In the growth stage, there is an increase in use of the service that is still promoted quite heavily, and staff may have to fine tune the service further to suit customer needs. The maturity stage is characterized by such services being seen as standard, a slowdown in growth and the spending of less time and money on advertising. In the decline stage, fewer people use the service, it is often superseded by other more appropriate services or deemed to have a low priority and plans are made to terminate it. Information technology

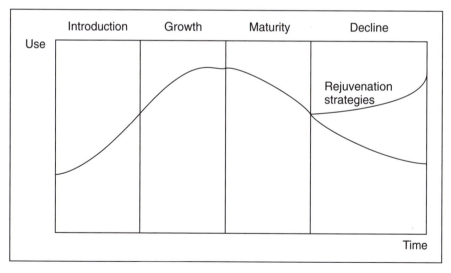

Figure 34.4   Product life cycle

shortens the life cycles of information services with many services quickly becoming obsolete as new applications emerge.

The life cycle concept has some drawbacks. Sometimes the stages in the life cycle cannot be clearly separated and may be difficult to distinguish. For information services, the maturity stage is the dominant stage and most services fall into this category. It is often difficult to predict when the next stage of the life cycle begins or how long it will last. Rejuvenation strategies may be used to stop the decline in the life cycle.

Whilst the product life cycle focuses upon growth dynamics, the product portfolio matrix emphasizes market growth (attractiveness) and relative competitive position (strength) of products or services. As information services become more competitive the significance of the product (service) portfolio matrix increases.

The most widely used product portfolio matrix is that developed by the Boston Consulting Group. Known as the BCG portfolio matrix, it classifies each business unit according to its potential for growth and its relative competitive position. In the information service, work units may be substituted for business units. The BCG matrix classifies products, services or markets into four groups and uses circles, with areas proportional to the sales volumes for each, to give a visual image of an organization's current products. In information services, usage rates could be substituted for sales volumes to provide an image of its current services (see Figure 34.5).

According to the BCG matrix:

- 'Star' products have a high market share and high growth (stars) and are roughly self-sufficient in terms of cash flow. They have the highest profit margins. In terms of the information service, these are the important information products or services and should be expanded if possible. Eventually the 'stars' become 'cash cows' as they reach the maturity stage of the product or service.
- 'Cash cows' are valuable assets; they have a high share in a low growth market. As products they generate more cash than is necessary to maintain a market position and should be protected at all costs. In information services, 'cash cows' would equate to the established products or services that have a high rate of usage and little competition. 'Cash cow' services maintain the value image of the information service and help to ensure its continued success and survival.
- 'Dogs' are products with low market share and slow growth. Their outlook for the future is usually bleak. 'Dogs' in information services comprise the information products or services that are declining in use and can often be superseded by new and better services. Alternatively, they are services that have failed to reach their potential.
- 'Problem children' are products with high growth potential but low

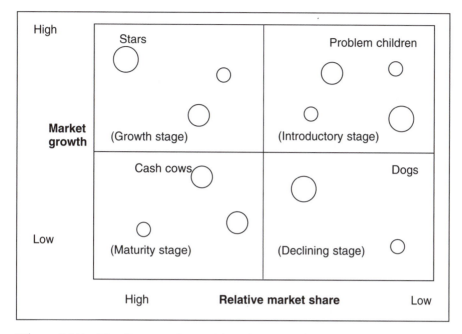

Figure 34.5   The Boston Consulting Group portfolio matrix

market share. They require large net cash outflows if their market share is to be maintained or increased. If successful these products become the new 'stars' that in the future become 'cash cows'. If unsuccessful they become 'dogs'. In information services, 'problem children' usually equate to new services that require fairly large funding allocations for their establishment and promotion. They may also be services that do not perform well. There can be a variety of reasons for their poor performance; they may have been inadequately managed, or have had inappropriate marketing strategies applied to them.

The information service can determine its information products' and services' use and standing by displaying these on the product portfolio matrix. They should also be linked to the product or service life cycle and its associated marketing and planning strategies.

The BCG matrix is useful in that it recognizes that products and services have differential growth rates and emphasizes the relative share of market held by products and services in the same stage of growth.

Use of the competitive portfolio analysis in managing library stock

In a multi-branch library system the concept of the product life cycle can be used to extend the life of the stock by identifying the point in time when stock can be transferred to another branch library. Certain types of stock are either more popular or are used more than others. Fiction books, for example, have different life cycles. Some authors' works are more popular than others and their books quickly become worn out, whilst others have a limited market appeal and become read out.

A book with a limited market appeal has a rising issue rate when it is first introduced into the library. At some point the issue rate begins to fall as the product (book) passes through the maturity stage into the decline stage. If, at this stage, the book is transferred to another library it will be subject to a rejuvenation strategy. A new audience (customers) will be found for the book and the product life cycle begins again, prolonging the life and value of the book.

The BCG portfolio matrix is an important tool for assessing the quality of stock in a library or information centre. 'Best sellers' are 'stars'. They become 'cash cows' when their original price has been justified by their large issue rate, by their use in strategic decision-making or when their presence creates an image of the library or information centre having good, current stock. 'Dogs' are stock that no one wants. All libraries and information centres have some 'dogs'; the result of a mistake in stock selection, when the market for an item has been misjudged, or the blurb was misleading. 'Problem children' comprise the stock that contains valuable information but is often overlooked by customers or library staff because of format, appearance or lack of knowledge of the contents. 'Problem children' stock can become 'stars' through education of library staff or promotions that draw attention to such stock in interesting ways. If left alone they become 'dogs'.

Diversification and service rejuvenation

There comes a time when it appears that an information service can no longer expand its services in its basic market. Growth has stabilized through the market being saturated and, if growth is to continue, new services or markets must be sought. The information service has four options at this stage:

- to remain in a stable situation and to accept the *status quo;*
- to look for new markets;
- to diversify into new areas; or

● to provide new services to its existing markets.

Changes in consumer behaviour, competitor behaviour, technology or government policies may also influence the information service to adopt one of the above strategies.

Rejuvenation strategies can overcome some lack of use of services, or, stop the decline in the product life cycle. Lazer et al. (1984, pp. 21–8) have identified four rejuvenation strategies. These are recapturing, redesigning, refocusing or recasting services.

Recapturing strategies

Recapturing strategies attempt to revive the old market. They concentrate on previous and existing customers without modifying the service. Displays and promotions that focus attention on existing services are recapturing strategies.

Redesigning strategies

Redesign involves marketing a modified version of a service that has been declining or has previously been abandoned. The original reasons for customer rejection may no longer prevail and it may be possible to rekindle interest among present customers. In information services and the publishing industry, redesign often occurs when particular authors go out of fashion but are brought back into vogue in new formats such as glossy paperbacks. Television and the film industry often act as the catalyst for redesign of a library's stock, creating demands for authors who have been unpopular for some time.

Recasting strategies

Recasting strategies are used in marketing a modified service to new customers. The object is to capitalize on the organization's strengths and experience, although some adjustments to the service and market have to take place. An example of a recasting strategy in a public library may be where the population has aged; and story-telling sessions, once aimed at preschoolers have taken on a slightly different format and are now used as bibliotherapy with the aged.

Refocusing strategies

Refocusing involves marketing an abandoned or declining service to new customers. Such an example may be marketing an archive or local history collection, which may have been established through legislation or demand for school project material, to the local newspaper for a series of articles on local identities or places of interest. Such a strategy may result in greater usage of the service by the general public.

The information service's decision to rejuvenate or diversify services should be based upon its resource requirements and capabilities. The potential of the rejuvenated or diversified services to contribute to the profile and value of the information service, the cost involved and predicted extended life span on a cost-benefit basis must also be assessed. In selecting the most appropriate strategy, the extent of service modification and degree of marketing effort needed to stimulate demand need to be evaluated.

Marketing is often mistaken for promotion. Marketing includes consideration of promotion strategies but it is more closely aligned to strategic planning. Marketing strategies ensure viable market positions and programmes that meet the objectives of the parent organization, customer information needs and ultimately, contribute to the success of the information service.

References

Kotler, P., FitzRoy, P. and Shaw, R. (1980), *Australian Marketing Management*, Sydney: Prentice Hall.

Lazer, W., Luqmani, M. and Quraeshi, Z. (1984), 'Product rejuvenation strategies' *Business Horizons*, November–December, 21–8.

McCarthy, E. J. (1971), *Basic Marketing: a Managerial Approach*, 4th edn, Homewood, IL: Irwin.

35 Quality control

Introduction

The provision of consistently higher quality services or products than those of competitors is an excellent way to differentiate an organization's services. To achieve this, senior management must show a commitment to quality by making it a self sustaining way of life within the organization.

Like beauty, quality is in the eye of the beholder. Customer expectations and perceptions of quality often vary as it is an individual judgement. There are also cultural differences in customer expectations and perceptions of quality, that impact on the service delivery. Gaps in service delivery can influence the perception of the level of quality offered in products or services. Customers also judge quality according to certain determinants of service quality.

An important component of quality is to get the steps in the value chain, right first time every time. If any part of the process falls down, then the remaining processes in the value chain will build upon an inferior product or service. Differentiation at the end of the value chain can be what distinguishes one product or service from another in terms of quality.

Roles and responsibilities

All employees should be given responsibility for quality and be made accountable for the quality of their individual output. They should be aware of the products and services offered by the information service and its parent organization, and make an effort to understand their customers' needs. Individuals should be given training and skills development opportunities in quality management, measuring customer satisfaction and in any additional areas that may be needed to improve the service they deliver.

The information services manager needs to target customer requirements in terms of quality information products and services and set realistic expectations of services at levels that can be achieved. In the drive for efficiency, there is often the temptation to put quality specifications in second place. This is false economy.

Quality control should be a regular item on the agenda of senior management meetings. This serves two purposes. It sends a message about the level of senior management commitment to quality and the value that it places on quality goods and services. It also allows senior management to review progress and evaluate performance. The agenda items should cover customer and stakeholder relationships, a review of quality initiatives and programmes, identification of service delivery gaps and the strategies to close these, and a general evaluation of the current levels of service delivery.

Customer expectations and perceptions

Customer expectations and perceptions of quality often vary as this is based upon an individual judgement. Quality control is an internal process management issue, being an important part of the value chain. However, it is judged externally by customers and stakeholders who only see the outputs or outcomes of the internal processes. For example, quality is judged in terms of:

- timeliness of service delivery – in responding to requests for information, files, help desk queries or the ordering and supply of new equipment;
- a well-designed product or service – that fits the purpose for use and is superior to others in the market-place;
- a product that does not break down and is easy to use;
- value for money; and
- a service delivered by courteous, knowledgeable and accurate staff.

Expectations and perceptions of quality can also differ from a cultural viewpoint. For example:

- in Germany, the dominant element of quality is an acceptance of standards;
- in Japan, quality is measured through the pursuit of perfection;
- in France, quality is viewed as luxury;
- in the United States of America, quality means 'it works'; and

- in Australia, quality is found in the relationship between the customer and the provider of the product or service.

As a consequence, the delivery of information services may subtly differ between countries in the quest for a quality service or information product.

Service quality

Parasuraman et al. (1985) have developed a service-quality model that highlights the main requirements for delivering the expected service quality. The model identifies five gaps that cause unsuccessful service delivery:

- the gap between customer expectation and management perception. Management does not always perceive correctly what customers want or how customers judge the service components;
- the gap between management perception and service quality specification. Management might not set quality standards or very clear ones. They might be clear but unrealistic, or they might be clear and realistic but management might not be fully committed to enforcing this quality level;
- the gap between service quality specifications and service delivery. This includes factors such as poorly trained or under resourced staff, low morale, equipment breakdown or drives for efficiency at the expense of customer satisfaction;
- the gap between service delivery and external communications. Customer expectations may be driven to a higher level of service delivery through advertising or promotions than can actually be delivered;
- the gap between the perceived service and expected service. This gap results when one or more of the previous gaps occurs.

Parasuraman et al. (1985) have also developed a list of the main determinants of service quality. These include:

- access – the service is easy to obtain in convenient locations at convenient times with little waiting;
- communication – the service is described accurately in the customer's language;
- competence – the employees possess the required skill and knowledge;
- courtesy – the employees are friendly, respectful and considerate;
- credibility – the organization and employees are trustworthy and have the customer's best interests at heart;
- reliability – the service is performed with consistency and accuracy;

- responsiveness – the employees respond quickly and creatively to customers' requests and problems;
- security – the service is free from danger, risk or doubt;
- tangibles – the service tangibles correctly project the service quality; and
- understanding or knowing the customer – the employees make an effort to understand the customer's needs and provide individual attention.

This list of determinants of service quality is pertinent to information services and products.

Quality as part of the value chain

An important component of quality is to get the steps in the product or service development process, the value chain, right first time every time.

The value chain is the chain of activities through which the organization transforms its input resources such as raw data or incoming correspondence into products and services that it delivers to customers. Each of the activities in the chain should build upon the value of the previous activity and contribute to the value of the final product.

If any part of the process falls down, then the remaining processes in the value chain will build upon an inferior product or service. This is wasteful of resources and time. It is the quality of the total service that matters – the end product or service, and the process that creates it.

The value chain not only leads to process improvement, it can also differentiate the product by offering an additional service (see Figure 35.1). For example, raw data can be identified, captured and merged or manipulated in a series of steps to create a value-added information product. The product is marketed and can be further differentiated by offering it in either a value-added form, for example a choice of formats, or by providing consultancy expertise to assist the customer to make the most out of the value-added information product for their purposes. The area of differentiation can be what distinguishes the product from another in terms of quality of service.

Continuous improvement

Continuous improvement, *kaizen* in Japanese, is a crucial part of both quality-based and time-based competitive strategies. The idea being that organizations can continuously improve the cost, quality and timeliness of their output by making small, incremental process improvements.

The important feature is that the improvement is built into the

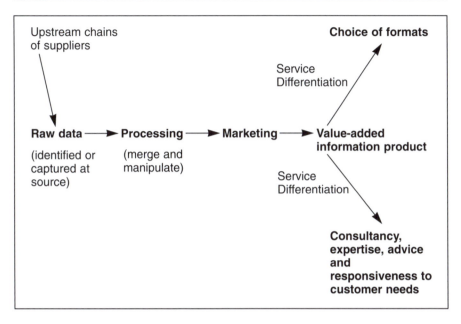

Figure 35.1   The value chain for a value-added information product

organization as a continuous process to which all staff have a sense of ownership and pride in improvements, rather than it being subject to a one-off improvement strategy that is initiated through a consultant.

Quality can be used to distinguish the information service from its competitors. This service-related strategy is dependent upon the information services manager being aware of customer expectations and perceptions of quality in order to tailor the services to meet their customers' quality values.

Reference

Parasuraman, A., Zeithaml, V. A. and Berry, Leonard L. (1985), 'A conceptual model of service quality and its implications for future research', *Journal of Marketing*, Fall, 41–50.

36 Customer focus

Introduction

The bottom line of customer focus is valuing the customer. This can be reflected in a management approach that fosters a culture that is service-driven and oriented to customer needs. The delivery of a service or product to the customer is only the beginning of the relationship between the information service and the customer. The service backup that supports the continual use of the service or product is of equal importance.

Technology can be used to enhance the relationship between the information service and the customer. It can also be used to provide competitive advantage in locking the customer into using the parent organization's products or services by offering the use of value-added services.

The customer approach to management

The customer approach to management is service-driven and quality oriented. It gives high priority to the efficiency and effectiveness of product and service delivery to the customers. Customers of information services can vary. For example, the customers of a public library will be a cross section of people who vary in age, interests and lifestyle. They may include local business entities, school children and tertiary students, the aged and those whose primary language is not English. The staff and elected members of the local authority may also be customers of the library.

The primary customers of an information service in a small entrepreneurial organization will be the management and employees of the organization. The information service will manage the information systems, keep the corporate records and deliver research services in such a manner so as to assist the management and employees maintain the parent organization's competitiveness. A secondary role may be to disseminate information about the organization's products to the external customers of the entrepreneurial organization.

The customer approach considers how the customers perceive the quality of the products and services and the total performance of the organization. This is instead of overemphasizing internal efficiencies, economies of scale and cost reduction. A competitive edge and profitability are achieved through closer customer relationships and needs rather than standardized products or services in an effort to save money. Close customer relationships can be built up by understanding the information needs of customers and the manner in which they require these needs to be satisfied.

Loyalty is a keystone to a successful customer approach. So is customer retention. There should be an openness and willingness to communicate with customers; to identify and resolve problems in service delivery and to ensure that the information products and services meet their needs. The organizational culture should reflect the customer approach. This should be reinforced in the values of senior management.

If information services fail in their ability to retain customers, then the parent organization may suffer in addition to the information service. If, for example, a special library or information service fails to provide the necessary customer service to the research and product development unit of the parent organization in terms of timeliness, level or appropriateness of information then the members of the unit may look elsewhere for their information needs. Not only will this be costly to the organization in terms of time and duplication of effort, the organization risks losing its intellectual property through the possible identification of the research being undertaken during the attempt to obtain the necessary information elsewhere.

The human resource, information and technology strategies should support customer services. The right person for the job should be selected. High-level performance in customer services should be recognized and mechanisms put in place to reward and reinforce customer-oriented behaviours. There should also be explicit budget provision for customer service initiatives.

Customer 'Rs'

An important strategy to achieve a customer focus is to concentrate on the 'Rs'.

Retention

The information service must develop services and strategies that keep the right customers from defecting to competitive services, or in ceasing to use services. Customers are retained through adding value and quality to standard products and services. An example may be that instead of seeing the Internet and other on-line public access systems as a competitor, advice services are provided on the best pages to access.

Requirements

Different customers have different requirements and the important part of service delivery is to tailor services to meet customer requirements. Information services should become astute in analysing both customer requirements and their trade-offs between preferences.

Refined segmentation

All information services have limited resources. By understanding customer preferences, a more refined segmentation can be achieved. This allows each segment to be serviced in a cost-effective manner that is valued by the customer.

Reach

Different customers need to be reached in different ways. These may be reflected by offering different mechanisms for the delivery or dissemination of information.

Response

Customers will also respond differently to different messages about services and products. Messages should be tailored and disseminated in a manner that communicates the right message to the right customer group.

Relationship

The relationship between the customer and the organization delivering the service is very important. Value can be added through having knowledgeable staff who make an effort to understand their customers' needs and provide individual attention.

Receptiveness

To build a true commitment to customer service, the information service must be receptive to feedback from customers and stakeholders about its services and product. A culture should be fostered that regards complaints as valuable information about systems failures rather than an annoyance. Formal suggestions and complaint procedures should be in place. The information service should also act on the feedback to improve quality or overcome shortfalls.

Regular consultation

There should be regular consultation with customers to establish their service and product requirements. This can be achieved through focus groups, surveys, interviews and forums.

Review

The customer approach to management requires a formal planning cycle of review, design, implement and improve systems. Complaints and service difficulties should be regularly analysed to identify recurrent problems.

Customer service backup

The delivery of a service or product to the customer is only the beginning of the relationship between the information service and the customer. What is of equal importance is the service backup that supports the continual use of the service or product. The customer's level of satisfaction or dissatisfaction with the quality and efficiency of the service backup will influence their perception of the product or service. Service backup can be found in the following areas.

Delivery or installation

Services and products should be delivered or installed at the customer's convenience. The delivery should be fast, on time and efficiently handled. For example, the opening hours for libraries and information services should be decided with customer convenience in mind, requests for paper records files to be brought up should be executed promptly, and an upgrade of software should be installed quickly at a time when there is not an urgent deadline being met by the operator of the personal computer.

After sales service

Follow-up should be made with the customer regarding the service or product. After sales service should be efficient and attentive. For example, public library staff may enquire about the success of material selected for a school project when a child returns the material; special library staff may follow up on a request for information to ensure that no additional information is required, or the help desk may ring a customer to ensure that no more trouble is being experienced with a personal computer.

Complaints handling

Complaints should be acted upon immediately and managed in a positive manner. Complaints should also be logged so that trends can be identified and rectified before there is an adverse effect on the product or service. This is particularly important when dealing with software.

Warranty repairs

Repairs under warranty should be efficiently handled.

Account management

Invoicing of accounts should be efficient and accurate. Account payment processes should be designed to be convenient for the customer. The account management aspect of service delivery is potentially the highest risk area in customer service. Inaccurate accounting systems that result in goods or services not being charged, being undercharged or in outstanding payments have a negative impact upon the cash flow and profitability of the organization. Conversely, the continued overcharging for products or services will sour customer relationships with the organization.

Customer service charters

Customer service charters articulate the organization's commitment to the customer. They contain statements on:

- who are the customers;
- the value that the organization places on the customer – 'the customer is the most important person to the information service';
- the relationship between the customer and the information service and how they may be expected to be treated – 'we will respect our customers'

requirements of confidentiality and privacy';
- the level of service that can be expected – 'we will respond to enquiries within ten minutes of receipt of the call';
- the value placed on employees and their roles in customer service – 'we respect our employees and encourage them to make creative suggestions that will further improve our service'.

Using technology for customer retention

Successful organizations retain customers through the strategic use of information-related technology. For example, they can develop and maintain their competitive advantage by placing terminals in customer sites or at convenient distribution points and linking these to their systems. These can be used for ordering goods, for providing access to library catalogues from remote sites or for locating file records.

This has advantages for the customer. The speed by which customer transactions are processed increases. Overheads may also be lessened, and management information about service demands can be collated and provided. Alternatively, in the case of a supply system, customers no longer need to keep a full inventory to support a 'just in case' scenario.

A close relationship is built with customers by offering them the technology, information on their own business activities, a saving of time and money, and more streamlined and tailored processes to fit their needs. A win-win situation develops as the organization is able to capture a profile of the customer's transaction requirements which increases their understanding of the customer's needs. This gives them the competitive edge over other firms in the market-place as the organization intimately knows the customer's business and can assist where needed.

Where the customers are external to the organization, there are additional competitive benefits. The customer's systems are increasingly built around and interact with the terminal or other technology application. The aim is to make the dependence on the service so great that they are unlikely to obtain terminals from competitors. A further strategy for maintaining the customer's allegiance to the organization is to make the exit costs from the terminal arrangement high enough to discourage the customer from moving to another competitor's terminal.

A further step is for the organization to offer value-added services such as extending the on-line access to decision support systems. The manner in which the decision support systems are set up also provides competitive advantage. For example, they can be designed so that access to the organization's product or service information is made easier than those of the other competitors, or, the information and function screens relating to the organization's products and services are the first to be presented.

The customer focus strategy is based around a knowledge of and attention to detail when dealing with the nine customer 'Rs' of retention, requirements, refined segmentation, reach, response, relationship, receptiveness, regular consultation and review.

37 Outsourcing service delivery

Introduction

Outsourcing is the contracting out of services to a third party (the vendor or service provider) to manage on the organization's behalf. In most instances it involves the transfer of ownership and responsibility for assets (including the people) from the organization (the customer) to the vendor.

Traditionally, the decision to outsource is based on the vendor's ability to offer economies of scale or specialization at a higher level than that achievable by the organization itself. An emerging concept is that of partnering in which both parties leverage their competitive advantage in the market-place through each other.

The outsourcing of information-related technology has increased dramatically over the last few years as organizations restructure and concentrate their activities on their core business. Other drivers for outsourcing are to reduce overhead costs, improve service levels, to gain access to know-how, or to take advantage of new technology directions.

Scope of outsourcing

Outsourcing can be applied to any service; from window cleaning to security services. Applied to information-related technology, outsourcing includes information technology, data centre and telecommunications network maintenance and facilities management, personal computer support, infrastructure development, systems maintenance, systems integration, systems development and design, training, end-user support, and service delivery, such as the delivery of value-added information products.

Within the functions of archives, records management and library services the following could also be considered for outsourcing:

- storage and retrieval of records and archives;
- delivery of specialized information services; and
- processing of journals and other stock (including accessioning, assigning the bibliographic description, binding, attachment of bar codes and security tags).

The concept of outsourcing is also being applied to business strategy and change management, business and process re-engineering.

The extent of outsourcing varies and includes:

- shared services – where customers pay monthly fees for certain transactions or services. These are provided for, or run on the service provider or vendor's systems, alongside transactions of other customers;
- remote computing – where a specific part of the vendor's installation is reserved for a particular customer;
- total outsourcing – where the service provider takes over all, or nearly all of the services and equipment.

Whilst the provision of information services can be outsourced, accountability for service levels and strategic decisions relating to service provision cannot. The role of the information services manager changes from being a provider of services to a purchaser of services. The fundamental responsibility and accountability for the quality of the end product or service still rests with management.

Outsourcing is a relatively long-term proposition. The length of the contract is usually between three and ten years. This is for two reasons:

- the service provider needs to be assured of a long-term contract in order to achieve a return on investment for the infrastructure they provide; and
- the initial expenses of handover and change mean that the cost savings for the organization are not realized until the third or fourth year of the contract.

Pros and cons of outsourcing

Reasons for outsourcing

Outsourcing is a viable consideration where the goods or services can be provided more efficiently or effectively by an experienced third party. The outsourcing of information-related technologies or the storage of corporate records to a specialist in the field allows the information service and its parent organization to refocus upon its core business or re-engineering its business processes.

The goals for outsourcing can include:

- skills and knowledge transfer;
- technology development and acquisition;
- the migration to new platforms and infrastructure;
- the divestment of legacy systems;
- lessening of overheads associated with storage;
- expanding the delivery of specialized services; and
- access to new markets and services.

Small to medium-sized enterprises, in particular, gain. They can enjoy access to new technologies and improved services without a major up front capital outlay or being left with redundant equipment. They also have access to a higher level and greater range of expertise than they could afford by themselves. Existing services can be upgraded or new ones introduced to completely transform the organization's capabilities and services.

Outsourcing can reduce costs by cutting an organization's capital investment in equipment and staff, and it obviates the need for debt financing of expensive information-related technology. It also provides a mechanism to shift technologies, take on board new technology directions, or introduce new information services cheaper and faster than if the organization was locked into an investment in its own infrastructure. Organizational change, mergers and new business or programme start-ups can also be achieved cheaper and faster. There is also more flexibility for handling peaks and troughs in business cycles.

Reasons for not outsourcing

The main reasons that are given for not outsourcing are:

- a fear of loss of control;
- the lack of ability to trust another party with a strategic investment;
- there is not a strong business case;
- the cost and effort of contractual negotiations give little return on the investment in time and legal representation;
- it results in constraints on flexibility; or
- concerns over vendor capabilities.

The outsourcing process

The outsourcing process involves:

- determining the right objectives and strategy;
- determining what to outsource;
- assessing the benefits;
- determining the risks;
- selection of the vendor;
- negotiating the contract;
- structuring the relationship; and
- managing the risks.

Determining the right objectives and strategy

An inhibiting factor to the success of outsourcing is that organizations frequently do not take the time to determine their objectives for outsourcing and develop a strategy to match. The objectives for outsourcing may be to:

- reduce overhead costs in service delivery;
- improve service delivery levels;
- gain access to a higher level and greater range of expertise;
- upgrade or introduce new information services to transform the organization's capabilities;
- share the level of risk in the introduction of new capital intensive technologies;
- shift technologies;
- manage a new business or programme start-up;
- increased flexibility for handling peaks and troughs in service delivery; or
- focus on core activities.

Each objective will require a different outsourcing mix and strategy, contract and management mechanisms. For example, an outsourcing strategy that is based on allowing the organization to focus on its core business will require a totally different partnership arrangement than one that is focused on a shift in technology or the sharing of risks.

Determining what to outsource

The information services that have been the most successful at outsourcing are those that have invested their time and energies into making a thorough examination of their options for outsourcing. The decision as to what to outsource should be based on a number of technology and management issues. These will include criticality of the service to the business needs of the organization, an assessment of in-house capabilities and available skills and expertise, financial situation, market opportunities, business and technology direction, the rate of change and complexity in the external environment, risk factors and benefits.

Assessing the benefits

Many senior management personnel have taken the decision to outsource their information-related technology based upon their belief that they would then be able to refocus on the core business of the organization, rather than being side-tracked by information-related technology issues. This assumption is incorrect. They are merely shifting responsibility for the delivery of services from an in-house source to an external source. The time, energy and expense taken in selecting the right service provider or vendor, establishing the contract conditions, and monitoring performance mean that the true benefits must come from elsewhere.

The benefits should be assessed according to the business need of the information service and its parent organization. These may include:

- the ability to spread the costs over a number of years or share risks;
- removing assets from the balance sheet with the ability to reinvest in other business-critical areas;
- jointly developing capabilities commercially;
- flexibility in the technology to support continued innovation, an upgrade or to introduce new services as and when required; and
- gaining access to a higher level and greater range of expertise than could be recruited or is available within the information service.

Determining the risks

The risks associated with outsourcing include:
- loss of expertise, key competencies and skills of staff within the information service. There can also be considerable damage to the productivity within the information service through a low level of morale within the staff who remain;
- costs are not actually reduced, they are only deferred. The internal changes within the organization that are required as part of the transition process may be higher than expected, or the time spent in negotiating the contract negates any financial gain in the outsourced agreement;

- lack of contract negotiation and continued contract management skills within the organization;
- incorrectly specified service delivery outcomes. This can result in incompatible or inappropriate services being offered, leading to loss of customers;
- poor vendor selection. This can occur either because the vendor or service provider is less competent than believed, or the co-ordination requirements are higher than expected. In addition, the vendor must be able to understand and contribute to the organization's business and corporate culture. Finally the vendor should also be financially stable and knowledgeable about the services offered;
- inadequate or unclear contracts;
- problems of getting different contractors and vendors to work together, especially in areas where the integration of systems is managed by different parties;
- vendors may lack flexibility and responsiveness to the customer; and
- outsourcing worsens rather than fixes existing problems. Problems remain unsolved. Only the responsibility for them has changed.

Improved telecommunications and lower labour market rates have resulted in a number of outsourcing venture operations being moved offshore. This can expose the organization to a number of risks that need to be managed as part of the contract negotiations. Examples being where:

- personal information residing on databases housed offshore (or in another commercial environment) is not subjected to the same level of privacy protection as the in-house systems;
- the same levels of security over confidential or commercially sensitive information are not applied in the outsourced environment, particularly where the information resides on shared services; or
- any intellectual property rights that the organization may have are not protected in the outsourced environment.

The failure of security systems can cause considerable embarrassment and the loss of commercially sensitive information may set back an organization's competitive advantage for a considerable length of time.

Selection of the vendor

The selection of the vendor should be based upon:

- their credibility and capability to provide the services being outsourced;
- size and shape, including whether the vendor is able to concentrate on

the information service's needs or whether it has other business interests to attend to;

- financial strength to remain in business for the life of the partnership (and longer);
- proven technical and service capability and performance in similar information-related environments;
- the variety of platforms offered to support the requirements of the information service and its customers;
- their ability to be controlled in terms of future direction, so that the information service shapes its future needs rather than being manipulated by the vendor;
- security and risk management issues;
- tender conformance;
- full cost of the proposal;
- strategic perspective;
- understanding and ability to contribute to the organization's business; and
- compatibility with the organization's corporate culture.

Negotiating the contract

The contract should meet the organization's business needs and objectives rather than the vendor's. A detailed specification for the outsourcing contract should be drawn up with legal advice. It should include:

- the business objective of the outsourcing arrangement;
- the areas to be outsourced;
- the service levels required. For example hours of operation, minimum service factors, and, the penalties if these service levels are not met;
- the level of service and contribution required of the organization and its management staff;
- costs, including those for maintenance and support;
- intellectual property rights and copyright. Including ownership of systems and developments, data and indemnities against the intellectual property rights of third parties;
- risk management, including: data redundancy, procedures and responsibilities, distribution of risk between the parties, security, confidentiality and backup, privacy protection;
- transfer of assets, including: details of assets, date of transfer, value at date of transfer, disposal of surplus assets, outstanding liabilities on assets;
- staff, including: staff development, transfer of staff and transfer conditions, outstanding liabilities in terms of accrued leave payments,

superannuation or other contractual obligations, use of contractors, availability and costs of additional staff, backup arrangements for key or critical staff, minimum proficiencies, poaching of staff;

- disputes and damages settlements, including: problem escalation procedures, formal and informal dispute resolution procedures. A third party arbitrator should be specified;
- termination, back out and change requirements for both parties. Termination clauses should cover the termination of the contract in the event of a dispute or violation of the contract, and the assistance to be provided at the end of the contract life. The contract should also cover the circumstances in which the contract conditions may be altered;
- performance measures. For example, response times, turnaround time, throughput;
- review and monitoring, including: third party review on physical security, disaster recovery, operations controls;
- indemnities and liabilities, including: provision for indemnity insurance or other indemnity provisions against contractual default and liability provisions for the vendor or service provider;
- other issues, including: notices, relationships of parties, successors or assignments, approvals or similar actions, contract variation procedures, waivers, publicity, governing law.

This list is not inclusive but covers the main points of the contract.

Structuring the relationship

The structure of the relationship between the organization (the customer) and the vendor will depend upon the objective of the outsourcing exercise. Each party should be very clear about:

- the objective and purpose of the outsourcing exercise;
- their role in the partnership arrangement;
- the organization's business and corporate culture;
- the distribution of risk between the parties;
- the ownership of the assets; and,
- the required outcomes and outputs;
- the roles of any third parties to the agreement.

Managing the risks

Senior management must be involved in contract negotiation and ongoing monitoring of performance levels. Legal advice should be obtained before and during the negotiation of the contract.

It is very important how the transition is managed and that thought is also given to managing the transition period at the end of the contract. The agreement should provide that on termination the service provider or vendor will assist the organization in taking back control of the service or in handing over the service to another vendor.

Whilst it is likely that the numbers of staff will be significantly reduced, the information service must be prepared to keep some expertise to oversee the contract and to evaluate performance and service delivery. As much thought should be given to the capabilities and skills of those who remain, as to the management of the staff who will transfer or leave.

Any reduction in staff within the information service may harm general morale and cause termination and severance for many employees. Change management strategies should be put in place to manage the transition stage. Whilst the service provider may hire a number of staff, others may face a job loss, early retirement or significant readjustment and retraining. Staff should be kept informed of progress and likely outcomes in terms of job security at all times.

There needs to be a high level of trust between the partners and a cultural fit between the organization and the service provider.

There should also be a post implementation review to determine the effectiveness of the outsourcing process, and to provide ongoing evaluation and monitoring of activities.

Outsourcing is a partnership between the information service, its parent organization and the third party service provider (the vendor). Whilst the emphasis in the literature and corporate environment has been associated with outsourcing information-related technology, the reasons for outsourcing, risk and contract management strategies, and relationships issues apply equally to any outsourcing venture in the other work units that belong to the information service.

38 Performance measurement and evaluation

Introduction

Performance measurement and evaluation are important management activities. They serve two purposes: as an assessment of how the information service is performing and as an accountability factor to the stakeholders.

Outputs and outcomes are two of the most common means of measuring and evaluating an information service's performance and value. Information services often experience difficulty in designing quantitative and qualitative measures that prove their value, as many of the benefits are intangible or linked to other outcomes for which they cannot be directly accountable.

In order to measure performance, information needs to be collected and analysed. The information services manager must determine what pieces of information are needed to evaluate or measure the service's performance. These are called performance indicators. They provide the formula through which measurement can be made.

Performance evaluation

Performance evaluation is the process by which the information service determines whether it is on course towards the achievement of the parent organization's objectives. The process includes:

- establishing an appropriate evaluation process;
- measuring and evaluating the performance; and
- adopting procedures for acting upon the outcomes and recommendations of the evaluation.

The establishment of the evaluation process requires the development of specific objectives and the establishment of performance indicators to measure progress. The specific objectives define the intended level and quality of the service, the outcomes to be achieved, and the time frame and resources available to achieve the outcomes.

The timing and format of the evaluation depends on whether management is evaluating the continuous performance of the information service as a whole, of each of the work units, or a specific project or aspect of the service. In the case of the latter, the performance of the service should be evaluated prior to and at the completion of a specific project. Finally, actions should be initiated in response to any findings or recommendations that arise out of the evaluation.

Measuring performance

Outputs and outcomes

Outputs and outcomes are two of the most common means of measuring and evaluating an information service's performance and value. Outputs provide a simple focal point for measuring the cost-effectiveness of the information service. They can be compared with inputs to measure efficiency, and with the corporate objectives to measure effectiveness. Examples of output measures include the average number of help desk enquiries successfully handled by an individual within a 15-minute response time, or the number of missing files or records located within the organization over a period of time.

Services are evaluated or appraised through outcomes. These measure the impact of the outputs on the target market and the environment. They are the intended consequences of the information service's activities and are found in changes in circumstances or behaviour, or needs that are satisfied.

The customer's ability to utilize the services offered by the information service to create further output is an outcome measure of its performance. The outcome can be measured in four separate value areas.

Value of the service to the parent organization in assisting competitiveness

Information services units identify and manage technology and systems to assist in the internal and external functioning of the organization. Their measures of performance are linked to how successful the organization is in achieving its objectives and its level of competitiveness. Specialized scientific or technical information centres add value to the quality of knowledge within the organization by acquiring, organizing and disseminating accurate and timely information. Their outcomes are found in the added values to knowledge and information within the organization that can help with new product development and to make it successful against its competitors.

Social value of information

Access to information is an important component of democracy. Public libraries add value to the quality of life of individuals, and occasionally commerce, through the provision of educational, informational, recreational and cultural services. The outcome measures used to evaluate their performance are linked to the societal marketing concept of customer satisfaction and the creation of an informed society by the most cost-effective methods.

Value of information as a commodity or resource

Information utilities and value-added information providers trade in information products and services. They add value and create new information products and services by manipulating, merging and redistributing information in a value-added form. The outcomes lie in their creating new markets for information and new (and profitable) value-added information products and services to meet customer and prospective customer needs.

Economic value of information

Information has unique economic properties that can affect its value at any one time. It can be stored and used at the same time. It can be reused without diminishing in value or, in the case of competitive information, its value lies in no one else having access. Information has different values to different customers, and more than one customer can use it at the same time. The outcome is that information has different values to different people in different situations and at different times.

Quality and value

One of the problems that information services managers have is in proving their worth or value in quantitative and qualitative terms. Many of the benefits are intangible. The quality of the service may be recognized by customers and stakeholders or senior management, but it is often difficult to apply concrete measures that can be directly attributed to the information service.

Sometimes an attempt is made to assume some sort of qualitative measure by applying a time-scale to the quantitative measures, for example the number of enquiries or advice taking 15 minutes or more. The assumption is that the longer the period of time taken, the more in-depth and valuable the service given. However, there are two problems with performance measures of this type:

- there is not necessarily a correlation between time and quality; and
- they do not measure the impact or outcome of the advice and how it was used in the value chain.

For example, the customer may be dissatisfied with the advice, but out of politeness and consideration for the staff, have made them feel helpful and successful.

The measures of quality (capability) and value (benefit) that arise out of the above example are much more difficult to measure directly. Indirect measures have been used, but as Orr points out (1973, p. 320), the relationship between capability and utilization is mediated through demand, which is itself a highly complex variable.

There are three measures of performance common to all services. These are efficiency and two other aspects: 'how good is the service?' and 'how much good does it do?' The latter can be expressed as quality and value or effectiveness and benefit. Orr (ibid., p. 318) states:

> The ultimate criterion for assessing the quality of a service is its capability for meeting the user (client) needs it is intending to serve, and the value of a service must ultimately be judged in terms of the beneficial effects accruing from its use as viewed by those who sustain the costs.

If the work units that comprise the information service collectively supply pertinent and timely information in an efficient manner that enables the organization to take advantage of its competitors, it will be perceived as being a valuable asset by senior management and funded accordingly. Services that are efficient and reflect the needs of the customers are usually well supported. Customers convey positive feedback to senior management and tangible effects are felt upon the parent organization. This support is reflected in the level of funding that the information service receives. In contrast, a poorly focused, inefficient information service results in disillusionment for both the staff and customers. This is manifested in a lack of commitment by customers, senior management and other stakeholders. Unless the service is refocused to meet customer needs and the quality of service improved, the information service and its level of funding will invariably decline.

Performance and value of information

Information by itself is not necessarily useful. If it is not used, for example it sits unused on an information system because people do not know of its existence, or it is not useful to customers or the business because it does not meet their needs, then it has no value to the organization.

Burk and Horton (1988) have suggested five ways in which the performance and value of information may be measured:

- quality of the information itself – accuracy, comprehensiveness, credibility and currency;
- quality of the information holdings – accessibility, adaptability, ease of use, format;
- impact upon productivity – greater returns, improvement in decision-making, more efficient operations;
- impact on organizational effectiveness – new markets, improved customer satisfaction, meeting goals and objectives; and
- impact on financial position – cost savings, creation of new assets, improved profits.

They also go on to rank or rate the information resource according to its:

- effectiveness in supporting the activity it was designed to support;
- strategic importance of the information resource (or service) to the activities of the parent organization; and
- strategic importance of the activities being supported to the parent organization.

These generic measurements of performance and value for the information resource may also be applied to measure the value and performance of the individual work units within the information service as well as to the information service as a whole.

Cause and effect

Orr (1973, p. 318) has developed four basic propositions:

1. that, other things being equal, the capability of the service tends to increase as the resources devoted to it increase, but not necessarily proportionately;
2. that, other things being equal, the total uses made of a service (utilization) tend to increase as its capability increases, but not necessarily proportionately;

3   that, other things being equal, the beneficial effects realized from a service increase as its utilization increases, but not necessarily proportionately;

4   that, other things being equal, the resources devoted to a service increase as its beneficial effects increase, but not necessarily proportionately.

The cause and effect sequence is useful in that it points out that funds invested in different services or work unit activities may not necessarily have the same impact. There are other important interactions that have just the same, if not more, effect on the services. For example, in competitive, customer-oriented environments it is quality and innovation, not quantity, that distinguishes an information service. The knowledge, creativity and resourcefulness of the staff can have more impact on the quality and value of the service than the funding level. The level of resources and funding still has some bearing upon the output and performance of the information service. Without adequate resources, the services will gradually decline. However, funds alone do not constitute a good service. The effectiveness of the information service's policies and practices, staff competence and morale, and the leadership skills of management also impact the quality of the service.

Performance indicators

A performance indicator is the formula which management uses to measure progress, quality and level of service towards achieving the organization's objectives. It is the means of knowing whether a specific objective is being achieved (see Table 38.1). However, even success in producing outputs and achieving outcomes does not call for complacency. The results should be analysed to see if there are better ways of achieving the same results at lower cost.

Performance indicators combine the elements of inputs, outputs and outcomes. Generally three types of indicators are used. These are:

- workload indicators;
- efficiency indicators;
- effectiveness indicators.

Workload indicators are output oriented. They measure the amount of work achieved against set milestones. Efficiency indicators compare resource inputs against resulting outputs. They quantify the resources used to achieve the intended outputs (services or products) so that the ratio of outputs to inputs can be determined. Effectiveness indicators measure the

Table 38.1 Examples of performance indicators which may be found in information services

Category	Objective	Performance indicator
Workload	To scan 2,500,000 items into an image system over a period of three months as part of the take-up of a large image project.	Actual work progress in terms of the number of items accurately scanned at the end of each week of the project.
	To process 10,000 client requests for information per year.	Actual requests for information (reported monthly).
Efficiency	Provide a help desk service at a maximum cost of £100.00 per person per month.	The actual cost of providing the help desk service (based on unit cost).
	Electronic commerce system is to provide customer transactions at a maximum cost of £10.00 per transaction.	The actual average cost of customer transactions each month (value of resources used divided by total number of transactions per month)
Effectiveness	To provide an information service that satisfies 90% of customer demands for information within three days.	Analysis of information service against customer demand/ requests for information and time taken to provide information, summarized monthly.

extent to which services achieve objectives using qualitative and quantitative indicators.

Performance indicators must be relevant to the cause and should clearly relate to the specific objectives of the service. They should be measurable. The information used must be reliable, valid and verifiable. Data collection should be accurate, interpreted accurately, unbiased and collected in time for proper use to be made of it. It is important that the indicators are not subjective. They should be capable of being translated into meaningful information for use by those who require them.

Each indicator should be unique. It should reveal some important aspect of performance that no other indicator does. The value of the information should be weighed against the costs of the collector's and analyst's time, efforts and resources. The degree to which routine operations are impeded in collecting the data, and the acceptance levels of staff time and operating expenses should be balanced against the value of the information provided.

Taylor (1986, pp. 181–4) has defined several other qualities or attributes that can assist in producing meaningful indicators in information services. For example, the audit should be at a definable point in the process such as the number of abstracts completed or requests for information processed. The activities should be easy to count and be defined, for example, enquiries can be classified as taking under 1 minute, 1–3 minutes, 5–10 minutes, and so on.

A defined output should also be consistent with existing information systems and, if possible, covered by historical data. Like should be compared with like. The historical context is important as it allows for comparisons over a period of time. The output should have a terminal quality. It should be isolated and counted at the point where it changes function and status. For example, the issue of a library book changes the status of the book from an asset or library resource to a source of information, education, culture or recreation for the customer. By counting issue transaction statistics, public libraries are counting one of the sources of added value to the quality of life in their communities. The outputs are the result of a process in which value is added.

Information services may be measured according to the value of the service it contributes to organizational competitiveness, in their social value and contribution to a community, in providing a commodity or resource for use in the creation of other goods and services, and in the economic value that differs according to the user. Other mechanisms through which the performance of the information service (and its information resource) may be valued include accuracy, comprehensiveness, accessibility, adaptability, ease of use, impact on productivity, impact on organizational effectiveness and impact on financial position.

References

Burk, C. F. and Horton, F. W. (1988). *Info Map: a Complete Guide to Discovering Corporate Resources*, Englewood Cliffs, NJ: Prentice Hall.

Orr, R. H. (1973), 'Measuring the goodness of library services: a general framework for considering quantitative measures', *Journal of Documentation*, **29**(3), September, 315–22.

Taylor, R. S. (1986), *Value Added Processes in Information Systems*, Norwood, New Jersey: Ablex.

Epilogue

Epilogue

39 The final strategy

Introduction

This chapter brings together the nine parts of the book; reflecting the role of the information services manager in today's competitive and changing environment, their skills requirements and the nature of their work. Each part describes a significant management activity that the information services manager undertakes to deliver a leading edge information service that meets the business objectives of the parent organization and customer information needs.

Understanding the role of manager

Successful information services managers understand that traditional management roles have changed. Their new management roles require them to be inspirational, visionary and leaders in a world that is continually changing. In short they have to 'learn to dance on a moving carpet'.

In addition to achieving more with less resources, information services managers have to manage risk, quality processes, contracts, the information service's image and the customer and stakeholder interface.

They must plan, develop and drive competitive business strategies that take into account the internal and external environments and the available resources. The environments are continually changing, so the managers and their strategies must be flexible enough to cope with changing conditions whilst still concentrating on the objectives of the information service and its parent organization. They must use their networks, communicating and political roles to sell the benefits of the information service within the parent organization, and with customers and stakeholders.

The objective of the information service is to assist the parent organization to utilize its information and supporting technologies for competitive advantage, and to deliver services that meet customer needs. To do this, the information services manager develops creative information services and products and uses the supporting technology in innovative ways to achieve customer satisfaction, market domination and increased profitability for the parent organization.

Understanding the environment

The information services manager must understand and manage the environment in which the information service operates. They must understand the strategic influences that impact on the organization. Global competitiveness, the drive for flexibility in the use of resources, and, a customer focus are three of the more strategic influences on organizations today.

Managing the environment through integrated planning

As a senior manager, the information services manager must demonstrate a personal involvement and commitment to the strategic planning process. Strategic planning recognizes that organizations cannot achieve everything that they would like to. Instead, it enables the information service to choose strategies and initiate new activities and services on a priority basis. These are chosen to meet customer needs. It introduces a systematic approach to managing dynamic environments and enables the information service to respond effectively to new situations with the available resources.

As part of the strategic planning process, the information services manager is the champion of an integrated approach to planning human, financial, information and technology resources. The strategic planning process also assists in the development of marketing strategies for the information service.

In managing the organizational unit with direct responsibility for driving and managing the use of the information and technology resources within the parent organization, the information services manager is consultative in their planning approach. They consult on business and information needs with management and employees of the parent organization (the internal customers), external customers and stakeholders such as suppliers and other entities that interact with the parent organization. To achieve maximum benefit they ensure that:

- the planning process takes into account the size, structure, culture and type of organization; and
- the technology and processes are aligned to fit the present and future business needs.

Creating the corporate environment

An important role for the information services manager is to create or modify the corporate culture so that it is innovative and able to respond positively to change. As a service organization, the information service's culture needs to espouse values of quality services leading to customer satisfaction. Integrity and ethical behaviour should also be valued, particularly where the information service is dealing with commercially sensitive or personal information.

To survive in a competitive environment, it is important that the information services manager is politically astute and able to control and manage the organizational politics for the benefit of the information service. Political behaviour can drive change and move forward items on the corporate agenda. The information services manager understands what the parent organization wants and positions the information service to provide creative solutions to important problems. They stay focused on achieving the vision and are not distracted by operational tasks.

In the policy-making role, the information services manager ensures that the policies are well planned and thought out in terms of strategic timing, costs, the issues at stake, the values and attitudes within the parent organization, and those of their customers and stakeholders. Their policies are future oriented and anticipate new demands and developments.

In developing a creative and innovative corporate culture, the manager shows a willingness to take risks and allow their staff to make mistakes as part of the learning process. They encourage those in the organization to value flexibility and adaptability. Their management practices, rewards systems and performance reviews support and encourage ideas generation and divergent thoughts in problem-solving.

Differentiations in expertise are recognized and valued for their contribution to the organization. The competitive elements associated with differentiation are managed so that they foster rather than hinder the organization's objectives.

Getting things done in the corporate environment

Managers achieve things through their interactions with people. Their ability to get things done in the corporate environment rests on their capacities to inspire and lead, influence and persuade, to delegate and involve others in decision-making. They actively seek input and participation, and provide continuous and timely feedback on performance.

Managers who have high-level leadership skills are able to articulate and clarify the organization's vision so that others can understand and want to be involved. They are also prepared to use their power and political skills to create and sell their vision for the information service and its future within the parent organization. Good managers provide clear instructions and expectations of what is required, and allocate responsibility to others.

Personal networks allow information services managers to seek and provide information, to obtain support and to positively influence outcomes. Many legitimate political tactics rely upon networks, and in belonging to others' networks valuable and competitive information can be obtained.

Information services managers continually work through groups of people. Some of these groups will be informal, whilst others will be formal units or teams. In working with groups, managers recognize that it is natural for individuals and groups to sometimes have conflicts. The most common reasons for this are individual dilemmas over roles that people play in groups, and the stages of group development that can lead to emotional tension. However, when the conflict spills over and becomes destructive, they do not leave it unchecked.

In building teams, the role of the manager is to facilitate the group's management of its members rather than manage the members as individuals. As a team-builder, the manager improves the co-ordination between the team members and gets the members of the team to work together to achieve a higher level of outcome. They encourage the leadership capacities to be shared amongst all the members of the team at different times.

To obtain the best out of people, managers must motivate them. Inspirational managers ensure that they continuously extend and develop individuals, coaching them to achieve greater levels as well as responding to their aspirations. They put strategies in place at organizational and individual levels to motivate their people. Organizational-level strategies include flexible work arrangements, performance-based compensation, job enrichment and job enlargement. At the individual level, managers acknowledge that there are different factors that can affect motivation levels and job satisfaction. Individuals have differing values and needs. They ensure that the motivational and rewards strategies are flexible enough to meet these differences.

Conflict and change are closely related. Information services managers manage conflict so that it remains healthy enough to encourage competition between individuals and groups without becoming destructive. Conflict occurs naturally and leads to change. In today's turbulent environment, information services managers must be able to champion, drive and manage change. As a champion of continuous change, the information services manager must promote new ideas and build support in order to implement the change. Where discontinuous or radical change occurs, the manager must be able to manage the resulting chaos with strong and direct leadership. In each case they will need to deal with individual resistance to change.

Many of the activities mentioned above rely upon the information services manager's negotiation and networking skills. Information services managers who are good negotiators are articulate, creative, yet determined and disciplined. They also have a high frustration and tolerance level. They are sensitive to the behaviour of others and are able to anticipate and evaluate others' responses.

Managing and communicating information within the corporate environment

A key role for the information services manager is to manage the information within the corporate environment, that is, within the parent organization and externally to customers and other stakeholders. To do this, the information services manager requires highly developed communication skills in order to make judgements, listen, evaluate, reason, reassure, appease and provide advice to peers, customers, their bosses and stakeholders.

The information services manager must act as a change agent by persuading and influencing individuals about the way in which information is viewed within the organization. They must sell their concepts through formal and informal channels of communication. Their abilities to influence and get things done in the corporate environment is based on clear communications across organizational boundaries and with all levels of people within the parent organization.

The management of the organization's communications with the outside world is as important as managing the internal communications. Two important activities of the boundary spanning role of the information services manager are to manage the information service's corporate image, and to gather competitive intelligence. The art of managing the corporate image is in identifying the target audience, determining the communication objectives and choosing the right communication channels. The art of gathering competitive intelligence is in knowing what information is relevant, where to find it legally and how to convert it into intelligence for use in decision-making.

The primary role of the information services manager is to make appropriate information available for decision-making in a seamless and consistent manner, when and where it is needed. This requires a knowledge of the available information and its supporting technologies, the organization's business needs and the information needs of management, customers, employees and stakeholders. The role of the information services staff is to assess, select, manage, process and disseminate communication vehicles for customers according to these needs.

Effective information service managers ensure that the information and its supporting technologies are designed to complement the organizational structure. This is so that relevant information can be identified, retrieved, manipulated and made available to those authorized to use it. They employ a systematic approach so that diverse forms of information are managed and made accessible in a consistent manner. The artificial boundaries that occur by reason of format or media, location or work unit ownership are removed. The information is also managed according to its stage in the life cycle.

Managing the individual

The information services manager recognizes that managing the well-being of the individuals who work in the information service is as important, if not more important, as managing the financial, technical and information resources. They are aware of individual vulnerabilities to stress and assist their people to manage these so that they can function well. They encourage stress management strategies to be used at the organizational and individual levels. They act to reduce workplace stressors such as faulty equipment, job insecurity or bad working relationships, and assist individuals to manage their personal stressors. These acts reduce their employees' vulnerabilities to stress and help to create a more productive work environment.

Information services managers who display a duty of care for their staff sustain and increase individual productivity, prepare their staff for the future, and, support their own and their employees' career and life goals through career planning and personal development. They recognize that an individual's total lifestyle should be managed, as their sense of well-being is directly related to their levels of motivation and productivity. They encourage the idea that career and lifestyle planning are both an individual and organizational responsibility. The information services manager also accepts their responsibility for ensuring appropriate assignments, coaching and counselling in order to assist individuals in the realistic planning and attainment of their goals. They demonstrate their commitment to training and other personal development opportunities by making available the necessary funding, time and the provision of opportunities for all staff.

In doing the above, the information services manager points out to individuals that they also have to accept responsibility for their personal growth and development. They encourage them to identify their long-term career and lifestyle plans and put strategies in place to achieve these.

Managing risk

A main role of the manager is to anticipate, assess, manage and minimize risk. Information services managers make use of the return on investment principles as an indication on how the information service is using its resources. If their use of resources in projects is well planned, risk is minimized and the return on investment maximized.

A significant risk associated with the management of information services is that of security. Information services managers recognize that security is a management rather than a technical issue. They manage according to the level of risk, the potential threats to the organization, and the probability of these occurring. They recognize that the level of risk is influenced by the type of organization, its business and objectives, and manage accordingly.

In addition to security and the threat of a major outage (failure or disaster) the information services manager identifies the level of exposure of the service and its parent organization to other risks and puts appropriate strategies in place to manage these. These other risks include fraud, inefficiency and waste, legal exposures, loss of public reputation, loss of key staff and expertise, public liability, property and other damage, unlawful acts or terrorism and occupational health and safety issues.

Service delivery

The manager recognizes that the service delivery aspects of the information service are one of the most important components of their position. They undertake strategic marketing strategies to ensure a viable market position and programmes to support the success of the information service.

Managers seek to ensure that their staff provide consistently higher quality services or products than those of competitors in order to differentiate their services from their competitors. They and their senior management peers show a commitment to quality by making it a self-sustaining way of life within the parent organization. This includes ensuring that each of the steps in the value chain are managed so that the outputs are correct first time every time.

The information services manager recognizes that the customers are the final judge of quality; that the customers are the ones who are affected by the outputs and outcomes. As different customers have their own perspectives and perceptions of quality, the information services manager manages the quality of services and products according to customers' known requirements.

The delivery of the service or product to the customer is only the beginning of the relationship between the organization and the customer. Knowing this, the information services manager ensures that the service backup that supports the continual use of the product or service is of equal quality. He or she also ensures that the delivery of services, follow-up, complaints handling, repairs or corrective actions, and account management are handled efficiently and effectively.

The information services manager creates an environment where there is openness and willingness to communicate with customers concerning their problems, needs and preferences. They recognize that loyalty and customer retention are key components to the service's competitive edge. Knowing that information-related technologies can be used to maintain a competitive position, they look for innovative ways to build a close relationship with the customer that create a win-win partnership for the customer, the information service and the parent organization.

A changing role for the information services manager is from a provider of services to a purchaser of services. Increasingly their role will be as a contract manager for the contracting out (or outsourcing) of information-related services to a third party. The drivers for this are to enable the organization to concentrate on its core activities, to reduce overhead costs, to improve service levels, to gain access to knowledge, or to take advantage of new technology directions. These managers recognize that the success of outsourcing service delivery will depend upon their:

- determining the right strategy to meet the required objectives;
- correctly assessing the benefits and determining the risks;
- managing these risks through a good contract and contract management process; and
- correctly structuring the relationship with the third party.

Finally, the information services manager measures and evaluates the information service's performance. This is to assess how the service is performing and to provide a means of accountability to stakeholders. The information services manager develops specific objectives and sets service standards and performance levels. They also determine what information is required to evaluate and measure the service's performance, and put steps in place to collect this information in a meaningful form.

Conclusion

The focus for managing in changing and competitive environments is to create a vision and inspire others to work towards the achievement of the vision. Along the way, diverse issues such as the need for increased productivity, the development of flexible processes and structures to withstand change, and the efficient use of resources within the organization need to be managed in order to survive. Creativity and innovation must also be encouraged and change should be championed rather than feared. Specifically, the information service should deliver its products and services tailored to suit customer needs, and align information and its related technology to the business needs of the organization, its customers and stakeholders; differentiating and positioning its services with quality in mind.

Index